mad about food

A collection of recipes from
a city that's mad about food

Presented by the Junior League of Madison, Wisconsin

The Junior League of Madison, Inc. is an organization of women committed to
promoting voluntarism, developing the potential of women and improving the
community through the effective action and leadership of trained volunteers.
Its purpose is exclusively educational and charitable.

Recipes from a city that's **Mad About Food**
is a collection of favorite recipes gathered by the Junior League of Madison, Inc.
Recipes are not necessarily original.

Cookbook committee chair: Sara DeTienne
Co-chair: Sandi Gregoire
Art Director: Lynn Wood
Concept and Design: Karen Stakun, Designer, Wood Communications Group
Illustrations: Karen Stakun and Sarah Landgren
Design Team: Mary Jane Carpenter, Amy Windsor, Michael Stormberg

Manufactured by Favorite Recipes Press
an imprint of

FRP

P.O. Box 305142, Nashville, Tennessee 37230
800-358-0560

ISBN: 0-9759650-0-X
Manufactured in the United States of America
First printing: September 2004 • 10,000

The Junior League of Madison, Inc. is a not-for-profit organization whose purpose is
exclusively educational and charitable. Proceeds from the sale of **Mad About Food**
will be used for programs supported by the
Junior League of Madison in the Greater Madison area.

For additional copies, send $26.95 plus $4.00 shipping and handling to the Junior League of Madison
at the address above. Wisconsin residents, add 5.5% sales tax.

Welcome!

We hope you enjoy **Mad About Food**, the Junior League of Madison's first community cookbook. This book was designed not only to share hundreds of fabulous recipes with you, but also to give you a glimpse of some of the many reasons we are "Mad About Madison." Throughout the book we have sprinkled morsels of "local flavor" to demonstrate why Madison consistently receives top billing as one of the country's most desirable places to live. We've also tried to give you a glimpse of how the Junior League of Madison works to make a measurable difference in our community.

Every year, the Junior League of Madison serves hundreds of area families by developing and supporting responsive, effective programs that empower women to make a difference in the lives of those around them. Dedicated Junior League members work diligently to serve the physical, intellectual, emotional and social growth needs of women and children by volunteering their time and talents, building local coalitions and raising funds.

But we are more than a volunteer organization. While working to better our community, we are also helping our members grow – personally and professionally. Junior League of Madison members learn to be effective, professional community volunteers, develop valuable friendships and find personal fulfillment. As a result, members become long-term contributors to the community.

As you read on, we hope you find a few new favorite recipes to add to your own collection and a few good reasons to visit our city. Thanks for your support. With your help, the Junior League of Madison can continue its work to improve our wonderful community.

JUNIOR LEAGUE OF MADISON
Women building better communities

The Junior League of Madison is a member of the Association of Junior Leagues International which is comprised of more than 200,000 volunteers in nearly 300 Leagues in four countries.

79
Going Overboard
Spectacular soups that will rock your boat

table of contents

289
No Reservations
Dine in with local restaurant favorites

cookbook committee

A community cookbook was a dream of the Junior League of Madison since its establishment in 1988. **Mad About Food** took three years to develop and produce. Credit for its successful completion goes to the past and current presidents of the League who had the vision, the members who supported the project and to the dedicated committee who made **Mad About Food** a reality.

2001-2005 Cookbook Committee Members

Sara DeTienne, Chair; Sandi Gregoire, Co-Chair
Peggy Angevine, Jane Arduser, Sue Bakke, Mary Bartzen, Sheri Carter,
Karen Christianson, Susie Conely, Lisa Danford, Kitty Dettman,
Gail Docken, Sarah Duren, Tammy Earl, Liz Heinrichs, Louisa Enz,
Katherine Klinke, Darlene Kozarek, Nancy Latta, Nancy Lynch,
Margaret Maher, Blythe Marlow, Alison Matthias, Jennifer McKnelly-Ginn,
Connie Mills, Elizabeth Misel, Stephanie Monday, Kelly Mortrud,
Michelle Ogilvie, Sue Ossman, Marcia Philipps Hyzer, Kathi Preboske,
Meg Prestigiacomo, Laurel Rice, Tracie Rodman, Sue Joy Sobota, Liz Sax,
Jen Scheller, Penny Symes, Paula Thill, Ellen Thom, Donna Weihofen,
Suzie Wilkinson, Amy Windsor, Lynn Wood, Amy Zumwalt

Design/Layout

Sandi Gregoire, Chair
Peggy Angevine, Mary Jane Carpenter, Sheri Carter, Sara DeTienne,
Katie Kennedy, Darlene Kozarek, Connie Mills, Elizabeth Misel,
Michelle Ogilvie, Tracie Rodman, Amy Windsor, Lynn Wood

Editing Team

Peggy Angevine, Chair; Donna Weihofen, Nutritional Analysis
Michele Bonnarens, Sara DeTienne, Susan Luskin, Nancy Lynch,
Connie Mills, Sheree Paradise, Jodi Sweeney, Lynn Wood

Marketing & Media Relations

Meg Prestigiacomo, Chair
Candace Bangerter, Sara DeTienne, Sandi Gregoire,
Kim Lothe, Nancy Lynch, Liz Sax, Lynn Wood

Recipe Captains

Lisa Danford, Co-Chair; Donna Weihofen, Co-Chair
Sue Bakke, Lisa Danford, Sara DeTienne, Sarah Duren,
Sandi Gregoire, Shari Kuemmel, Margaret Maher, Kelly Mortrud,
Jen Scheller, Sue Joy-Sobota, Paula Thill, Donna Weihofen,
Amy Windsor, Sue Zaleski

Copywriting

Katie Kennedy, Chair
Elizabeth Misel, Peggy Angevine

❦ ❦ ❦ ❦ ❦ ❦

Artistic Design and Production

Wood Communications Group
Lynn Wood, Art Director
Karen Stakun, Lead Designer
Sarah Landgren & Karen Stakun, Illustrators
Michael Stormberg, Layout
Mary Jane Carpenter & Amy Windsor, Design Development

❦ ❦ ❦ ❦ ❦ ❦

Junior League of Madison Presidents

Laurel Rice, 1988-1990
Carmen Skilton, 1990-1992
Ginger Gant Scholz, 1992-1994
Mary Pat Berry, 1994-1995
Cindy Rogerson, 1995-1996
Gail Docken, 1996-1997
Suzie Wilkinson, 1997-1998
Melinda Pellino, 1998-1999
Vincia Carlstrom, 1999-2000
Laurel Rice, 2000-2001
Marcia Philipps Hyzer, 2001-2002
Mary Bartzen 2002-2003
Susan Luskin 2003-2004
Polly Duchow 2004-2005

Please see page 314 for recognition of the additional friends, family and members of the Junior League of Madison who contributed to this book.

the nuts & bolts

We hope **Mad About Food** becomes one of your favorite cooking resources. In an effort to make this book as user-friendly as possible, we've added the following special features:

- Each recipe includes total servings and most include a per-serving nutritional analysis.
- See left margins for general cooking tips, tricks and trivia and supplemental recipes.
- See page 306 for a glossary of handy cooking tips and tricks.
- See page 309 for a guide to herbs and spices.
- Each section includes a themed menu for your reference.

Watch for these symbols throughout the book to aid your selection:

 Chef's Tip: Notes preparation alternatives such as substitutions, variations or time-saving ideas.

 Quick 'N Easy: Indicates recipes that are tasty and can be prepared quickly.

 Plan Ahead: Denotes recipes that may require extra preparation time and should be planned ahead or CAN be made ahead for ease of preparation

 Freezable: Identifies recipes that can be made ahead and frozen for future use.

 Vegetarian: Signifies vegetarian dishes. Several meatless dishes are also listed in the main course section.

 Local Flavor: Designates Madison-area stories intended to provide a glimpse of our fine city.

 JLM Program: Provides information about current and past community programs supported by the Junior League of Madison.

cooking equivalents

MEASUREMENT		EQUIVALENT
1 TABLESPOON (TBSP)	=	3 TEASPOONS (TSP)
1/16 CUP	=	1 TABLESPOON
1/8 CUP	=	2 TABLESPOONS
1/6 CUP	=	2 TABLESPOONS + 2 TEASPOONS
1/4 CUP	=	4 TABLESPOONS
1/3 CUP	=	5 TABLESPOONS + 1 TEASPOON
3/8 CUP	=	6 TABLESPOONS
1/2 CUP	=	8 TABLESPOONS
2/3 CUP	=	10 TABLESPOONS + 2 TEASPOONS
3/4 CUP	=	12 TABLESPOONS
1 CUP	=	16 TABLESPOONS
8 FLUID OUNCES (FL OZ)	=	1 CUP
1 PINT (PT)	=	2 CUPS
1 QUART (QT)	=	2 PINTS
4 CUPS	=	1 QUART
1 GALLON (GAL)	=	4 QUARTS
16 OUNCES (OZ)	=	1 POUND (LB)
1 OUNCE	=	28.35 GRAMS
1 GRAM	=	.035 OUNCES

making a
scene

Show stopping appetizers & beverages

appetizers & beverages

APPETIZERS

Appetizer Meatballs 40

Asian Wing Dings 41

Athenian Artichoke Dip 8

Avocado & Goat Cheese 9

Bacon Tomato Cups 23

Baked Chinese Eggrolls 36

Baked Pita Chips 8

Beer Cheese Fondue 28

Blue Cheese Pecan Spread 15

Brie w/Port Wine & Cherry Sauce 19

Chicken Satay with Spicy Peanut Sauce 32

Chipotle Mayonnaise 17

Clam Puffs 30

Crab Wontons 31

Endive with Goat Cheese and Mandarin Oranges 21

Fiesta Dip 17

Guacamole 12

Homemade Hummus 13

Hot Crab & Shrimp Dip 14

Marinated Pork Tenderloin 35

Mediterranean Tapenade 18

Moroccan Beef Purses 38

Mushroom Strudel 27

Olive Salsa 11

Rose Bowl Cheddar Dip 10

Saganaki 20

Salsa 12

Shooting Stars 37

Shrimp Sweet Potato Cakes with Chipotle Mayonnaise 16

Spicy Pork Wonton Cups 34

Summer Ceviche 29

Swiss Cheese Zucchini Tart 24

Tantalizing Tomato Pesto Tartlets 26

Tenderloin Supreme 39

Tunarific Dip 31

West Coast Pizza 22

Yummy Stuffed Mushrooms 25

BEVERAGES

After Workout Guiltless Smoothy 46

Bloody Larry 42

Cranberry Orange Spice Cooler 45

Easy Sangria 42

Gin Fizz 46

Hot Spiced Cider 43

Irish Cream 46

Margarita Madness 44

Old Fashioned Sweet 45

Pear Liqueur 43

Pink Punch 44

photo courtesy of Wisconsin Dept. of Tourism

Concerts on the Square

Summer in Madison is a banquet of sights, sounds, and tastes. And, for six consecutive Wednesdays, the Capitol lawn is packed with people enjoying a healthy dose of all three.

The Wisconsin Chamber Orchestra provides the music – free for all within earshot. Restaurants and caterers offer delectable fare from light snacks to gourmet dinners. Picnic baskets are bursting with summertime favorites. Colorful blankets form a crazy quilt of color that covers virtually every inch of lawn. Tables, complete with linen tablecloths and crystal, provide a ribbon of contrast along Capitol walkways.

By mid-afternoon people begin scurrying for the best places to situate their blanket. By the time musicians begin tuning their instruments, offices that look out onto the Capitol are overflowing with enthusiastic music lovers.

For two glorious hours the audience is treated to favorite pieces from John Phillip Sousa, Tschaikovsky, Bach and Mozart to name a few. As the sun sets, people finish the last of their desserts, say goodbye to friends, fold up their blankets and head for home.

All in all, a classic and tasty Madison evening.

See "local flavor" for more about Madison's arts, cultural and entertainment offerings.

picnic lunch menu

Marinated Pork Tenderloin Appetizer
page 35

Clam Puffs
page 30

Cucumber Pasta Salad
page 128

Champagne Ham
page 208

Rolls

Carrot Cake
page 249

Wine

Local Beer

Athenian Artichoke Dip

1 (14 ounce) can artichoke hearts in water, drained and quartered
4 ounces feta cheese, crumbled (plain or herbed)
1/4 cup red or green bell pepper, chopped
1 garlic clove, pressed
1 cup mayonnaise
3 green onions with tops, thinly sliced
3/4 teaspoon dried oregano leaves
1/4 cup sliced almonds (optional)
dash white or cayenne pepper (optional)

Preheat oven to 350 degrees.

Using food processor, chop artichoke hearts; add cheese and bell pepper. Transfer to 1-quart bowl. Using garlic press, press garlic into bowl. Add mayonnaise, green onions and oregano; mix well. Spoon into 8-inch mini-baking dish. Top with almonds.

Bake 10 minutes, until golden brown and bubbly.

Serve with Baked Pita Chips (recipe below)

Serves: 10

Nutritional Information per Serving (for Athenian Artichoke Dip and Pita Chips)
Calories: 230, Fat: 20 grams, Protein: 4 grams, Carbohydrates: 9 grams, Cholesterol: 25 milligrams, Fiber: 3.3 grams

Baked Pita Chips

5 whole wheat pita bread rounds or a sourdough baguette

Preheat oven to 400 degrees.

Using a pizza cutter, cut each pita bread round horizontally in half. Cut each half into 8 triangles. Arrange triangles in single layer on flat baking stone.

Bake 8-10 minutes or until slightly browned and crisp.

Makes 80 pita chips

 You can also use a thinly sliced sourdough baguette or crackers for serving if pressed for time.

Notes:

Avocado and Goat Cheese Spread with Crostini

Spread
> 1 ripe avocado
> 3 1/2 ounces goat cheese, softened
> 1 tablespoon fresh lemon juice
> 1 teaspoon extra virgin olive oil
> 2 dashes of hot pepper sauce
> 3 oil-packed sun-dried tomatoes, drained and chopped
> garlic salt and fresh ground pepper to taste

Crostini
> 1 sourdough baguette, cut into 1/4-inch thick slices
> extra-virgin olive oil
> fresh garlic cloves

Mash avocado with a fork until smooth. Add goat cheese and mix until creamy in texture. Add remaining ingredients.

Refrigerate until ready to use. Bring to room temperature before serving.

Preheat oven on broil setting.

Brush baguette slices with extra-virgin olive oil and toast lightly in oven set on broil, approximately 1 minute per side. Rub the toasted bread with a fresh garlic clove.

Serves: 6

Nutritional Information per Serving
Calories: 325, Fat: 12 grams, Protein: 12 grams, Carbohydrates: 42 grams, Cholesterol: 20 milligrams, Fiber: 3.9 grams

 It is easiest to chop sun-dried tomatoes by snipping with a kitchen scissors. Sun-dried tomatoes can be purchased dry or packed in oil. When not packed in oil, they need to be re-hydrated before using.

THE OVERTURE CENTER FOR THE ARTS

Madison is passionate about the arts, and the Overture Center for the Arts epitomizes that fact. Located in the heart of downtown Madison, the Overture Center anchors Madison's vibrant downtown with a cultural arts district that is the envy of many cities. The Overture Center, a world class performing and visual art center designed by renowned architect Cesar Pelli, is a blend of new and renovated spaces which provides a variety of venues for resident groups and visiting artists.

The Overture Hall seats 2,250 and is home to the Madison Symphony Orchestra, Madison Opera, Wisconsin Chamber Orchestra and Madison Ballet. To the delight of Broadway-loving Madisonians, this facility also enables large-scale theater productions to add Madison to their touring lists. A dramatic, one-of-a-kind, hand-made pipe organ with more than 4,000 pipes was custom-designed specifically for the acoustics and architecture of Overture Hall.

The Overture Center for the Arts was made possible by a generous donation from resident businessman, Jerry Frautschi. His gift of $100 million is the largest single donation for an arts project in the U.S.

The Overture Center for the Arts joins the State Capitol and the Monona Terrace Community and Convention Center as the architectural icons of the City.

Rose Bowl Cheddar Dip

Can be made the night before, store in airtight container

3/4 cup white cheddar cheese shredded
4 ounces low-fat cream cheese, softened
1/4 cup plain non-fat yogurt or sour cream
1/4 cup bottled roasted red peppers, diced
2 teaspoons hot pepper sauce
salt to taste
2 pieces bacon, cooked and crumbled
4 green onions, sliced

Blend cheeses, yogurt, red peppers, pepper sauce and salt in a food processor or blender until smooth. Set aside some bacon and green onions for garnish. Fold in remaining bacon and green onions. Chill at least one hour for flavors to marry.

Garnish dip with extra green onions and bacon. Serve with breadsticks, vegetables or chips.

Serves: 8

Nutritional Information per Serving
Calories: 110, Fat: 7 grams, Protein: 6 grams, Carbohydrates: 6 grams, Cholesterol: 25 milligrams, Fiber: 2 grams

 To save time use precooked bacon.

Notes:

 # Olive Salsa

1 (6 ounce) can black olives, chopped
1 (6 ounce)jar green olives, chopped
5 green onions, chopped
1 small (4.5 ounce) can green chilies, chopped
6 plum tomatoes chopped (add more or less to taste)
2 tablespoons olive oil
1 tablespoon vinegar
1 clove garlic, minced

Place all ingredients in food processor and pulse to desired consistency. For best results, make this a day ahead to marry the flavors. Serve with tortilla chips.

Store in air tight container in the refrigerator.

Serves: 16

Nutritional Information per Serving
Calories: 55, Fat: 3 grams, Protein: 1.5 grams, Carbohydrates: 7 grams, Cholesterol: 0 milligrams, Fiber: 1.7 grams

 If you're in a hurry, or don't have fresh tomatoes, you may substitute 2 (14.5 ounce) cans of diced tomatoes, drained.

Guacamole Dip

This is a wonderful appetizer for tailgating at Badger Football games!

2 large avocados, peeled and pitted
1 lime, juiced
1/4 cup minced white onion
1/4 cup chopped green onion
1 tablespoon olive oil
1 teaspoon minced garlic
1 teaspoon chili pepper
1 teaspoon salt

EXTRA VIRGIN OLIVE OIL:

Extra virgin olive oil will give your recipe better flavor and a less oily taste.

In a medium bowl mash avocados. Add remaining ingredients and mix well.

Cover and refrigerate 1-2 hours before serving.

Serves: 6

Nutritional Information per Serving
Calories: 118, Fat: 10 grams, Protein: 1 gram, Carbohydrates: 6 grams, Cholesterol: 0 milligrams, Fiber: 0 grams

 To keep the guacamole from turning brown, place an avocado pit in the dip until just prior to serving.

Salsa

5 green onions, finely chopped
2 cloves garlic, finely chopped
1 jalapeno pepper, finely chopped
1 tablespoon cilantro, finely chopped
2 tomatoes, finely chopped
1/2 teaspoon lime juice
1/2 teaspoon Tabasco sauce
salt to taste

In a small bowl mix all ingredients. Refrigerate for at least 1 hour.

Serves: 6

Nutritional Information per Serving
Calories: 50, Fat: o grams, Protein: 2 gram, Carbohydrates: 11 grams, Cholesterol: 0 milligrams, Fiber: 3.75 grams

Homemade Hummus

6 garlic cloves
2 1/2 cups chickpeas
1/2 cup tahini (Middle Eastern sesame paste)
3 tablespoons fresh lemon juice
3 tablespoons water
2 teaspoons kosher salt
1 teaspoon hot sauce, or to taste
olive oil

Mince garlic in food processor. Add chickpeas, tahini, lemon juice, water and salt. Puree until very smooth.

Serve in shallow dish. Circle olive oil over top of hummus. Place a few chickpeas on top for presentation.

Serve with whole wheat or regular pita bread.

Nutritional Information per Serving
Calories: 125, Fat: 6 grams, Protein: 4 grams, Carbohydrates: 14 grams,
Cholesterol: 0 milligrams, Fiber: 2.8 grams

AMERICAN PLAYERS THEATRE

American Players Theatre (APT) is an outdoor amphitheatre located in Spring Green, 40 miles west of Madison. The classical theatre sits on 110 acres of woods, near the Wisconsin River.

Founded in 1979, APT has continuously grown in popularity and now is the second most popular outdoor classical theatre in the country.

The outdoor venue offers a scenic picnic area for patrons to gather with friends to enjoy pre-theater feasts of wines, cheeses and fruits. Grills allow more ambitious guests to cook up their own tasty meals. While some choose to be catered to by one of several local restaurants that offer upscale box lunches.

As summer turns into fall and the air becomes cooler, APT holds a chili feast to close the curtain on another season.

Hot Crab and Shrimp Dip

1 pound lump crab meat
1 pound medium cooked shrimp, chopped
1/4 cup chopped celery
1/4 cup chopped onion
1/4 cup chopped green pepper
3/4 cup mayonnaise
2 teaspoons Worcestershire sauce
1 teaspoon lemon juice
1/2 teaspoon salt
dash cayenne pepper
1/2 cup soft bread crumbs
2 tablespoons melted butter

Preheat oven to 400 degrees.

Combine crab and shrimp in a medium bowl and set aside.

In another bowl, combine the celery, onion, green pepper, mayonnaise, Worcestershire sauce, lemon juice and salt. Fold into the crab and shrimp.

Place mixture in a 1 1/2-quart casserole dish. Top with the bread crumbs and drizzle with the melted butter.

Bake for 20-30 minutes, until bubbly. Serve with crackers or on a sliced sourdough baguette.

Serves: 16

Nutritional Information per Serving
Calories: 160, Fat: 10 grams, Protein: 12 grams, Carbohydrates: 5 grams, Cholesterol: 75 milligrams, Fiber: 0.4 grams

Notes:

Blue Cheese Pecan Spread

3 ounces low-fat cream cheese
4 ounces blue cheese, crumbled
1 tablespoon white wine
1/4 cup chopped pecans
1/2 teaspoon onion powder
1/2 teaspoon dill weed
1/4 pint whipping cream, whipped
small sourdough baguette

Preheat oven to 325 degrees.

In a small bowl, blend cheeses, wine and spices. In another bowl, prepare whipping cream. Add whipped cream to cheese mixture; then add pecans. Chill in refrigerator for 2-3 hours.

Slice baguette into 3/4-inch slices. Spread cheese mixture on baguette slices and warm in oven for about 10 minutes, until cheese is melted.

Serve warm or at room temperature.

Serves: 8

Nutritional Information per Serving
Calories: 218, Fat: 14 grams, Protein: 7 grams, Carbohydrates: 16 grams, Cholesterol: 38 milligrams, Fiber: 1.0 grams

 If you do not have whipping cream on hand, substitute 3-4 squirts of canned whipped cream.

MADISON MUSEUMS

Museum buffs can have a field day in Madison. From history to art to children's exhibits, the list of local museums offers something for everyone.

On the UW campus, the Elvehjem Museum of Art is Wisconsin's second largest art museum with more than 1,700 objects including artworks from 2300 B.C. to the present and representing cultures around the globe.

The Madison Children's Museum is a hands-on museum for kids. Changing exhibits, programs and outreach activities teach kids about art, science, culture and technology.

Madison Museum of Contemporary Art is an independent, non-profit museum committed to enhancing the appreciation and understanding of modern and contemporary art. The Art Center's six galleries feature more than 20 changing exhibitions each year, representing a range of local to international artists.

The State Historical Museum on Madison's Capitol Square contains permanent exhibits which depict significant aspects of life in Wisconsin while the Wisconsin Veteran's Museum honors the men and women of Wisconsin who have served their country in conflicts from the Civil War to the Persian Gulf War.

All in all, these fine museums are a tribute to the talent and history that make Wisconsin great.

Shrimp Sweet Potato Cakes with Chipotle Mayonnaise

1 pound tan-skinned sweet potatoes
4 large garlic cloves, unpeeled
4 tablespoons (or more) vegetable oil
8 ounces peeled cooked large shrimp, coarsely chopped
3/4 cup chopped fresh cilantro
2/3 cup fresh white breadcrumbs
3 tablespoons minced jalapeño or poblano chili
3 tablespoons minced red onion
1 1/2 teaspoons Latin Spice Mix
all-purpose flour

SERVING SUGGESTION:

Use a hollowed out red bell pepper as your serving dish.

Preheat oven to 350 degrees.

Pierce potatoes all over with fork. Place on baking sheet. Toss garlic with 1 tablespoon oil in small bowl. Enclose garlic in foil; place on baking sheet with potatoes. Bake until potatoes and garlic are tender, about 30 minutes for garlic and 1 hour 15 minutes for potatoes. Cool garlic and potatoes slightly.

Remove peel from garlic. Remove skins from potatoes. Combine potatoes and garlic in a large bowl. Mash until smooth.

Add shrimp, cilantro, breadcrumbs, chili, onion and 1 1/2 teaspoons Spice Mix. Stir to blend well. Season with salt. Form mixture into 1-inch-diameter patties.

Preheat oven to 375 degrees.

Lightly coat cakes in flour. Heat 3 tablespoons oil in heavy large skillet over medium-high heat. Cook cakes in batches until brown, adding more oil if necessary, about 2 minutes per side. Place on baking sheet. Bake until heated through, about 5 minutes.

Place 1 cake on each plate. Serve Chipotle Mayonnaise (page 17) beside cakes; garnish with sprig of cilantro.

Serves: 20

Nutritional Information per Serving
Calories: 71, Fat: 3 grams, Protein: 3.3 grams, Carbohydrates: 7.5 grams, Cholesterol: 23 milligrams, Fiber: 0.8 grams

Chipotle Mayonnaise

1 cup reduced-fat mayonnaise
1 1/2-2 tablespoons fresh lime juice
1 tablespoon canned chipotle chilies, minced
salt

Mix all ingredients in medium bowl to blend. Season to taste with salt.

Serves: 6

Nutritional Information per Serving
Calories: 265, Fat: 29 grams, Protein: 0 grams, Carbohydrates: 1 grams, Cholesterol: 20 milligrams, Fiber: 0 grams

 Consider adding 3 tablespoons small capers and/or two tablespoons sweet pickle relish for a different taste.

Fiesta Dip

16 ounces cream cheese, softened
1/4 cup lime juice
1 tablespoon ground cumin
1/2 teaspoon salt
dash of black pepper
1/4 cup vegetable oil
1 (16 ounce) can whole kernel corn, drained
1 cup chopped pecans
1 small white onion, finely chopped
1/4 cup finely chopped red bell pepper
tortilla chips

Using an electric mixer, beat cream cheese, lime juice, cumin, salt, pepper and oil until blended. Fold in corn, pecans, onions and red pepper. Serve with tortilla chips. Unused portion may be stored in the refrigerator for up to 1 week.

Serves: 16

Nutritional Information per Serving
Calories: 180, Fat: 16 grams, Protein: 3 grams, Carbohydrates: 6 grams, Cholesterol: 30 milligrams, Fiber: 0.7 grams

Mediterranean Tapenade

1 (15 ounce) jar roasted red peppers, drained and chopped
1 (15 ounce) jar pitted kalamata olives, drained and chopped
1 (3.5 ounce) jar capers, drained
4 tablespoons chopped red onion
3 tablespoons balsamic vinegar
2 tablespoons extra virgin olive oil
oregano to taste
salt and pepper to taste
11 ounces goat cheese

Preheat oven to 350 degrees.

In a small bowl, combine red peppers, olives, capers, red onion, balsamic vinegar, olive oil and seasonings.

Place the goat cheese on an ovenproof platter and spoon tapenade over the top. Bake for 10 minutes.

Serve with sliced bread rounds or crackers with a spoon.

Serves: 20

Nutritional Information per Serving
Calories: 180, Fat: 14 grams, Protein: 10 grams, Carbohydrates: 3 grams, Cholesterol: 30 milligrams, Fiber: 0.5 grams

Notes:

Brie with Port Wine and Cherry Sauce

Can make sauce and bread toasts up to three days ahead.

48 slices of French bread, from a long baguette,
sliced approximately 1/4 inch thick

1 cup port wine
1/2 cup dried cherries
2 tablespoons sugar
1 (8-10 ounce) round of brie
1 egg, beaten
1/4 cup fine bread crumbs
2 tablespoons butter
2 ounces bleu cheese, crumbled (optional)
1 tablespoon chives or scallions, sliced

Preheat oven to 375 degrees.

Place bread slices in a single layer on a baking sheet. Toast for 10 minutes or until toasted and just turning golden near the edges. Remove from the oven; set aside.

In a heavy saucepan, boil the port wine and sugar for 10 minutes or until it starts to thicken into syrup. Add the dried cherries and cook for two minutes. Remove from heat.

Dip the round of brie in the egg to coat all sides. Coat with bread crumbs.

Melt butter in heated sauté pan. Add the brie and cook until golden brown on both sides.

Place brie on a serving platter or plate. Top with the port wine cherry sauce. Crumble bleu cheese on top and sprinkle the chives or scallions over for garnish.

Serve with French baguette slices.

Serves: 24

Nutritional Information per Serving
Calories: 80, Fat: 5 grams, Protein: 2.5 grams, Carbohydrates: 8 grams,
Cholesterol: 20 milligrams, Fiber: 0.2 grams

DINNER & A MOVIE

Need a fun party idea? Honor famous Madison-based, movies, actors, producers or directors by hosting a "Madison Movie Night." You'll have plenty of comedy classics to choose from.

Consider movies by UW-Madison classmates Jerry and David Zucker and Jim Abrahams who drew from their time in Madison's Kentucky Fried Theater to produce their first feature film, "Kentucky Fried Movie." The trio went on to create "Airplane" and the "Naked Gun" trilogy.

The late Chris Farley, former Saturday Night Live standout and star of several movies, was born and raised in Madison. View any of his movies including "Tommy Boy," "Black Sheep" and "Beverly Hills Ninja" for a heaping helping of laughter.

Or watch old reruns of the General Lee, Daisy Duke, Boss Hogg and the good old boys from "Dukes of Hazzard." Tom Wopat, a.k.a. Luke Duke, is a native of Lodi, located about 20 miles from Madison, and attended the University of Wisconsin.

The movie "Back to School" was filmed on the picturesque University of Wisconsin-Madison campus.

Saganaki

This is a fun, interactive appetizer which will get guests attention. Kasseri is a Greek cheese made from sheep or goat milk. It has a sharp, salty flavor and hard cheddar-like texture that's perfect for grating. If you cannot find it, substitute with Pecorino Romano cheese.

   1/2 pound Kasseri cheese
   1 ounce, or more, brandy
   1/4 cup olive oil
   1/2 cup flour
   1 lemon, cut into wedges
   1 loaf good quality French bread, sliced

Cut Kasseri cheese into 1/4-inch thick slices. Place flour on plate. Coat cheese with flour on both sides. In a medium, non-stick pan heat olive oil until hot. Fry cheese in olive oil for about 1 minute and flip to fry the other side.

After cheese has been fried, pour about 1 ounce of brandy in skillet. Quickly light match and ignite alcohol. Quickly put flame out with lemon wedges. Cheese will have crisped up and browned on the edges. Transfer cheese to plate and cut into sections that will fit nicely onto baguette.

Serves: 6

Nutritional Information per Serving
Calories: 440, Fat: 33 grams, Protein: 19 grams, Carbohydrates: 16 grams, Cholesterol: 60 milligrams, Fiber: 0 grams

 Serve this with a Greek salad and a bottle of wine for a great meal.

Notes:

Endive with Goat Cheese and Mandarin Oranges

1/3 cup coarsely chopped walnuts
2 tablespoons honey
cooking spray
1/4 cup balsamic vinegar
3 tablespoons orange juice
16 Belgian endive leaves, about 2 heads
11 ounce can mandarin oranges
1/3 cup (1 1/2 ounces) crumbled goat cheese
1 tablespoon minced fresh chives
1/4 teaspoon cracked black pepper

Preheat oven to 350 degrees.

Combine walnuts and 1 tablespoon honey. Spread on a baking sheet coated with cooking spray. Bake for 5 minutes; stir mixture and return to oven for 5 more minutes.

Combine 1 tablespoon honey, vinegar and orange juice in a small saucepan. Bring mixture to a boil over high heat and cook until reduced to 3 tablespoons, about 5 minutes.

Fill each endive leaf with 1 mandarin orange section. Top each section with 1 tablespoon cheese and 1 tablespoon walnuts; arrange on a plate. Drizzle the vinegar mixture evenly over leaves and sprinkle evenly with chives and pepper.

Serves: 8

Nutritional Information per Serving
Calories: 70, Fat: 3 grams, Protein: 3 grams, Carbohydrates: 12 grams,
Cholesterol: 5 milligrams, Fiber: 2.5 grams

THE RINGLING BROTHERS CIRCUS

Ringling is one of the most famous circus names in America, along with Barnum and Bailey. It was in Baraboo, Wisconsin, a small town a short drive from Madison that the Ringling tent circus began in 1884.

Alf T. Ringling, Al Ringling, Charles Ringling, John Ringling, and Otto Ringling soon became known as Kings Of The Circus World. By 1889 two additional brothers had joined the show, which was now playing cities in Wisconsin and Illinois. This was also the year that the brothers decided to purchase railroad cars and become a railroad circus. At that time admission was 50¢ for adults and 25¢ for children.

In 1907, the Ringlings purchased Barnum & Bailey Circus and eventually merged the two shows creating, beyond a doubt, the "Greatest Show on Earth."

Today the Circus World Museum is located at the site of the original Ringling Brothers Circus Winter Quarters in Baraboo. Nearly 100,000 circus lovers visit the museum each year to relive the magic and enjoy an educational and fun family experience.

West Coast Pizza

A great new way to prepare pizza - on the grill!

Dough
- 1 cup warm water (105-115 degrees F)
- 1 tablespoon sugar
- 1 envelope dry yeast
- 3 tablespoons olive oil
- 3 cups (or more) flour
- 1 1/2 teaspoons salt
- 1 tablespoon chopped fresh rosemary

Sauce
- 3/4 cup olive oil
- 6 tablespoons balsamic vinegar
- 3 tablespoons minced garlic
- 2 tablespoons chopped fresh rosemary
- 2 yellow or red bell peppers, cored, quartered lengthwise
- 1 large red onion, peeled, cut through root end into 1/2 inch thick wedges

Topping
- 2 cups grated mozzarella cheese
- 1-1/2 cup freshly grated Parmesan cheese
- 2 cups crumbled chilled soft fresh goat cheese
- 4 plum tomatoes, seeded and chopped

Dough:
Combine water and sugar in processor. Sprinkle yeast over, let stand until foamy, about 10 minutes. Add oil, then 3 cups flour and salt. Process until dough comes together, about 1 minute. Turn dough out onto floured work surface. Sprinkle with rosemary. Knead until dough is smooth and elastic, adding more flour by tablespoonfuls if dough is sticky, about 5 minutes. Lightly oil large bowl. Add dough; turn to coat with oil. Cover bowl with plastic, then towel. Let stand in warm draft-free area until dough doubles, about 1 hour.

Punch down dough. Knead dough in bowl until smooth, about 2 minutes.

Sauce:
Whisk first 4 ingredients in medium bowl. Let vinaigrette stand 15 minutes at room temperature or refrigerate up to 2 hours.

Prepare barbeque to medium heat. Arrange peppers and onions on baking sheet. Brush with some of vinaigrette. Sprinkle with salt and pepper. Grill until slightly charred and crisp-tender, turning and basting occasionally, about 8 minutes. Transfer to a cutting board and cut peppers and onions into thin strips.

Divide dough into 4 equal pieces. Stretch out each piece on floured surface to

Notes:

9-inch round. Place 2 dough rounds on grill. Keep remaining 2 rounds covered until ready to grill. Grill over medium heat until top of dough puffs and underside is crisp, about 3 minutes. Turn rounds over. Grill 1 minute. Transfer to baking sheet with well-grilled side up. Repeat with remaining 2 dough rounds. Sprinkle each with 1/4 of mozzarella and Parmesan. Top each with 1/4 of the peppers and onions, then with 1/4 of goat cheese and tomatoes. Drizzle each with 1 1/2 tablespoons vinaigrette.

Using large metal spatula, return 2 pizzas to grill. Close grill or cover pizzas loosely with foil. Grill until cheese melts and dough is cooked through and browned, using tongs to rotate pizzas for even cooking, about 5 minutes. Transfer to plates. Repeat grilling for remaining 2 pizzas.

Serves: 8

Nutritional Information per Serving
Calories: 650, Fat: 43 grams, Protein: 20 grams, Carbohydrates: 45 grams, Cholesterol: 55 milligrams, Fiber: 1.4 grams

Bacon Tomato Cups

9 bacon slices (1/2 pound), cooked and crumbled
1 large tomato, finely chopped
1/4 cup finely chopped white onion
3/4 cup shredded Swiss cheese
1/2 teaspoon minced garlic
1/2 cup mayonnaise
1 teaspoon dried basil
1 (7.5 ounce) can refrigerated flaky biscuits

Preheat oven to 375 degrees. Grease mini-muffin pans.

Combine bacon, tomato, onion, cheese, garlic, mayonnaise and basil. Separate each biscuit into 3 thinner ones. Press biscuit pieces into miniature muffin pan cups. Fill biscuit shells evenly with tomato mixture.

Bake 10-12 minutes or until bubbly.

Makes 24 appetizers

Nutritional Information per Serving (2 cups)
Calories: 195, Fat: 15 grams, Protein: 7 grams, Carbohydrates: 8 grams, Cholesterol: 20 milligrams, Fiber: 0.2 grams

Swiss Cheese Zucchini Tart

Pastry
1 1/2 cups flour
6 teaspoons fresh thyme or 1 teaspoon dried thyme
1/2 teaspoon black pepper
1/2 teaspoon salt
8 tablespoons chilled butter
2-4 tablespoons ice water

Filling
1 tablespoon olive oil
1 tablespoon butter
1 cup sliced onions
3 cups zucchini, cut in fine julienne
1 1/2 tablespoons fresh basil or 1 1/2 teaspoons dried basil
1/2 teaspoon thyme
2 cloves garlic, minced
salt and pepper to taste
1 cup grated Swiss cheese

Preheat oven to 400 degrees.

Blend flour, thyme, pepper and salt in a processor. Using on/off turns, cut in butter until pea-size pieces form. With machine running, add enough ice water by tablespoonfuls to form moist clumps. Gather dough into ball; flatten into disk. Chill, wrapped in plastic wrap, until firm, at least 1 hour. (May refrigerate in an airtight container up to 3 days.)

For the filling, heat the oil over medium heat; add the butter. Once butter has melted add the onions and zucchini. Cook over medium heat until the onions are translucent and the liquid from the zucchini has nearly evaporated, 5-8 minutes. Add basil, thyme and garlic and stir for 2 minutes. Salt and pepper to taste. Set aside. (May refrigerate in an airtight container up to 3 days.)

On a floured surface, roll the dough into a circle approximately 12 inches in diameter. Place in a 10-12-inch tart pan. If you do not have a large enough tart pan, place on a cookie sheet. (If the cookie sheet is not Teflon-coated, use parchment paper to cover it.) Crimp the edges and prick the bottom with the tines of a fork approximately 20 times. Bake until a light golden brown, approximately 15 minutes.

Notes:

Remove from the oven and reduce oven temperature to 350 degrees.

Sprinkle the cheese evenly over the pastry. Top with the zucchini mixture. Spread evenly. Bake until well heated and cheese has melted, approximately 15 minutes.

Garnish with fresh thyme or basil.

Serves: 6

Nutritional Information per Serving
Calories: 385, Fat: 25 grams, Protein: 10 grams, Carbohydrates: 30 grams, Cholesterol: 60 milligrams, Fiber: 1.4 grams

 During its off season, zucchini may be bitter. In this recipe you can counteract the bitterness of the zucchini by peeling off the skin and adding the two teaspoons of lemon juice.

Yummy Stuffed Mushrooms

This easy microwave recipe makes the mushrooms very tender in a fraction of the time!

1/2 pound large fresh mushrooms
4 slices bacon, cooked and crumbled
4 ounces cream cheese, softened
2 tablespoons minced onion
1/2 cup bread crumbs
2 tablespoons melted butter

Wash and dry mushrooms. Twist stems off and chop to make 1/2 cup; set aside.

In a small bowl, cream the cheese; add bacon, onions and chopped mushroom stems. Drop butter by 1/8 teaspoon in the bottom of each mushroom cap and then fill with mixture.

Place in microwave safe dish and cover. Cook on high power for 5 minutes. Allow to rest for 3-5 minutes, covered.

When ready to serve, remove cover and microwave 2-3 more minutes until bubbly.

Serves: 6

Nutritional Information per Serving
Calories: 170, Fat: 13 grams, Protein: 4 grams, Carbohydrates: 9 grams, Cholesterol: 35 milligrams, Fiber: 0.9 grams

Tantalizing Tomato-Pesto Tartlets

Great for unexpected company. A hit every time!

1/3 cup reduced-fat mayonnaise
1/4 cup grated mozarella cheese
3 tablespoons grated Parmesan cheese
2 teaspoons basil pesto
1/8 teaspoon cracked black pepper
2 plum tomatoes, chopped
1 package mini tart shells (2.1 ounce shells)

Preheat oven to 375 degrees.

Mix first five ingredients in small bowl. Fold in tomatoes; mix well. Spoon mixture into mini tart shells.

Bake for 10-12 minutes, until bubbly and golden brown.

Makes 15 tarts

Nutritional Information per Tart
Calories: 265, Fat: 18 grams, Protein: 4 grams, Carbohydrates: 22 grams, Cholesterol: 5 milligrams, Fiber: 0.2 grams

 If you don't have time to make fresh pesto, substitute prepared.

Notes:

 # Mushroom Strudel

2 leeks, cleaned thoroughly
2 tablespoons plus 1/4 cup melted butter
12 sheets phyllo dough, thawed
1/2 pound shiitake mushrooms, finely chopped
1/2 pound brown mushrooms, finely chopped
1/2 pound portabella mushrooms, finely chopped
1 tablespoon fresh thyme or 1 teaspoon dried
3/4 cup beef stock
1/2 cup cream
1/2 cup hazelnuts, finely chopped
3 tablespoons fresh parsley, finely chopped
1 cup sour cream

Finely chop white portion of leeks to make 2 tablespoons. Sauté leeks in 2 tablespoons butter for 5 minutes in large pan. Add all the mushrooms to the leeks with thyme and salt and pepper to taste. Sauté until mushrooms have rendered all their juices. Add beef broth and cook over high heat until liquid is reduced. About 7 minutes. Add cream and cook until cream thickens and binds mixture together. Remove from heat and stir in parsley. Set aside to cool.

Place sheet of phyllo dough on flat surface and brush with melted butter. Top with another sheet of phyllo dough and brush with butter. Sprinkle with 1/4 of the nuts. Repeat this pattern until all the dough and nuts have been used. Spread the mushroom mixture in the middle of the strudel and leave a 3 inch boarder around the edge. Roll up the dough jelly roll style. Brush seams with butter to seal. Place roll on a cookie sheet. Cover with plastic wrap and chill for 1 1/2 hours. Slice chilled roll in 1/2 inch slices and place on a cookie sheet and bake flat at 375 degrees. for 30 minutes or until golden brown. Serve hot or at room temperature. Serve with sour cream as a garnish.

Serves: 10

Nutritional Information per Serving
Calories: 355, Fat: 22 grams, Protein: 8 grams, Carbohydrates: 31 grams, Cholesterol: 40 milligrams, Fiber: 1.6 grams

 This is a very elegant and tasty appetizer but it is time consuming. When time is a factor the filling can be made in advance and then warmed up in the microwave and served as a dip for crackers. The filling can be used in frozen puff pastry shells too.

Beer Cheese Fondue

This appetizer highlights the great local cheeses from Wisconsin.

1 clove garlic
1 pound well-aged sharp cheddar cheese
3 tablespoons flour
2 teaspoons Worcestershire sauce
1/2 teaspoon dry mustard
2 cups beer
hot sauce to taste
2 tablespoons chopped chives
1 sourdough baguette, cubed

Rub the inside of your fondue pot with garlic then discard.

Toss the cheese in flour until lightly coated. Pour 1 1/2 cups of beer into fondue pot and heat until almost boiling.

Add the cheese by handfuls making sure that each addition has melted and blended completely before adding more. Add remaining 1/2 cup beer if fondue is too thick. When all cheese has melted and the mixture is smooth and thick, stir in the Worcestershire sauce, dry mustard and hot sauce.

Garnish with chives. Serve with bread cubes for dipping.

Serves: 8

Nutritional Information per Serving
Calories: 260, Fat: 19 grams, Protein: 15 grams, Carbohydrates: 7 grams, Cholesterol: 60 milligrams, Fiber: 0.2 grams

Notes:

Summer Ceviche

2 pounds medium-small shrimp, peeled and deveined
kosher salt
1 cup fresh lime juice (about 4 limes)
1 cup fresh lemon juice (about 4 lemons)
1/2 cup fresh orange juice (about 1 orange)
2 large tomatoes, diced
1 red onion, diced
1/2 bunch cilantro, stemmed and roughly chopped
1 serrano chili, finely chopped
2 large avocados, peeled and diced
1 large cucumber, peeled and diced
tortilla chips for garnish

Add the shrimp to a large pot of boiling, salted water and simmer until just cooked through (approximately 5 minutes). Using a slotted spoon transfer the shrimp to a bowl of ice water to chill.

Drain the shrimp; cut into bite-size pieces and transfer to a large bowl. Add the juices, stir to combine and refrigerate for at least 4 hours and up to 6.

Add the tomato, onion, cilantro and chili to the shrimp mixture and let sit at room temperature for about 20 minutes.

When ready to serve gently stir in the avocado and cucumber. Line the sides of 8 chilled martini glasses with tortilla chips and add the ceviche using a slotted spoon.

Serves: 8

Nutritional Information per Serving
Calories: 300, Fat: 12 grams, Protein: 26 grams, Carbohydrates: 23 grams, Cholesterol: 175 milligrams, Fiber: 4.2 grams

 You can substitute frozen, uncooked shrimp if fresh is not available.

Clam Puffs

12 ounces cream cheese, softened
1/2 teaspoon hot pepper sauce
1 teaspoon Worcestershire sauce
1 tablespoon lemon juice
1 tablespoon clam juice
1 clove garlic, minced
3 (8 ounce) cans of chopped clams, drained, juice reserved
1/2 cup butter
1 cup flour
4 large eggs, room temperature

Preheat oven to 400 degrees.

In a medium bowl mix the cream cheese, hot pepper sauce, Worcestershire sauce, lemon juice, clam juice and garlic. Fold in the clams and set aside.

Notes:

Heat 1 cup of the reserved clam juice (add water if you do not have enough for a cup) in a pan over low heat; add the butter and bring to a boil. Add the flour all at once and stir vigorously over low heat until mixture leaves sides of pan. Add the eggs one at a time beating after each egg.

Drop batter by rounded teaspoons 1 1/2 inches apart onto ungreased baking sheets.

Bake for 10 minutes. Reduce the heat to 300 degrees and bake for an additional 20-25 minutes.

Transfer puffs to rack and cool. Cut puffs in half and fill with cream cheese and clam mixture. Puffs can be frozen. Defrost and fill just prior to serving.

Makes about 72 puffs

Nutritional Information per Serving (2 puffs)
Calories: 100, Fat: 6 grams, Protein: 6 grams, Carbohydrates: 4 grams, Cholesterol: 50 milligrams, Fiber: 0 grams

 Tunarific Dip

Make a day in advance for best flavor.

6 ounce can albacore tuna, drained
8 ounces cream cheese, softened
1 tablespoon grated onion
1/2 cup mayonnaise
1 tablespoon Tabasco sauce
2 tablespoons chopped fresh parsley
1 teaspoon lemon pepper seasoning
1 tablespoon Worcestershire sauce
1 tablespoon fresh lemon juice
1 tablespoon grated Parmesan cheese

Mix all ingredients together. Chill 8-10 hours or overnight. Serve cold with crackers.

Serves: 16

Nutritional Information per Serving
Calories: 110, Fat: 10 grams, Protein: 4 grams, Carbohydrates: 1 grams,
Cholesterol: 20 milligrams, Fiber: 0.1 grams

Crab Wontons

8 ounces crabmeat
8 ounces cream cheese, softened
1/4 teaspoon garlic powder
1/4 teaspoon seasoned salt
1 (12 ounce) package wonton wrappers
water for moistening wonton wrappers
2 cups vegetable oil for frying
sweet & sour sauce or mustard sauce for dipping

Combine the crabmeat, cream cheese, garlic powder and salt.

Lay 1 wonton wrapper on work surface. Place 1/2 teaspoon of crabmeat mixture in the middle of each wonton wrapper. Fold points of wrapper over to form a triangle, sealing the last point with a touch of water on your fingertip. Deep fry until light golden brown.

Serve hot with sweet and sour sauce or hot mustard sauce.

Makes 45 wontons

Nutritional Information per Serving (2 wontons)
Calories: 120, Fat: 8 grams, Protein: 4 grams, Carbohydrates: 8 grams,
Cholesterol: 20 milligrams, Fiber: 0 grams

Chicken Satay with Spicy Peanut Sauce

These delicious appetizers disappear fast.

Marinade

1 1/4 pounds boneless, skinless chicken breast
1/4 cup sherry
1/4 cup soy sauce
2 tablespoons corn oil
2 tablespoons sesame oil
2 tablespoons lemon juice
2 teaspoons minced garlic
2 teaspoons minced ginger
1/4 teaspoon salt
1/4 teaspoon fresh ground black pepper
2 dashes hot pepper sauce

Notes:

Peanut Sauce

4 teaspoons corn oil
2 teaspoons sesame oil
2 tablespoons minced garlic
1/2 tablespoon minced red onion
1 1/2 teaspoons minced ginger
1 tablespoon red wine vinegar
1 tablespoon brown sugar
1/3 cup creamy peanut butter
1/2 teaspoon ground coriander
3 tablespoons soy sauce
1 tablespoon fresh lime or lemon juice
1/2 teaspoon fresh ground pepper
1 dash hot pepper sauce
1/3-1/2 cup hot water
1/2 teaspoon turmeric for color (optional)

16 wooden skewers, soaked in water 30 minutes

Marinade:
Cut the chicken into 1/2 inch wide by 3 inches long strips. Combine remaining ingredients and pour over over chicken. Marinate in the refrigerator for 1-3 hours.

Preheat the oven to 375 degrees.

Sauce: Heat the corn and sesame oils in a small saucepan. Add the garlic, onion and ginger. Sauté over medium heat until softened. Add the vinegar and brown sugar, continue to cook and stir until sugar dissolves. Remove from heat and stir in remaining ingredients (or combine in a food processor for a completely smooth sauce).

Thread each piece of chicken onto skewers and arrange on baking sheets. Discard marinade. Bake for 5-10 minutes or until just cooked. Serve hot with bowl of room temperature sauce for dipping.

Makes 16 skewers

Nutritional Information per Serving
Calories: 115, Fat: 8 grams, Protein: 8 grams, Carbohydrates: 3 grams, Cholesterol: 16 milligrams, Fiber: 0.4 grams

 Since the sauce can be made in advance, it may thicken or separate before you use it. Whisk in a little hot water until the sauce is the consistency you desire.

ART FAIR ON THE SQUARE

For over forty-five years, Madisonians have been flocking to the scenic Capitol Square to enjoy the warm July weather and vibrant works of art at the annual Art Fair on the Square.

Each summer over 200,000 enthusiastic art collectors gather the second weekend in July to experience a unique and large selection of fine, handcrafted work including ceramics, glasswork, drawings, jewelry, leather, paintings, photography, sculptures and woodwork.

In addition to the works of over 500 artists from across the country, fairgoers enjoy live music, succulent ethnic food and several family-oriented activities.

This spectacular cultural event is one of the top-rated art fairs in the country. Proceeds go to support the Madison Museum of Contemporary Art's year-round free exhibitions and programs.

 Spicy Pork Wonton Cups

Sauce

- 1/2 cup hoisin sauce
- 3 tablespoons frozen orange juice concentrate, thawed
- 2 green onions, minced
- 1 tablespoon chili-garlic sauce
- 1 teaspoon (packed) grated orange peel

Filling

- 1 1/4 pounds ground pork, browned, drained
- 2 large green onions, chopped
- 3 large garlic cloves, finely chopped
- 2 tablespoons hoisin sauce
- 1 1/2 tablespoons fresh ginger, minced and peeled
- 1 tablespoon soy sauce
- 1 tablespoon sesame oil
- 1 1/2 teaspoons (packed) grated orange peel
- 1 teaspoon salt
- 1 large egg yolk

- 1 12 ounce package wonton wrappers
- vegetable oil

PEELING GINGER:

To peel ginger, use a small, sharp paring knife or potato peeler.

Preheat to 475 degrees.

Sauce: Mix all ingredients in a small bowl. Season to taste with salt and pepper. (Can be prepared up to 2 days ahead; cover and refrigerate.)

Filling: Mix first 10 ingredients in medium bowl.

Position rack in bottom third of oven.

Place a wonton wrapper on a flat work surface; brush one side with vegetable oil. Fill wonton with 1 heaping teaspoon of pork filling. Gently press sides of wonton up and together, pinching into four corners, so that a square-shaped cup is formed. Do not fully enclose pork mixture. Repeat process for each wonton.

Place wontons on baking sheets and bake until wonton is crisp and filling is cooked through, about 15 minutes. (Can be made 1 day ahead. Refrigerate until cool, then cover and chill. Re-warm uncovered on a baking sheet in 475 degree oven until heated through, about 12 minutes.)

Transfer to platter. Spoon orange-hoisin sauce atop wonton cups.

Makes 24 wonton cups

Nutritional Information per Serving (2 wonton cups)
Calories: 300, Fat: 16 grams, Protein: 16 grams, Carbohydrates: 24 grams, Cholesterol: 60 milligrams, Fiber: 1.4 grams

Marinated Pork Tenderloin

2 pork tenderloins (about 1 1/2 – 2 pounds total)
1/2 cup soy sauce
3 tablespoons sugar
4 tablespoons minced onion
4 cloves garlic, minced
2 teaspoons ground ginger
3/4 cup sesame seeds
2 tablespoons oil

Preheat oven to 375 degrees.

Trim the fat from the tenderloins. If thick, split lengthwise. Place in a large glass baking dish.

Combine soy sauce, sugar, onion, garlic, ginger and sesame seeds in a small bowl. Pour over pork. Marinate the pork in the mixture 3 hours in the refrigerator, turning and basting frequently. Remove pork and transfer the marinade to a small saucepan.

Transfer the pork to an oiled roasting pan and roast until tender, about 45 minutes.

Simmer the marinade 10 minutes. Cut the pork into thin slices and serve on cocktail picks with the marinade in a small bowl.

Serves: 20

Nutritional Information per Serving
Calories: 170, Fat: 8 grams, Protein: 23 grams, Carbohydrates: 3 grams, Cholesterol: 40 milligrams, Fiber: 0.1 grams

Baked Chinese Egg Rolls

This is a wonderful appetizer that will be a big hit at your next get-together!

Filling
> 1 cup coarsely chopped celery
> 1 cup coarsely chopped carrot
> 1/2 cup chopped water chestnuts
> 2 cups shredded cabbage
> 1/2 teaspoon vegetable oil
> 1 cup onion, finely chopped
> 1/2 teaspoon fresh ginger, minced and peeled
> 1 clove garlic, minced
> 1/2 pound ground pork sausage
> 2 tablespoons low-sodium soy sauce
> 1/4 teaspoon black pepper
> 16 egg roll wrappers
> cooking spray
> 1 egg white

Notes:

Sauce
> 3/4 cup low-sodium soy sauce
> 6 tablespoons rice vinegar
> 2 tablespoons dark sesame oil
> 1 tablespoon fresh ginger, minced and peeled
> 1/3 cup thinly sliced green onions

Preheat oven to 425 degrees.

Combine celery, carrots and water chestnuts in food processor and pulse 10 times or until finely chopped. Transfer celery mixture to a medium, microwave-safe casserole with lid; add cabbage. Microwave at high for 5 minutes; drain. Set aside.

Heat oil in a large nonstick skillet over medium-high heat. Add onion, 1/2 teaspoon ginger and garlic; sauté 2 minutes. Add pork; cook 5 minutes. Remove from heat. Transfer to large bowl. Stir in cabbage mixture, 1 1/2 tablespoons soy sauce and pepper. Cover and chill 15 minutes.

Place one egg roll wrapper on work surface with one corner pointing toward you, in a diamond shape. Spoon 3 tablespoons sausage filling into center of wrapper. Fold the bottom corner over the filling and roll upwards one turn so the filling is completely encased. Moisten the left and right corners of the triangle with egg white, fold in the corners and press down firmly to seal, creating an envelope. Moisten the top corner of the skin with beaten egg and give one more turn, sealing the cylinder. Repeat procedure with remaining wrappers, sausage filling and egg white.

Place egg rolls seam side down on baking sheet; lightly coat egg rolls with cooking spray. Bake for 16 minutes or until golden brown.

In a small bowl, combine all sauce ingredients. Serve with egg rolls.

Serves: 16

Nutritional Information per Serving
Calories: 80, Fat: 3 grams, Protein: 4 grams, Carbohydrates: 9 grams, Cholesterol: 10 milligrams, Fiber: 1.0 grams

Fresh unpeeled gingerroot, tightly wrapped, can be kept in your freezer for up to 6 months. To use, slice off a piece of the unthawed root and return the rest to the freezer.

Shooting Stars

2 cups (1 pound) cooked crumbled sausage, drained
1 1/2 cups grated sharp cheddar cheese
1 1/2 cups grated Monterey Jack cheese
3/4 cup prepared ranch dressing
1/2 (2.25 ounces) can sliced black olives
1/2 cup chopped red pepper
24 wonton wrappers, thawed if frozen
vegetable oil

Preheat oven to 350 degrees.

In a medium bowl combine sausage with cheeses, salad dressing, olives and red pepper. Lightly grease a regular muffin tin and press 1 wonton wrapper in each cup. Brush each wrapper with oil.

Bake 5 minutes or until golden. Remove wontons from tins and place on baking sheet. Fill with sausage mixture. Bake 5 minutes or until bubbly.

Makes: 24 stars

Nutritional Information per Serving (2 stars)
Calories: 400, Fat: 34 grams, Protein: 14 grams, Carbohydrates: 10 grams, Cholesterol: 60 milligrams, Fiber: 0.1 grams

For a more delicate appetizer, cut the wontons on a diagonal and place them in mini muffin tins.

Moroccan Beef Purses with Chutney Sauce

These are labor intensive, but can be made in advance and are worth the time.

1/2 cup plain low-fat yogurt
1/2 cup mango chutney
1 pound ground chuck
1/2 cup chopped onion
1/3 cup dried currants
1/2 teaspoon salt
1/2 teaspoon ground cumin
1/4 teaspoon ground nutmeg
1/4 teaspoon ground cinnamon
1/8 teaspoon ground red pepper
1/8 teaspoon black pepper
1/2 cup water
1 tablespoon cornstarch
15 sheets frozen phyllo dough, thawed
butter-flavored vegetable cooking spray

CURRANTS:

If you do not have currants, substitute raisins.

Combine yogurt and mango chutney in a bowl; stir well and refrigerate until ready to use.

Cook ground beef and onion in a large nonstick skillet over medium heat until browned, stirring to crumble. Drain meat mixture in a colander; wipe drippings from skillet with a paper towel.

Return meat mixture to skillet. Add currants, salt, cumin, nutmeg, cinnamon and both peppers; stir well. In a small bowl, combine water and cornstarch; stir well. Add to the meat mixture. Cook over medium heat 2 minutes, stirring constantly. Remove from heat; set aside.

Preheat oven to 400 degrees.

Working with 1 phyllo sheet at a time, cut each sheet lengthwise into 4 (3 1/2-inch-wide) strips; lightly coat strips with cooking spray (cover remaining phyllo dough to keep it from drying out). Stack 2 strips and spoon about 1 tablespoon meat mixture onto one end of stack. Fold the left bottom corner over mixture, forming a triangle; keep folding back and forth into a triangle to end of strip. Repeat with remaining phyllo and meat mixture. (Can be made up to 1 week in advance. Freeze or refrigerate. Bring to room temperature before cooking.)

Place triangles, seam sides down, on a baking sheet lightly coated with cooking spray. Bake for 12 minutes or until golden. Serve warm with chutney sauce.

Makes: 60 triangles

Nutritional Information per Serving (2 triangles)
Calories: 130, Fat: 6 grams, Protein: 6 grams, Carbohydrates: 12 grams, Cholesterol: 10 milligrams, Fiber: 0.4 grams

Tenderloin Supreme

2 pounds beef tenderloin
1/4 cup red wine vinegar
2 teaspoons Dijon mustard
2 teaspoons salt
1/4 cup vegetable oil
1/4 cup olive oil
1 medium red onion
1 avocado
1/4 cup chopped parsley
1 sourdough or French baguette

Preheat oven to 375 degrees.

Cook tenderloin on a broiler pan for 30 minutes for medium-rare, up to 45 minutes for medium-well.

Cool tenderloin for about 10 minutes and slice thin. While meat is cooling, prepare marinade.

Place vinegar, mustard, salt and half of sliced red onion in bowl. Whisk in oils until well mixed.

Arrange meat in shallow container or place in a large zip-lock bag and pour marinade over meat. Cover and refrigerate several hours or overnight, spooning marinade over meat several times.

Thinly slice remaining red onion and avocado. On a large serving platter, arrange meat and then layer with onions and avocados.

Garnish with chopped parsley and serve with sliced baguette. This makes a festive and heartier appetizer, or main dish for special gatherings.

Serves: 8

Nutritional Information per Serving
Calories: 590, Fat: 34 grams, Protein: 38 grams, Carbohydrates: 33 grams, Cholesterol: 90 milligrams, Fiber: 3.2 grams

Appetizer Meatballs

Meatballs:

1 pound ground beef
1 egg
1/2 cup soft bread crumbs
1/4 cup milk
1/3 cup finely chopped onion
1 teaspoon Worcestershire sauce
salt and pepper to taste

Sauce:

1 teaspoon cayenne pepper
1 clove garlic, minced
1/2 cup ketchup
1/2 cup chopped onion
1/3 cup sugar
1/3 cup balsamic vinegar
1 tablespoon Worcestershire sauce
1/8-teaspoon pepper

Preheat oven to 350 degrees.

Combine the first 7 ingredients; mix well. Shape into 1-inch balls. In a skillet over medium heat, brown meatballs; drain. Place in a 2-1/2 quart baking dish.

In a small bowl combine sauce ingredients. Pour over meatballs.

Bake, uncovered for 50-60 minutes or until meatballs are done.

Makes 48 meatballs

Nutritional Information per Serving (3 meatballs)
Calories: 120, Fat: 5 grams, Protein: 7 grams, Carbohydrates: 12 grams, Cholesterol: 30 milligrams, Fiber: 0.6 grams

HEART HEALTHY TIP:

For heart healthy eating you can use 1/4 cup egg substitute in place of one egg

Asian Wing Dings

This version of chicken wings is great for a party when you need something substantial. It has a unique flavor!

12.5 ounces oyster sauce
2-3 tablespoons crushed pineapple
8 cloves garlic, minced
2 tablespoons hot pepper sauce
2 tablespoons balsamic vinegar
3/4 cup brown sugar
1/2 tablespoon ginger, minced
6 green onions, sliced
3 cups peanut oil
6 pounds chicken wings (24-28)

Combine first 7 ingredients in a medium sized bowl. Place sauce in large wok or saucepan. Heat on medium heat until sauce caramelizes and becomes gooey, approximately 10-15 minutes.

Heat peanut oil in deep fryer or large heavy saucepan. Deep fry chicken wings in batches until golden brown. Using a slotted spoon transfer to paper towels to drain.

Place cooked chicken wings in saucepan with sauce and stir until well coated. Transfer wings and extra sauce to a serving dish. Sprinkle with green onions and serve. (Can be made a day ahead and re-heated in oven.)

Makes 24 wings

Nutritional Information per Serving
Calories: 200, Fat: 14 grams, Protein: 12 grams, Carbohydrates: 8 grams,
Cholesterol: 50 milligrams, Fiber: 1.0 grams

KEHL SCHOOL OF DANCE

The Kehl School of Dance has been instructing students of all ages in the Madison community for over a century. Frederick W. Kehl started the school in 1880, and Kehl's has been the place where generations of families have taken their children to be instructed in the fine arts of dance, discipline and stage performance.

Frederick's son, Leo Kehl, taught many great dancers, including Gene Kelly and Ginger Rogers, and did choreography for Shirley Temple. Leo's daughters kept the dancing tradition strong in the Madison community, holding the annual dance recitals at the old Orpheum Theater.

Fourth generation Kehl family continue the tradition with studios throughout the greater Madison area.

Kehl School of Dance has always been active in community events through participation in festivals, school fine arts programs, assisted living communities and more.

Easy Sangria

1.5 liters (49.8 ounces) dry red wine
2 tablespoons brandy
2 tablespoons triple sec
1/3 cup sugar
2/3 cup orange juice
2 tablespoons fresh lime juice
2 tablespoons fresh lemon juice
5 whole cloves
1 (3-inch) cinnamon stick
2 cups sparkling water, chilled
8 orange wedges
5 lemon slices
5 lime slices

Notes:

Combine 1/2 cup wine, brandy, triple sec and sugar in a 2 quart glass measure. Microwave on high 2 minutes or until mixture is warm. Stir to dissolve sugar. Stir in the remaining wine, juices, cloves and cinnamon. Chill at least two hours.

Strain mixture into a pitcher and discard spices. Just before serving, stir in water and the fruit slices.

Serves: 8

Bloody Larry

ice cubes
2 1/2 ounces vodka
5 ounces tomato juice
1/2 ounce lemon juice
1/8 teaspoon black pepper
1/8 teaspoon celery salt
3 dashes Worcestershire sauce
1 dash Tabasco sauce
1 lime wedge
1 stalk of celery

In a shaker half-filled with ice cubes, combine vodka, tomato and lemon juice, celery salt, pepper, Worcestershire and Tabasco sauce. Shake well. Strain into a highball glass almost filled with ice cubes. Garnish with the celery and lime wedge.

Serves: 1

Hot Spiced Cider

1 quart apple cider
1 pint cranberry juice
1 cup orange juice
3/4 cup lemon juice
1/2 cup sugar
1 teaspoon whole allspice
1 teaspoon whole cloves
3 cinnamon sticks

Combine apple cider, cranberry, orange and lemon juice in an automatic percolator. Place sugar, allspice, cloves and cinnamon in percolator basket. Allow beverage to go through the percolator cycle. Serve hot.

Serves: 16 (1/2 cup serving size)

Alternative Stove Top Method:
If you do not have a percolator you can prepare this on the stove top. Wrap your spices in a cheesecloth sack and add the sugar to the other liquids. Cook over medium heat until it comes to a slow boil then serve.

 # Pear Liqueur

1/2 pound mature firm pears
2 apples, peels only
1 clove
1/2-inch cinnamon stick or pinch of cinnamon
pinch nutmeg
2 coriander seeds
1 cup granulated sugar
1 1/2 cups vodka or brandy

Cut the pears in strips, do not pare, and place in a jar with all peels, clove, cinnamon stick, nutmeg, coriander and sugar. Add vodka or brandy to cover. Steep 2 weeks. Shake the jar every 2 days to mix the ingredients.

Strain and filter. If you like the liqueur sweeter, add sugar syrup in small quantities. (about 1 ounce to 4 ounces liqueur) to establish the sweetness ratio. Then add to the whole batch accordingly. Matures in about 2 months.

Makes 2 cups

Pink Punch

This pink punch is perfect for bridal and baby showers.

2 (46 ounce) bottles of cranberry-raspberry juice
1 (32 ounce) bottle Pina Colada mix
1 (2- liter) bottle of raspberry ginger ale soda

In a large plastic container combine cranberry-raspberry juice with Pina Colada mix. Freeze overnight.

Remove from freezer 30 minutes before serving. Place frozen slush in punch bowl and slowly add raspberry ginger ale.

Serves: 24

Margarita Madness

These are especially great poolside on a hot summer day.

Notes:

6 ounces frozen limeade, we recommend a high quality brand such as Minute Maid
6 ounces tequila
3 ounces triple sec
ice
margarita salt for glasses
sliced limes

Combine limeade, tequila and triple sec in blender with ice. Continue to add ice to desired consistency. If you prefer a less slushy drink, place the mix, in the blender, in the refrigerator for 5 minutes. This will give it a creamier texture.

Rub a sliced lime around the rim of your glass and dip in margarita salt. Place lime over the rim of the glass and add margarita mixture.

Makes 4 drinks

Old Fashioned Sweet

This is an all time favorite cocktail for Wisconsinites. Many variations have been used with whiskey or Southern Comfort. Traditionally, this drink is made with brandy.

1/2 teaspoon sugar
4 dashes of aromatic bitters (such as Angostura)
1 splash maraschino cherry juice
1 maraschino cherry
1 orange slice
4 ice cubes
1.5 ounces of brandy, whiskey or Southern Comfort
3 ounces lemon-lime soda

Place sugar, bitters, cherry juice, cherry and orange slice in the bottom of a tumbler. Using a wooden mortar, muddle all ingredients until well mashed.

Place ice cubes and brandy, whiskey or Southern Comfort in tumbler. Top off with soda. Stir well, until drink is well blended.
Serves: 1

Cranberry-Orange Spice Cooler

4 bags orange spice tea
2 cups water
2 tablespoons sugar
1/3 cup dried cranberries
4 strips orange zest
juice of 1 orange
cold sparkling water

Combine tea bags and water in saucepan. Boil down to about 1 1/2 cups. Discard tea bags. Stir in sugar. Add cranberries and orange zest. Chill.

Pour into 4 tall iced glasses. Add orange zest and cranberries. Top with sparkling water.

Serves: 4

BREAST CANCER RECOVERY FOUNDATION (BCRF)

"The Breast Cancer Recovery Foundation is so grateful to have the support of the Junior League of Madison.

I'm not sure what we would do without the JLM! Their members have volunteered at many BCRF events, helping with registration, set-up, marketing and taking care of those last-minute details that are so crucial for a successful event.

Moreover, the generous financial support of the JLM has helped ensure that the BCRF can continue to carry out its mission of providing environments for women to heal emotionally, physically and spiritually from breast cancer."

The Junior League of Madison is truly a Madison treasure."

Sue E. Abitz
Executive Vice President
Breast Cancer Recovery Foundation, Inc.

After Workout Guiltless Smoothie

1/2 cantaloupe, diced (about 2 cups)
1/3 cup lemon sorbet
2 teaspoons frozen orange juice concentrate
1 teaspoon fresh lemon juice
4 ice cubes, crushed
pinch of salt

Combine all ingredients in a blender. Blend until smooth.

Serves: 2

Irish Cream

1 cup brandy
1/2 cup milk
1 tablespoon chocolate syrup
1 teaspoon instant coffee
1 pint whipping cream
1 can sweetened condensed milk

Blend all ingredients together in a blender. Pour into a decorative bottle and refrigerate. Will keep up to 3 weeks.

Serves: 6

Gin Fizz

2 1/2 ounces gin
1 ounce orange or lemon juice
1 teaspoon superfine sugar
4 ounces club soda
ice

Blender Method: Combine first 4 ingredients in a blender and blend. Add ice until mixture reaches a foamy consistency.

Shaker Method: In a shaker half-filled with ice cubes, combine gin, juice and sugar. Shake well. Strain into a Collins or similar glass almost filled with ice cubes. Add the club soda. Stir well.

Serves: 1

Notes:

rise
'n shine

Breads & breakfasts to jump start your day

breads & breakfasts

Banana Scones with Walnuts 52

Blueberry Lemon
Scones 50

Breakfast Berry
Pudding 67

Bubble Bread 62

Chili Cheese Breakfast Casserole 75

Chocolate Chip
Banana Bread 60

Cinnamon Apple
Muffins 53

Cranberry Orange
Bread 59

Cranberry Streusel
Coffee Cake 56

Crème Brûlée
French toast 65

Deep Dish Crab Bake 70

Dilly Bread 63

Dutch Pancakes 68

Easy Caramel
Orange Ring 57

Egg & Sausage Bake 69

German Potato Pancakes 78

Grandma's Easy
Quiche 71

Leek Tart 74

Morning Brunch Casserole 73

Morning Spread 58

Poppy Seed Bread 61

Pumpkin Chocolate
Chip Muffins 54

Rainbow Baked Fruit 68

Raspberry Crepes 66

Sour Cream
Coffee Cake 55

Steamin' Cornbread 64

Tart Cherry and
Vanilla Scones 51

Tomato, Watercress
and Chive Butter Sandwich 77

Tortilla de Patata 72

Vanilla Granola 76

photo courtesy of Wisconsin Dept. of Tourism

Paddle & Portage

Madison is a city perfectly suited to outdoor fun. Located on a narrow isthmus, downtown Madison sits between Lake Mendota and Lake Monona, with the state Capitol as its centerpiece. Lake Mendota is approximately 26 miles around, and Lake Monona, the smaller of the two, is 13 miles around.

The summer Paddle & Portage competition attracts sport lovers of all kinds to take advantage of this unique location while thousands of spectators cheer on the four legged canoes as they race across the Capital lawn. Competitors launch canoes from James Madison Park on Lake Mendota to paddle through a 1.5 mile course before carrying their boats 1.5 miles across the Isthmus and around the Capitol. On the other side, they launch their boats once more and row the last 1.5 miles on Lake Monona to finish on the shores of Olin-Turville Park on the south end of the lake.

In Madison, the lakes, rolling hills and wooded parks provide plenty of opportunity to enjoy the outdoors running, biking, boating and just getting together with family and friends for food and fun. Paddle and Portage is one of the most popular excuses to enjoy the scenic beauty of this lovely city.

hearty breakfast menu

Blueberry Lemon Scones

1 cup plus 1 tablespoon all-purpose flour
1 cup sifted cake flour
2/3 cup sugar
2 teaspoons baking powder
1/2 teaspoon baking soda
1/4 teaspoon salt
3 tablespoons chilled butter, cut into pieces
3/4 cup fresh blueberries
2 teaspoons grated lemon rind
3/4 cup vanilla nonfat yogurt
Vegetable cooking spray
2 teaspoons sugar

Raspberry Butter
1/2 cup butter
1/2 cup raspberry preserves

Notes:

Preheat oven to 450 degrees.

In a large bowl, combine 1 cup flour, cake flour, sugar, baking powder, baking soda and salt.

Cut in butter with a pastry blender or two knives until mixture resembles coarse meal. Place blueberries in a small bowl and coat with 1 tablespoon of flour. Add blueberries and lemon rind to flour mixture; toss well. Add yogurt, stirring just until dry ingredients are moistened (dough will be sticky).

Spray hands with cooking spray and turn dough onto a lightly floured surface, knead 4 or 5 minutes. Pat dough into an 8-inch circle on a baking sheet coated with cooking spray. Cut dough into 8-12 wedges, cutting into but not through. Sprinkle 2 teaspoons of sugar over the dough.

Bake 12 minutes, or until golden.

For Raspberry Butter, mix the butter until creamy, add raspberry preserves and blend well. Chill until ready to serve. Serve with warm scones.

Makes 12 scones

Nutritional Information per Serving
Calories: 260, Fat: 10 grams, Protein: 3 grams, Carbohydrates: 40 grams, Cholesterol: 30 milligrams, Fiber: 0.6 grams

Tart Cherry and Vanilla Scones

3/4 cup dried tart cherries
1/4 cup boiling water
1 3/4 cup all-purpose flour
1/3 cup sugar
1/4 cup yellow cornmeal
2 teaspoons baking powder
1/4 teaspoon salt
2 tablespoons chilled butter, cut into pieces
2 tablespoons vegetable shortening
1/3 cup plain yogurt
1/4 cup evaporated milk
1 teaspoon vanilla extract
1/4 teaspoon butter extract
cooking spray
1 large egg white
2 teaspoons sugar

Combine cherries and boiling water in a bowl; cover and let stand for 10 minutes, or until softened. Drain, set aside.

Preheat oven to 400 degrees.

Combine flour, sugar, cornmeal, baking powder and salt in a large bowl. Cut in butter and shortening with pastry blender until it resembles coarse meal.

Combine cherries, yogurt, milk and extracts; add to flour mixture, stirring just until moist. Dough will be sticky.

Turn dough out onto a lightly floured surface; knead lightly 4 times with floured hands. Pat dough into an 8-inch circle on a baking sheet coated with cooking spray. Brush with egg white and sprinkle with sugar. Cut dough into 8 wedges, cutting into but not through.

Bake at for 15-18 minutes, or until golden.

Makes 8 scones

Nutritional Information per Serving
Calories: 255, Fat: 7 grams, Protein: 4 grams, Carbohydrates: 44 grams,
Cholesterol: 15 milligrams, Fiber: 0.9 grams

DEVIL'S LAKE

For many Madison area residents, there is no better way to spend a sunny weekend than at Devil's Lake State Park in Baraboo. Devil's Lake provides a picturesque setting for a wide variety of recreational activities. Quartzite bluffs and mammoth cliffs make this location one of the most popular spots in the region for rock climbing. Biking, skiing and camping are just a few of the other pursuits in which visitors to the park can engage.

The park also offers various events during the summer, such as dances in the historic chateau building along the lake and weekends during which fishing or entrance to the park is free.

This beautiful spot is the perfect destination for families seeking a day filled with picnicking, swimming and hiking as well as for groups looking to enjoy some heart-pounding athletic activity. Devil's Lake State Park is a venue that everyone can enjoy.

Banana Scones
with Walnuts

3 cups all-purpose flour
1/2 cup plus 1 tablespoon packed brown sugar
2 teaspoons baking powder
1/2 teaspoon salt
1/4 teaspoon baking soda
3 tablespoons chilled butter, cut into pieces
1/4 cup buttermilk
1 teaspoon vanilla extract
1 large egg
1 cup mashed ripe banana (about 2)
Cooking spray
1/3 cup coarsely chopped walnuts, toasted

BUTTERMILK
SUBSTITUTE:

Add 3/4 teaspoon vinegar to
1/4 cup milk for a buttermilk
substitute.

Preheat oven to 400 degrees.

In a large bowl, combine the flour, 1/2 cup brown sugar, baking powder, salt
and baking soda. Cut in the butter with a pastry blender or 2 knives until the
mixture is crumbly.

In a small bowl, whisk together buttermilk, vanilla and egg. Add buttermilk
mixture and banana to flour mixture, stirring just until moist. Dough will be wet
and sticky.

Turn dough out onto a lightly floured surface; with floured hands, knead lightly
4 times. Pat the dough into a 9-inch circle on a baking sheet coated with
cooking spray. Sprinkle the walnuts and 1 tablespoon brown sugar over dough,
pressing gently into dough. Cut dough into 12 wedges, cutting into but not
through.

Bake 20 minutes, or until golden.

Makes 12 scones

Nutritional Information per Serving
Calories: 185, Fat: 4 grams, Protein: 4 grams, Carbohydrates: 33 grams, Cholesterol: 25
milligrams, Fiber: 0.3 grams

Cinnamon Apple Muffins

Muffins
- 3/4 cup firmly packed brown sugar
- 1/2 cup vegetable oil
- 1 egg, beaten
- 1 teaspoon vanilla
- 1 1/2 cups flour
- 1/2 teaspoon baking soda
- 1/4 teaspoon salt
- 1 cup peeled, chopped apple
- 1/2 cup buttermilk

Topping
- 1/4 cup firmly packed brown sugar
- 1/2 teaspoon cinnamon
- 1/4 cup chopped walnuts

Preheat oven to 325 degrees. Grease or line 12 muffin cups.

In a large bowl, blend 3/4 cup brown sugar, oil, egg and vanilla.

In another bowl mix flour, baking soda and salt, then add to the sugar mixture. Blend in apple and buttermilk and mix thoroughly. Place batter in muffin cups.

Mix 1/4 cup brown sugar, cinnamon and walnuts. Sprinkle over the muffin batter.

Bake 30-35 minutes, or until muffins are browned.

Makes 12 muffins

Nutritional Information per Serving
Calories: 185, Fat: 9 grams, Protein: 2 grams, Carbohydrates: 23 grams, Cholesterol: 15 milligrams, Fiber: 0.3 grams

 When using dark baking pans reduce cooking time by at least five minutes and watch closely.

Pumpkin Chocolate Chip Muffins

3 cups sugar
1 1/8 cup vegetable oil
3 eggs
1 tablespoon vanilla
3 cups flour
1 1/2 teaspoons cinnamon
1 teaspoon cloves
1 teaspoon nutmeg
1 teaspoon ginger
1 teaspoon salt
1 teaspoon baking powder
1/2 teaspoon baking soda
1 (15 ounce) can pumpkin
1 cup miniature chocolate chips

Preheat oven to 325 degrees. Grease or line 24 muffin cups.

In a large bowl blend together sugar, oil, eggs and vanilla.

In another bowl combine flour, cinnamon, cloves, nutmeg, ginger, salt, baking powder and baking soda. Add to the sugar mixture. Add pumpkin and chocolate chips. Mix well.

Fill muffin cups about 2/3 full.

Bake 40-45 minutes until golden and tester comes out clean.

Makes 24 muffins

Nutritional Information per Serving
Calories: 300, Fat: 13 grams, Protein: 3 grams, Carbohydrates: 43 grams, Cholesterol: 25 milligrams, Fiber: 1.1 grams

 If you beat muffin batter too long the muffins will turn out tough. Mix muffin batter by hand just long enough to bring moisture to dry ingredients.

Notes:

Sour Cream Coffee Cake

1 cup butter
2 3/4 cup sugar, divided
2 teaspoons vanilla extract
4 eggs
3 cups flour
2 teaspoons baking powder
1 teaspoon baking soda
1 teaspoon salt
2 cups sour cream
2 tablespoons cinnamon
1/2 cup chopped nuts

Preheat oven to 350 degrees. Grease a 10-inch (10-12 cup) bundt pan.

Using an electric mixer, cream butter and 2 cups of sugar. Add vanilla and eggs. In a separate bowl combine flour, baking powder, baking soda and salt. Add flour mixture and sour cream alternately to the creamed ingredients; mix well. Spoon 1/3 of the batter into the prepared bundt pan.

Combine cinnamon, nuts and remainder of sugar. Divide this mixture in 1/4 and 3/4 parts.

Sprinkle half of the 3/4 cinnamon mixture over the first 1/3 of the batter; cover with second 1/3 of batter and then the remaining half of the 3/4 cinnamon mixture. Cover with last 1/3 of the batter and end with the 1/4 cinnamon mixture.

Bake for 1 hour. Cool for 20 minutes. Remove from pan and serve warm.

Serves: 16

Nutritional Information per Serving
Calories: 425, Fat: 20 grams, Protein: 5 grams, Carbohydrates: 55 grams, Cholesterol: 90 milligrams, Fiber: 0.6 grams

Cranberry Streusel Coffee Cake

Cake
- 1/2 cup unsalted butter, room temperature
- 1 cup granulated sugar
- 2 large eggs
- 1 teaspoon vanilla extract
- 1 tablespoon grated orange zest
- 2 cups unbleached all-purpose flour
- 1 teaspoon baking powder
- 1 teaspoon baking soda
- 1/2 teaspoon salt
- 1 cup sour cream
- 2 1/2 cups whole fresh cranberries

Topping
- 3/4 cup packed, light brown sugar
- 1/2 cup unbleached all-purpose flour
- 2 1/2 teaspoons cinnamon
- 1/4 cup unsalted butter
- 1/2 cups walnuts, chopped (optional)

Notes:

Preheat oven to 350 degrees. Grease and flour a 13x9-inch baking pan.

Using an electric mixer, cream the butter and sugar together until light and fluffy. Beat in the eggs one at a time, then add the vanilla and orange zest.

Mix the flour, baking powder, soda and salt together. Add the flour mixture to the creamed mixture, alternating with the sour cream to make a smooth, thick batter.

Spread the batter evenly in the prepared pan. Sprinkle the cranberries over the top.

In a small mixing bowl toss the sugar, flour and cinnamon together. Cut in the butter with 2 knives or pastry blender until the mixture is crumbly. Stir in the walnuts. Sprinkle the streusel evenly over the cranberries on the coffee cake.

Bake 45 minutes, or until a tester inserted in the center comes out clean. Serve warm or at room temperature, cut into squares.

Serves: 10

Nutritional Information per Serving
Calories: 450, Fat: 21 grams, Protein: 5 grams, Carbohydrates: 60 grams, Cholesterol: 85 milligrams, Fiber: 1.4 grams

Easy Caramel Orange Ring

1 tablespoon butter, softened
1/2 cup orange marmalade
2 tablespoons chopped nuts
1 cup firmly packed brown sugar
1/2 teaspoon cinnamon
2 (7.5 ounce) packages buttermilk flaky biscuits
1/2 cup melted butter

Preheat oven to 350 degrees.

Grease a 12-cup bundt pan (do not use an angel food tube pan) with 1 tablespoon of butter. Drop teaspoonfuls of orange marmalade in pan. Sprinkle with nuts.

Combine brown sugar and cinnamon and set aside.

Separate biscuits. Dip each biscuit in melted butter then in sugar mixture. Stand biscuits on edge of pan, spacing evenly. Sprinkle the remaining sugar mixture and drizzle with butter.

Bake 30-40 minutes, or until tester comes out clean. Cool for 5 minutes, then invert onto serving plate.

Serves: 12

Nutritional Information per Serving
Calories: 245, Fat: 10 grams, Protein: 2 grams, Carbohydrates: 37 grams, Cholesterol: 25 milligrams, Fiber: 0.1 grams

HENRY VILAS ZOO

In 1904, Col. William F. and Anna M. Vilas gave a large parcel of land to the Madison Park and Pleasure Drive Association "for the uses and purposes of a public park and pleasure ground." From 1905 through 1910, the Vilas family donated an additional $42,000 for improvements, and public donations of $10,000 were raised for the enlargement and improvement of the park. The park was named in memory of the Vilas' son, Henry. In 1911, the first animal exhibits were created, representing the start of the Henry Vilas Zoo.

Today, Madison's Henry Vilas Zoo is one of the oldest free zoos in America. Every summer the zoo draws thousands of visitors who are entertained by the many exhibits the zoo has to offer. Some of the zoo's most popular attractions are the children's zoo, a penguin exhibit, the "Discovering Primates" complex and the "Big Cat" complex.

Morning Spread

8 ounces cream cheese, softened
1/2 cup butter, softened
1/4 teaspoon vanilla
3/4 cups powdered sugar
2 tablespoons brown sugar
3/4 cup miniature semi-sweet chocolate chips
1 cup finely chopped pecans

Using an electric mixer, beat cream cheese, butter and vanilla until fluffy. Add sugars and mix well. Fold in the chocolate chips. Place in refrigerator for two hours and then form into a ball. Refrigerate another hour and roll in pecans before serving. Great with cinnamon bagels or breakfast toast.

Serves: 20

Nutritional Information per Serving
Calories: 150, Fat: 12 grams, Protein: 1 gram, Carbohydrates: 10 grams, Cholesterol: 25 milligrams, Fiber: 0.6 grams

 This spread is a sweet treat for your morning bagel.

Notes:

Cranberry Orange Bread

2 cups all-purpose flour
1 cup sugar
1 1/2 teaspoons baking powder
1 teaspoon salt
1/2 teaspoon baking soda
1/4 cup butter
1 egg, beaten
1 teaspoon grated orange peel
3/4 cup orange juice
1 1/2 cups dried cranberries
1 1/2 cups fresh or frozen cranberries, chopped

Preheat oven to 350 degrees. Grease a 9x5-inch loaf pan.

Sift flour, sugar, baking powder, salt and baking soda into a large bowl. Cut in the butter with a pastry blender or 2 knives until the mixture is crumbly. Add egg, orange peel and orange juice all at once; stir just until mixture is evenly moist. Fold in cranberries. Spoon into prepared pan.

Bake for 1 hour and 10 minutes or until a toothpick inserted in center comes out clean. Remove from pan; cool on a wire rack.

Makes 1 loaf

Nutritional Information per Serving
Calories: 250, Fat: 4 grams, Protein: 3 grams, Carbohydrates: 50 grams, Cholesterol: 25 milligrams, Fiber: 1.2 grams

Chocolate Chip Banana Bread

This recipe has the added health bonus of bananas and whole wheat flour!

1 cup whole wheat flour
1 cup all-purpose or unbleached flour
1 teaspoon cinnamon
1 teaspoon baking soda
1/8 teaspoon salt
1/2 cup mini chocolate chips
1/2 cup chopped pecans
2 eggs
1/2 cup firmly packed brown sugar
1/4 cup unsalted butter
1 teaspoon vanilla
3 ripe medium bananas, mashed
1/4 cup plain yogurt

Notes:

Preheat oven to 350 degrees. Grease two 7 1/2x3 1/2-inch loaf pans.

In a large bowl, combine flours, cinnamon, baking soda, salt, chocolate chips and pecans. In a separate bowl, beat eggs, sugar, butter, vanilla, bananas and yogurt together until well blended. Stir into dry ingredients just until all ingredients are moistened. Spoon batter into greased pans, filling each 2/3 full.

Bake 50-60 minutes, or until deep golden brown and wooden pick inserted in the center of the loaf comes out clean. Cool in pan for 10 minutes; remove loaves to a wire rack and let cool completely.

Serve immediately, or wrap in plastic wrap and refrigerate for up to four days.

Serves: 12

Nutritional Information per Serving
Calories: 210, Fat: 8 grams, Protein: 4 grams, Carbohydrates: 30 grams, Cholesterol: 40 milligrams, Fiber: 2.4 grams

Poppy Seed Bread

Bread

3 cups flour
2 1/2 cups sugar
1 1/2 cups milk
3 eggs
1 1/2 teaspoons salt
1 1/2 teaspoons baking powder
1 1/2 teaspoons almond flavor
1 1/2 teaspoon vanilla
1 1/3 cups vegetable oil
1 1/2 teaspoons poppy seeds

Glaze

3/4 cup white sugar
1/4 cup orange juice
1 teaspoon vanilla
1/2 teaspoon almond flavoring
2 tablespoons melted butter

Preheat oven to 350 degrees. Grease and flour 2 9x5-inch loaf pans.

Bread: In a large mixing bowl, beat all bread ingredients at low speed for 30 seconds until combined. Blend at medium speed for 2 minutes until well mixed.

Bake for 70-75 minutes, until tester comes out clean. Cool for 10 minutes on a rack. Gently remove from pan.

Glaze: In a small bowl beat all glaze ingredients.

Pour glaze over top and sides of bread.

Makes 2 loaves.

Nutritional Information per Serving
Calories: 360, Fat: 17 grams, Protein: 3 grams, Carbohydrates: 48 grams, Cholesterol: 30 milligrams, Fiber: 0.1 grams

UNIVERSITY OF WISCONSIN ARBORETUM

The UW-Madison Arboretum is a 1260-acre horticultural facility that serves as a University field research facility and a community recreation center. Visitors enjoy more than 20 miles of trails for walking, jogging and biking.

In spring, neighbors for several blocks surrounding the Arboretum enjoy the sweet and welcome scents of lilacs and other flowering shrubs. During summer, the park-like setting teems with wildlife in woodland, prairie and wetland ecosystems. Fall's brilliant colors are most spectacular in the Arboretum's woods. In wintertime, the trails in the Arboretum draw cross-country skiers to a stunning, snow-blanketed world.

The Arboretum is a nationally recognized leader in restoration research that has become a model for land management practices and ecological restoration.

Students and visitors can observe and study several distinct ecological communities, numerous horticultural collections, effigy mounds and historic artifacts. The arboretum's collection of restored ecosytems is the oldest and most extensive such collection.

Bubble Bread

16 frozen dinner rolls
1 cup brown sugar
1 (3 1/2 ounce) package cook-and-serve butterscotch pudding mix (not instant)
1/4 cup sugar
1 teaspoon cinnamon
1/2 cup pecans, chopped
1/2 cup butter, melted

Grease and flour bundt cake pan. Place frozen rolls in bottom of the pan.

In a small bowl, mix brown sugar and pudding mix and sprinkle over rolls. In another bowl mix granulated sugar and cinnamon. Sprinkle over brown sugar and pudding mixture. Spread pecans over the top and pour melted butter over pecans.

Place on counter overnight. Do not cover.

Bake in a 350 degree oven for 30 minutes. Let rest in pan 10-15 minutes, before turning out. Slice, or pull apart.

Serves: 12

Nutritional Information per Serving
Calories: 290, Fat: 12 grams, Protein: 3 grams, Carbohydrates: 42 grams, Cholesterol: 20 milligrams, Fiber: 1.4 grams

Notes:

Dilly Bread

Serve with Sumptuous Seafood Gumbo (page 92) for a complete meal.

2 packages dry yeast
1/2 cup warm water
2 cups creamed cottage cheese, heated to lukewarm
1/4 cup sugar
2 tablespoons instant minced onion
4 tablespoons dill seed
2 tablespoons salt
1/2 teaspoon baking soda
2 tablespoons butter, softened
2 unbeaten eggs
4 1/2 cups flour
additional butter and salt

Dissolve yeast in warm water, set aside for 5 minutes.

In a large bowl, combine yeast mixture with cottage cheese, sugar, onion, dill seed, salt, baking soda, butter and eggs. Mix well.

Add 4 1/2 cups flour to form a soft, non-sticky dough, mixing/kneading well after each addition.

Place dough in a large oiled bowl and let rise until barely doubled in size, about 1-1 1/2 hours.

Punch dough down and knead to remove air. Turn into 2 well greased round casseroles (1 1/2 quart Pyrex bowls work). Let rise in a warm place until doubled in size, about 30-40 minutes.

Preheat oven to 350 degrees.

Bake bread in casserole dishes at for 40-50 minutes, or until golden brown. Brush with soft butter and sprinkle with kosher salt.

Serves: 16

Nutritional Information per Serving
Calories: 195, Fat: 4 grams, Protein: 8 grams, Carbohydrates: 32 grams, Cholesterol: 30 milligrams, Fiber: 0.8 grams

 1/2 whole wheat and 1/2 white flour may be used if desired.

Steamin' Cornbread

2 cups yellow cornmeal
2 cups flour
1 cup sugar
2 tablespoons baking powder
1 1/2 teaspoons salt
2 1/2 cups milk
1 cup vegetable oil
5 eggs

CAST IRON SKILLET:

Regular cast iron requires seasoning so that it won't react with or absorb the flavors of some foods cooked in it. Seasoning, which is a simple process of rubbing the inside of a pan with cooking oil and heating it for an hour in a moderate oven, gives cast iron a natural nonstick finish. Clean cast iron pans by first wiping them clean with a paper towel or soft cloth and, if necessary, gently scrubbing with a nylon pad.

Preheat oven to 350 degrees. Grease a 9x13-inch pan or 9-inch cast iron skillet.

In a large bowl stir together the cornmeal, flour, sugar, baking powder and salt. Set aside.

In another large bowl, beat together the milk, oil and eggs. Add the cornmeal mixture and stir just until combined. Pour into prepared pan.

Bake 40-45 minutes, or until a toothpick comes out clean. Cool in pan and then cut into squares.

Serves: 12

Nutritional Information per Serving
Calories: 440, Fat: 22 grams, Protein: 8 grams, Carbohydrates: 53 grams, Cholesterol: 80 milligrams, Fiber: 1.7 grams

 Consider adding in 4 ounces of chopped green chilies and/or 15 ounces of whole kernel corn for a heartier bread.

Crème Brûlée French Toast

6 tablespoons unsalted butter
1 cup brown sugar, packed
2 tablespoons corn syrup
1 loaf challah bread or baguette
5 large eggs
1 1/2 cups half and half
1 teaspoon Grand Marnier or orange flavored liqueur
3/4 teaspoon vanilla
1/4 teaspoon salt

In a small saucepan, melt butter with brown sugar and corn syrup until smooth. Pour into a 9x13-inch pan.

Cut six 1-inch-thick slices from center portion of bread. Trim crust (optional). Arrange in casserole squeezing to fit. Do not overlap.

In a bowl, whisk eggs, half and half, vanilla, Grand Marnier and salt. Pour evenly over bread. Chill eight hours or overnight.

Preheat oven to 375 degrees.

Bring mixture to room temperature. Bake 35-40 minutes or until bread is puffed and edges of bread are brown. Serve immediately. This looks prettiest if slices are brown sugar side up.

Serves: 6

Nutritional Information per Serving
Calories: 580, Fat: 28 grams, Protein: 12 grams, Carbohydrates: 70 grams, Cholesterol: 215 milligrams, Fiber: 1.8 grams

Raspberry Crepes

Crepes
- 1 egg
- 1 cup milk
- 1 tablespoon sugar
- 1 tablespoon brandy
- 1 teaspoon vanilla
- 1/4 teaspoon salt
- 1 cup flour
- vegetable oil

Raspberry Filling
- 1 pint raspberries
- 3/4 cup sugar
- 3/4 cup water
- 1 tablespoon butter
- 1 cup ricotta cheese

Notes:

Crepes: In a medium bowl, whisk egg with milk. While whisking, add sugar, brandy, vanilla and salt. Blend well. Add flour slowly, beating constantly. Chill 15 minutes or longer.

Brush an 8-inch crepe pan or small non-stick skillet lightly with the oil. Heat over medium heat. Tilting the pan, coat evenly with 2-3 tablespoons of the batter. Bubbles should form right away. Cook until sides peel away from pan, approximately 30 seconds. Turn and cook briefly on other side. (Crepes can be made ahead and frozen.)

Filling: In a small saucepan add 1/2 pint of the raspberries, sugar and water and bring to a boil. Reduce mixture until the sauce coats the back of the spoon. Add remaining raspberries and butter. Turn off heat when the butter is melted, stirring carefully so as to keep the remaining raspberries whole. Reserve half of the mixture for topping the crepes; set aside.

Add the ricotta cheese to the sauce in the pan and blend carefully. Fill crepes, rolling gently. Top with reserved raspberry filling.

Serves: 8

Nutritional Information per Serving
Calories: 300, Fat: 9 grams, Protein: 9 grams, Carbohydrates: 46 grams, Cholesterol: 60 milligrams, Fiber: 0 grams

Breakfast Berry Pudding

8 slices day-old white bread
6 ounces cream cheese
3 tablespoons sugar
1 teaspoon cinnamon
2 cups fresh raspberries, blueberries
1/2 cup brown sugar
8 eggs
2 cups milk
2 teaspoon vanilla extract

Preheat oven to 350 degrees.

Spread each slice of bread with cream cheese. Mix sugar and cinnamon together and sprinkle over bread. Cube bread and place in bottom of 9x13-inch pan. Distribute berries evenly over bread. Sprinkle half the brown sugar over cubes.

In a large bowl, beat together eggs, milk and vanilla; pour over cubes. Sprinkle with remaining brown sugar.

Bake 50-60 minutes, or until knife inserted in center comes out clean.

Serves: 10

Nutritional Information per Serving
Calories: 250, Fat: 12 grams, Protein: 9 grams, Carbohydrates: 26 grams, Cholesterol: 170 milligrams, Fiber: 2.2 grams

Consider topping each serving with a dollop of sour cream and a teaspoon of sliced strawberries.

HUNTING IN WISCONSIN

Offering a wide variety of game from white-tailed deer and wild turkey to ducks and geese, Wisconsin is a favorite choice of hunters for both its abundance of wildlife and breathtaking natural landscape. Hunting is seen as the perfect way to commune with nature and spend some quality time with family members and friends. For many hunters, bringing home a deer or turkey is only an added bonus.

The hunting season also helps to manage the size of the wildlife population and maintain more healthy herds.

While most hunters gravitate toward the northwoods of Wisconsin, hunting is an activity that occurs throughout the state, giving hunters their choice of scenic locations and terrain.

Dutch Pancakes

1/3 cup butter
4 eggs
1 cup flour
1 cup milk
2 lemon wedges

Preheat oven to 425 degrees.

Place butter in 9x13-inch glass baking pan. Melt butter in oven while pre-heating. Watch butter closely, being careful not to burn.

In a blender or food processor combine eggs, flour and milk. Blend until all ingredients are smooth. Pour mixture into prepared pan.

Bake for 20-25 minutes or until edges are golden brown.

Remove from oven and squeeze lemon over Dutch Pancakes. Sprinkle with powdered sugar for a nice presentation and serve with syrup, or Rainbow Baked Fruit (below).

Serves: 6

Nutritional Information per Serving
Calories: 225, Fat: 14 grams, Protein: 7 grams, Carbohydrates: 18 grams, Cholesterol: 150 milligrams, Fiber: 0 grams

Notes:

Rainbow Baked Fruit

3 peaches, pitted and sliced
2 plums, pitted and sliced
1/2 cup maple syrup
1/2 cup fresh raspberries
1/2 cup fresh blueberries

Preheat oven to 425 degrees.

Place peaches and plums in 9x12-inch baking dish. Drizzle maple syrup over fruit and toss. Bake along with Dutch Pancakes (above) about 20 minutes.

Toss berries in. Spoon inside Dutch Pancake and garnish with a dollop of sour cream.

Serves: 6

Nutritional Information per Serving
Calories:110, Fat:0 grams, Protein:.5 grams, Carbohydrates:28 grams, Cholesterol:0 milligrams, Fiber: medium

Egg & Sausage Bake

5 home-style white bread slices, crusts trimmed and cut into cubes
6 eggs
2 cups milk
1 teaspoon salt
1 teaspoon dry mustard
1 cup grated cheddar cheese
1 pound mild bulk sausage, browned and drained

Grease an 8x12-inch glass dish or soufflé dish.

In a large bowl beat eggs; add milk, salt and mustard. Add cubed bread and stir. Fold in cheese and sausage; blend well.

Pour into prepared pan. Refrigerate overnight, covered.

Bake at 350 degrees for 45 minutes, uncovered. Let stand a few minutes before serving.

Serves: 6

Nutritional Information per Serving
Calories: 550, Fat: 44 grams, Protein: 23 grams, Carbohydrates: 15 grams, Cholesterol: 260 milligrams, Fiber: 0.5 grams

 Deep Dish Crab Bake

4 slices bread, with crusts removed
1 cup grated cheddar cheese
2 (6 ounce) cans of crab meat, drained
5 eggs
1 cup milk
1/4 teaspoon mustard
1/2 teaspoon finely chopped onion
1/4 teaspoon Worcestershire sauce
1/4 teaspoon paprika
1/4 teaspoon salt
1/4 teaspoon pepper

Grease an 8x8-inch pan.

Remove crusts from bread and cube each slice. Put half of the bread in the bottom of prepared pan.

Sprinkle with half of the cheese, top with half of the crab. Repeat.

Beat eggs, add milk, onion and spices. Pour over top of the dish. Refrigerate overnight, covered.

Bake at 350 degrees for 1 hour and 10 minutes, or until top is golden.

Serves: 6

Nutritional Information per Serving
Calories: 370, Fat: 18 grams, Protein: 35 grams, Carbohydrates: 16 grams, Cholesterol: 340 milligrams, Fiber: 0.6 grams

Notes:

Grandma's Easy Quiche

This is a wonderful 'no crust' quiche.

1/2 cup biscuit baking mix
4 eggs
1 cup shredded cheddar cheese
1/3 cup onion, finely chopped
1/3 cup mushrooms and/or green peppers
2 cups milk or half and half
1/4 teaspoon salt
1/4 teaspoon pepper

Preheat oven to 350 degrees. Grease a 9-inch quiche pan or a deep dish pie plate.

Put all ingredients into a blender and mix for 30 seconds. Pour into a prepared pan.

Bake for 50-55 minute, or until golden brown.

Let stand 5 minutes before cutting.

Serves: 6

Nutritional Information per Serving
Calories: 205, Fat: 13 grams, Protein: 11 grams, Carbohydrates: 11 grams, Cholesterol: 150 milligrams, Fiber: 0.2 grams

 Consider adding chicken or crab for a heartier quiche.

Tortilla de Patata

This classic egg and potato dish from Spain is terrific for brunch, lunch or dinner.

1 3/4 cups vegetable or olive oil for frying
1 3/4 pounds Yukon Gold potatoes (about 5 potatoes), thinly sliced
2 1/4 teaspoons kosher salt
1 pound onions (about 2-3 onions), thinly sliced
5 cloves garlic, minced
6 eggs
1/8 teaspoon pepper

In a 10 1/2-inch nonstick skillet, heat the oil on medium high.

In a large bowl toss the potatoes with 2 teaspoons of salt. When oil is hot, slip the potatoes into the pan with a slotted spoon. Fry the potatoes, turning occasionally, and adjust the heat so that they continue to sizzle but do not crisp or brown, about 10-12 minutes.

Place a sieve or paper towels over a plate. Using a slotted spoon transfer potatoes to sieve or paper towels to drain.

Return pan to stove, but lower heat slightly. Add onion and garlic to the pan. Sauté until the onions are very soft and translucent, about 7 minutes. Remove pan from heat and transfer onions and garlic to sieve or paper towels with potatoes. Drain the oil, reserving 1 tablespoon. Wipe out the pan with a paper towel so it's clean.

In a large bowl, beat the eggs, 1/4 teaspoon of salt and pepper with a fork until blended. Add the potatoes, onion and garlic to the egg mixture. Mix gently, being careful not to break the potatoes.

Heat the skillet on medium-high. Add the reserved 1 tablespoon of oil to pan. When pan is very hot, pour in the potato-egg mixture. Cook for 1 minute, then lower the heat to medium-low, cooking until the eggs are completely set at the edges and halfway set in the center, about 8-10 minutes.
To flip the tortilla, slide onto a large flat plate, then invert skillet over tortilla and flip it back into skillet. Round off edge of tortilla with plastic spatula and cook over low heat, covered, about 7 minutes.

Transfer tortilla to a platter. Cool slightly. Serve warm or at room temperature.

Serves: 6

Nutritional Information per Serving
Calories: 250, Fat: 22 grams, Protein: 6 grams, Carbohydrates: 7 grams, Cholesterol: 180 milligrams, Fiber: 1.3 grams

 For a golden top, place the patata under the broiler for 3-5 minutes.

Morning Brunch Casserole

1 (6 ounce) box of wild rice mixture
1 (10 ounce) package of frozen broccoli, cooked and drained
3 cups of cubed cooked ham
1 (4 ounce) jar of drained sliced mushrooms
1 cup grated cheddar cheese
1 cup of cream of celery soup
1 cup of mayonnaise
2 teaspoons of spicy mustard
1/2 teaspoon of curry powder
1/4 cup Parmesan cheese

Preheat oven to 350 degrees.

Cook rice according to package.

Layer the rice, broccoli, ham, mushrooms and cheddar cheese in a greased 9x13-inch pan.

In a medium bowl, mix the soup, mayonnaise, mustard and curry powder. Spread over the top of the casserole. Sprinkle Parmesan cheese over the top. Can be made one day ahead.

Bake 45 minutes. Let stand 5-10 minutes and serve.

Serves: 10

Nutritional Information per Serving
Calories: 335, Fat: 25 grams, Protein: 11 grams, Carbohydrates: 17 grams, Cholesterol: 40 milligrams, Fiber: 2.3 grams

Leek Tart

pie crust for a 12-inch pie dish or removable-bottom tart tin
1 tablespoon olive oil
6 ounces bacon, cut into 1/4 inch pieces
6 leeks, white and pale green parts, carefully cleaned and diced
salt and freshly ground black pepper
6 large eggs
2/3 cup whole milk
1/3 cup half and half
1 cup shredded Fontina cheese

Line the pie dish of your choice with the pastry and chill in the freezer for 30 minutes.

Preheat oven to 400 degrees.

Prick the pastry all over with the tines of a fork or a sharp knife, then line it with aluminum foil and fill it with dry beans or pastry weights to keep it from bubbling up. Bake it in the lower third of the oven until the edges of the pastry are golden brown, about 10 minutes. Remove from the oven and set aside.

Put olive oil and bacon in a large skillet over medium heat and cook until the bacon is slightly golden but not crisp, 2-3 minutes. Add leeks; stir so they are coated with fat and cook, covered, until they are tender, about 15 minutes, stirring occasionally so they don't stick to the bottom of the pan. Season with salt and pepper and remove from the heat.

In a medium bowl whisk together the eggs until they are broken up, then whisk in the milk and the half and half. Season with salt and pepper.

Arrange the leeks and the bacon evenly over the pastry. Sprinkle the cheese over leeks and bacon. Pour the custard mixture over the top.

Place pastry pan on a cooking sheet and bake it in the bottom third of the oven until the top is golden and puffed and the custard is cooked through, 25-30 minutes.

Remove the edge of the tart tin if you've used a removable bottom tart tin and serve. You may also let stand and serve at room temperature.

Serves: 6

Nutritional Information per Serving
Calories: 610, Fat: 45 grams, Protein: 27 grams, Carbohydrates: 24 grams, Cholesterol: 260 milligrams, Fiber: 1.0 grams

Notes:

 Chili Cheese Breakfast Casserole

Make this one day before serving.

3 English muffins, split in half
1 tablespoon butter, softened
1 pound ground pork sausage
1 (4.5 ounce) can chopped green chilies,
    drained and divided
3 cups (12 ounces) cheddar cheese, shredded
12 large eggs, lightly beaten
1 1/2 cups light sour cream

Spray a 13 x 9-inch baking dish with cooking spray.

Spread English muffin halves with butter and place buttered side down in prepared baking dish. Set aside.

Brown sausage in a skillet, stirring until it crumbles; drain. Layer half each of sausage, chilies and cheese over English muffins.

Combine eggs and sour cream, pour over casserole. Top with remaining sausage, chilies and cheese; cover casserole and chill
8 hours.

Let stand at room temperature for 30 minutes.

Bake at 350 degrees for 35-40 minutes.

Serves: 12

Nutritional Information per Serving
Calories: 383, Fat: 31 grams, Protein: 18 grams, Carbohydrates: 9 grams, Cholesterol: 240 milligrams,
Fiber: 0.1 grams

 Vanilla Granola

non-stick vegetable spray
4 cups old fashioned oats
1 cup sliced almonds
1/2 cup packed golden brown sugar
1/4 teaspoon salt
1/8 teaspoon ground cinnamon
1/3 cup vegetable oil
1/4 cup honey
2 tablespoons sugar
4 teaspoons vanilla extract

Preheat oven to 300 degrees. Lightly spray large baking sheet with non-stick spray.

Mix next 5 ingredients in a large bowl. Combine oil, honey and sugar in a small saucepan; bring to simmer over medium heat. Remove from heat; stir in vanilla. Pour hot liquid over granola mixture.

Spread granola on prepared cookie sheet. Bake until golden brown, stirring occasionally, about 30 minutes. Transfer sheet to rack; cool granola completely.

Nutritional Information per Serving
Calories: 350, Fat: 17 grams, Protein: 8 grams, Carbohydrates: 41 grams, Cholesterol: 0 milligrams, Fiber: 4.5 grams

 Can be made two weeks ahead. Store in an airtight container at room temperature.

Notes:

Tomato, Watercress and Chive Butter Sandwich

These slender sandwiches really highlight the sweet, tart flavor of tomato.

4 tablespoons butter, softened
3 tablespoons lemon juice
1/2 bunch fresh chives, sliced
12 slices thinly sliced white or wheat bread
1 tomato very thinly sliced
salt and pepper
watercress, stems trimmed, washed and dried

In a small bowl, mix together butter, lemon juice and chives to make a paste. Spread thinly over all the bread.

Arrange one layer of tomatoes over half the bread slices and season with salt and pepper. Top with 2 or 3 watercress leaves and top with slice of buttered bread. Press to seal, trim crusts and cut into fingers or triangles.

Serves: 6

Nutritional Information per Serving
Calories: 200, Fat: 9 grams, Protein: 4 grams, Carbohydrates: 26 grams, Cholesterol: 20 milligrams, Fiber: 1.4 grams

SOUTH MADISON HEALTH AND FAMILY CENTER (HARAMBEE)

"The Junior League of Madison and the Early Childhood Family Enhancement Center are kindred spirits when you talk about family support and interest in the well being of children in this community. Historically, our partnership has implemented fun and creative initiatives that educated and informed families about child development, play as learning and the important role that parents play in the lives of their children. Madison and Dane County are fortunate to have the leadership of these women."

Betty Banks, Director Early Childhood Family Enhancement Center
South Madison Health and Family Center

German Potato Pancakes

A delicious way to use your leftover potatoes.

2 beaten eggs
1/4 cup flour
1 tablespoons minced onion
1/8 teaspoon baking powder
1/2 cup milk
3 tablespoons butter, softened
1/2 teaspoon salt
1/2 teaspoon pepper
3 cups finely grated potatoes, about 4 medium potatoes

Using a blender or food processor, beat eggs. Add flour, onion, baking powder, milk, butter, salt and pepper. Pulse blender until ingredients are well blended. Mix potatoes in last for chunkier styled pancakes or pulse potatoes for smoother style pancakes.

Heat griddle and melt butter until well coated. Pour pancakes and fry until golden brown and turn once until golden brown on both sides.

Serves: 6

Nutritional Information per Serving
Calories: 150, Fat: 8 grams, Protein: 4 grams, Carbohydrates: 15 grams, Cholesterol: 80 milligrams, Fiber: 0.9 grams

Notes:

going
overboard

Spectacular soups that will rock your boat

SOUPS

Asian Ginger Chicken Soup 94

Asparagus and
Mushroom Soup 88

Autumn Squash Soup 83

Beef Burgundy Stew 98

Black Bean Soup 91

Chestnut Soup with Cognac Cream 86

Chicken Florentine Soup 93

Cold Cucumber Soup 106

Corn Chowder 87

Easy Lobster Stock 85

Firehouse Chili 96

Gazpacho 105

Lamb & Pasta Stew 99

Lentil Stew 100

Lobster Bisque 84

One Pot Sausage Soup 97

Peanutty Chicken Stew 103

Potato Leek Soup 90

Southwestern Chicken
and Lime Soup 89

Sumptuous Seafood Gumbo 92

Summertime Avocado
and Tomato Soup 104

Tomato Basil Bisque 82

Turkey Wild Rice Soup 95

White Chicken Chili 101

Vegetarian Chili 102

photo by Zane Williams

Madison— A Gathering of Waters

The name "Wisconsin" originates from a Native American term meaning "gathering of the waters."

About 13,000 years ago the last glacier retreated from the four lakes region of Wisconsin, leaving behind 37 lakes, 475 miles of streams and rivers and 14 miles of the Wisconsin River in Dane County alone. Madison's own chain of lakes includes Lake Mendota, Monona, Waubesa, Wingra and Kegonsa.

Where there are lakes, there will be fishermen - sun or snow. Walleye, bass, pike, muskellunge, panfish and perch are some of the many fish caught during this favorite pastime of Madison residents.

The lakes also lend themselves to various boating events. The Midwest Rowing Championships are held yearly on Lake Wingra. This regatta is one of the largest and longest running regattas in the nation with nearly 1,500 participants.

Lake Mendota hosts regattas of a different breed. The large body of water makes for perfect sailing conditions and regattas are held almost weekly - weather permitting.

In addition, Madison's many water venues provide a plethora of other recreational activities for every season.

Tomato Basil Bisque

A gourmet soup that is easy to make and delicious.

3 tablespoons butter
3 medium white onions, chopped
2 large carrots, chopped
2 cloves garlic, minced
1 cup water
12 tomatoes peeled, seeded and diced (or 48 ounces canned,
 diced tomatoes)
2 cups half and half
1 cup fresh basil, chopped
salt and pepper, to taste

In a large stockpot or saucepan, melt butter over medium heat. Add onions, carrots and garlic. Cook 5 minutes. Add 1 cup water, tomatoes, and salt and pepper. Cook uncovered over medium heat for 40 minutes, stirring occasionally. Cool slightly.

Blend in a blender or food processor, in batches if necessary. Stir in half and half. Sprinkle with fresh basil and blend again until completely pureed.

Serves: 8

Nutritional Information per Serving
Calories: 170, Fat: 11 grams, Protein: 4 grams, Carbohydrates: 13 grams, Cholesterol: 35 milligrams, Fiber: 2.6 grams

 For a little extra wow, add crème fraîche or sour cream with a little basil when serving.

Notes:

Autumn Squash Soup

2 pounds butternut squash
3 tablespoons olive oil
2 tablespoons butter
1 medium onion, chopped
2 medium leeks (white parts only), sliced
3 garlic cloves, minced
1 tablespoon fresh sage, minced
1/4 teaspoon nutmeg
1/2 cup white wine
5 cups chicken broth
1/2 teaspoon lavender (optional)
salt and pepper to taste

Preheat oven to 350 degrees.

Cut the butternut squash in half, discarding the seeds. Drizzle with 1 tablespoon of oil and place face down on a baking sheet. Bake for 35 minutes. When squash has cooled, scoop out the flesh and set aside.

Heat 2 tablespoons olive oil and the butter in a 4-quart heavy saucepan. Add the onion and leek and sauté over medium-high heat until tender, about 5 minutes. Add the garlic and nutmeg, continuing to sauté for an additional 3 minutes. Add the white wine and sage; reduce sauce over medium heat for about 10 minutes.

Add the prepared squash and 2 cups chicken broth. Cook for 10 minutes. Remove from heat; cool slightly.

Puree in a blender or food processor, in batches if necessary. Return to the saucepan and heat over medium-low heat. Add the lavender and remaining 3 cups chicken broth. Continue cooking until heated through. Season to taste with salt and pepper.

Serves: 8

Nutritional Information per Serving
Calories: 175, Fat: 9 grams, Protein: 8 grams, Carbohydrates: 15 grams, Cholesterol: 10 milligrams, Fiber: 0.5 grams

 Garnish with a dollop of sour cream.

Lobster Bisque

Your guests will never forget the time you served this treat.

3 tablespoons butter
8 shallots, peeled and thinly sliced
2 cloves garlic, minced
1 cup brandy or cognac
6 sprigs fresh thyme
4 bay leaves
4 cups lobster stock
2 tablespoons tomato paste
1/4 cup basmati rice
3 cups heavy cream
salt to taste

Notes:

In a large saucepan, melt the butter over medium heat; sauté the shallots and garlic until soft, stirring often to prevent from browning. Remove pan from heat and add the brandy or cognac; allow to steam for a few seconds.

Return pan to medium heat and add thyme and bay leaves; reduce mixture until pan is almost dry. Add the lobster stock and tomato paste and increase heat to high; cook until mixture is reduced by half.

Add rice and reduce heat to medium, stirring often while rice cooks and begins to fall apart. Add cream and bring to a simmer, stirring often to prevent rice from scorching on the bottom of the pan. Simmer for 30 minutes. Remove from heat.

Pass mixture through a sieve into another saucepan and re-heat on low until warmed through.

Serves: 6

Nutritional Information per Serving
Calories: 670; Fat grams 53; Protein 4; Carbohydrates 19;
Cholesterol 190 milligrams.; Fiber 1.1 grams.

 It is possible to purchase lobster stock from some specialty seafood stores. Or use the recipe on page 85 and reserve the lobster meat for the bisque.

Easy Lobster Stock

shells and heads from 2 cooked 1 1/4-pound lobsters
1 large carrot, chopped
1 onion, chopped
1/4 cup vegetable oil
2 tablespoons tomato paste
1 cup dry white wine
8 cups water

With back of a heavy knife crush lobster shells and heads. Chop carrot and onion. In an 8-quart heavy kettle heat oil over moderate heat until hot, but not smoking. Brown lobster shells and heads, mashing with a wooden spoon to help break up, about 15 minutes. Stir in carrot, onion, tomato paste and wine, and simmer until most of wine is evaporated.

Add water and simmer until liquid is reduced to about 4 cups, about 1 1/2 hours. Pour stock through a fine sieve into a heat-proof bowl. (Stock may be made 3 days ahead. Cool, uncovered, before chilling. Freeze stock up to 3 months.)

Makes 4 cups.

Nutritional Information per Serving
Calories: 170, Fat: 11 grams, Protein: 4 grams, Carbohydrates: 13 grams,
Cholesterol: 35 milligrams, Fiber: 2.6 grams

WATER, WATER EVERYWHERE!

Did you know Minnesota, Wisconsin's neighbor to the northwest, bills itself as the "Land of 10,000 lakes," but Wisconsin is the real leader with over 15,000 lakes throughout the state?

Much of Wisconsin's geography was shaped by Ice Age glaciers and it borders two of the Great Lakes — Lake Superior and Lake Michigan. Wisconsin's western border is demarcated by the St. Croix and Mississippi rivers.

Chestnut Soup with Cognac Cream

Rich and delicately flavored, this soup makes an elegant start to any holiday meal.

2 tablespoons butter
1 tablespoon olive oil
1 celery stalk, chopped
1 small carrot, chopped
1/2 medium onion, chopped
1 teaspoon minced fresh thyme or 1/4 teaspoon dried
4 cups canned low-salt chicken broth
2 cups boiled chestnuts or 2 cups (10 ounces) vacuum-
packed chestnuts, halved
1/4 cup whipping cream
2 teaspoons cognac
pinch salt

BOILED CHESTNUTS:

1 pound chestnuts
Use a small, sharp knife to cut an "X" in each chestnut. Cook chestnuts in a large saucepan of boiling water until just tender, about 15 minutes. Working with batches use slotted spoon to transfer several chestnuts to work surface. Remove and discard the hard shell and papery brown skin while chestnuts are still warm. Makes 2 cups.

Melt butter with oil in heavy large saucepan over medium heat. Add celery, carrot, onion and thyme and sauté until vegetables are tender, about 10 minutes. Add broth and chestnuts. Cover partially and simmer until chestnuts are very tender, about 30 minutes. Puree soup in batches in blender. Season to taste with salt and pepper. Can be prepared 1 day ahead. Cover and chill.

Whisk cream, cognac and pinch of salt in medium bowl until thickened but not stiff. Set aside.

Bring soup to simmer over low heat. Ladle into bowls. Swirl spoonful of Cognac cream into each bowl and serve.

Serves: 4

Nutritional Information per Serving
Calories: 335, Fat: 18 grams, Protein: 13 grams, Carbohydrates: 30 grams, Cholesterol: 40 milligrams, Fiber: 5.3 grams

Corn Chowder

Make a double batch of this for football parties like the Playoffs or the Super Bowl.

Soup
   2 tablespoons butter
   1 large onion, chopped
   3 cloves garlic minced
   1 teaspoon salt
   1/2 teaspoon pepper
   1/4 teaspoon dried oregano
   2 tablespoons flour
   2 (12 ounce) cans undrained corn
   2 cups chicken stock
   1/4 cup fresh parsley
   2 cups half and half
   1 jalapeño chili pepper, seeded, finely chopped

Topping Options
   shredded cheddar cheese
   chopped tomatoes
   chopped cooked chicken
   crumbled tortilla chips
   chopped avocado
   crumbled bacon

Melt the butter in a large saucepan and sauté onion over medium-low heat, about 3 minutes. Add the garlic, salt, pepper and oregano and sauté an additional 2 minutes. Blend in flour, remove from heat.

Add 1/2 of the corn, chicken stock and parsley to the saucepan, stirring to mix. Blend in batches in a blender or food processor. Return to saucepan.

Add half and half and remainder of the corn. Bring to a boil, then reduce to a simmer. Add jalapeño and simmer until ready to serve.

Serves: 6

Nutritional Information per Serving (without toppings)
Calories: 270, Fat: 15 grams, Protein: 10 grams, Carbohydrates: 24 grams, Cholesterol: 40 milligrams, Fiber: 3.8 grams

 Consider serving the soup with any or all of the topping options. Let your guests be creative!

Asparagus and Mushroom Soup

Soup
3 tablespoons olive oil
5 ounces shiitake mushrooms, stems removed, thinly sliced
3/4 teaspoon salt
1/4 teaspoon fresh ground pepper
1 medium onion, chopped
1 cup water
2 cups chicken broth
2 tablespoons long grain rice
1 pound asparagus, trimmed and cut into 1 inch slices

Garnish - Cheese Toast
8 (1/2 inch) baguette slices
2 tablespoons olive oil
2 ounces Gruyere cheese, shredded

Notes:

In a medium saucepan, heat 2 tablespoons olive oil over medium-high heat until hot. Add mushrooms, 1/4 teaspoon salt and pepper. Cook for 5 minutes or until the mushrooms are golden brown, stirring occasionally. Remove the mushrooms with a slotted spoon to a bowl, reserving the pan drippings. Reduce heat to medium-low.

Add 1 tablespoon olive oil to the reserved pan drippings. Add the onion. Cook for 5 minutes or until tender, stirring occasionally. Stir in water, broth, rice and 1/2 teaspoon salt. Bring to a boil. Continue boiling for 10 minutes, stirring occasionally.

Stir in asparagus and cook for 5 minutes longer, until the asparagus is tender, stirring occasionally.

Puree the soup in a blender or food processor until smooth. Return the soup to the saucepan. Stir in the mushrooms. Cook until just heated through. Remove from heat. Cover to keep warm.

Cheese Toasts: Brush both sides of the bread slices with the 2 tablespoons olive oil. Arrange the slices in a single layer on a baking sheet. Broil for 2 minutes or until brown; turn over. Sprinkle with the cheese and broil an additional 2 minutes or until the cheese is melted.

Ladle into soup bowls and sprinkle with additional cheese. Serve with bread slices.

Serves: 4

Nutritional Information per Serving
Calories: 175, Fat: 11 grams, Protein: 8 grams, Carbohydrates: 11 grams, Cholesterol: 0 milligrams, Fiber: 2.3 grams

Southwestern Chicken and Lime Soup

1 cup plus 2 tablespoons olive oil
4 flour tortillas, cut into strips
6 cups chicken broth
2 tablespoons fresh cilantro, minced
1 tablespoon fresh oregano, minced
1 teaspoon apple cider vinegar
1/2 teaspoon ground cumin
2 tablespoons fresh lime juice
Salt and pepper, to taste
1 chicken breast, sliced thinly crosswise
1/2 cup chopped seeded tomato
1/2 cup chopped green bell pepper
1/2 cup chopped white onion
1 avocado, diced and tossed with 1 tablespoon lime juice
6 lime slices

Heat 1 cup oil in medium skillet over medium heat. Working in batches, add tortilla strips and fry until golden, about 30 seconds per side; transfer to paper towels to drain.

In a large stock pot mix broth, cilantro, oregano, vinegar and cumin; bring to a boil. Reduce heat and simmer 15 minutes. Add lime juice and season with salt and pepper.

Heat remaining 2 tablespoons oil in large skillet over medium-high heat. Sprinkle chicken strips with salt and pepper. Add chicken to skillet, sauté 3 minutes. Add tomato, bell pepper and onion. Sauté until chicken is cooked through, about 2 minutes longer.

Place 1 lime slice in each bowl and ladle soup over. Mound chicken mixture in the center of each bowl, topping with tortilla strips. Garnish with diced avocado.

Serves: 6

Nutritional Information per Serving
Calories: 225, Fat: 15 grams, Protein: 15 grams, Carbohydrates: 7 grams, Cholesterol: 10 milligrams, Fiber: 2.2 grams

 Serve with Steamin' Cornbread (page 64) and a Sunshine Salad (page 116).

 # Potato Leek Soup

1 tablespoon butter
1 onion, thinly sliced
4 leeks (white part only), sliced
2 garlic cloves, thinly sliced
2 quarts chicken or vegetable stock
6 potatoes, peeled and diced
1 bay leaf
2 sprigs fresh thyme or 2 teaspoons dried thyme
2 teaspoons salt
1 teaspoon black pepper
1 cup half and half
1 tablespoon chopped chives

SERVING SUGGESTION:

Try serving any hearty soup or dip in a sourdough bread bowl. Simply hollow out a round loaf of bread and ladle in soup.

Heat the butter in a stockpot and sauté the onion, leeks and garlic until translucent. Add the stock, potatoes, bay leaf, thyme, salt and pepper. Simmer 40 minutes.

Remove the vegetables; pureé them in a blender or food processor, working in batches, if necessary. Return pureéd vegetables to soup.

Simmer another 10 minutes. Add the cream. Serve hot and garnish with chopped chives.

Serves: 6

Nutritional Information per Serving
Calories: 265, Fat: 10 grams, Protein: 18 grams, Carbohydrates: 26 grams, Cholesterol: 23 milligrams, Fiber: 2.6 grams

 Place peeled potatoes in water to prevent potatoes from turning brown.

Black Bean Soup

1/2 pound bacon
10 large carrots, peeled, chopped
6 cloves garlic, minced
2 medium onions, finely chopped
1/4 teaspoon ground cumin
1/4 teaspoon dried oregano
1/4 teaspoon cayenne pepper (to taste)
6 (15 ounce) cans black beans, rinsed and drained
5 quarts chicken broth
1/2 cup sherry
salt and pepper to taste
sour cream
chopped green onions for garnish

Fry bacon in a large stock pot. Remove with a slotted spoon and drain on paper towels. Crumble bacon. Reserve bacon fat.

Mince carrots in a food processor. Transfer to stock pot and sauté in bacon fat over medium heat. Add onions and garlic and continue to sauté over medium heat until tender, about 15 minutes, stirring occasionally. Add cumin, oregano and cayenne, and sauté 5 minutes, stirring often. Add the beans and the chicken broth. Simmer uncovered for at least 1 hour, until soup thickens. Add additional chicken broth, if necessary.

Stir in sherry and reserved bacon. Simmer 5 minutes longer. Season to taste with salt and pepper.

Ladle into bowls and garnish each serving with a spoonful of sour cream and green onions.

Serves: 12

Nutritional Information per Serving
Calories: 450, Fat: 16 grams, Protein: 37 grams, Carbohydrates: 40 grams, Cholesterol: 20 milligrams, Fiber: 13.8 grams

Sumptuous Seafood Gumbo

Perfect for a casual fall dinner party.

1/4 cup bacon drippings (from 1/2 pound bacon) or olive oil
1/4 cup flour
1 pound fresh or frozen okra
1 1/2 teaspoon paprika
1 cup chopped onion
1/2 cup chopped green pepper
1/2 cup chopped celery
1/2 cup chopped fresh parsley
1 (8 ounce) can tomato sauce
1 (14.5 ounce) can tomatoes with green chilies
8 cups chicken broth
1 bay leaf
1 teaspoon thyme
3 teaspoons pepper
1 tablespoon Worcestershire sauce
2 teaspoons salt
2 teaspoon dried oregano
dash Tabasco sauce
1 pound cooked shrimp, peeled and deveined
2 cups prepared white rice

Notes:

In a large stock pot, heat the bacon drippings and add the flour; whisk until a thick, dark paste forms. Add okra and paprika and cook until the okra is tender and well coated with the flour and bacon drippings.

In a separate large frying pan, sauté the onions, pepper, parsley and celery. Add to the stock pot. Add remaining ingredients, except the shrimp, and cook over low heat for 2 hours.

About 1/2 hour before serving, add the shrimp.

Serve with 1/3 cup white rice in the middle of the bowl.

Serves: 6

Nutritional Information per Serving
Calories: 445, Fat: 14 grams, Protein: 37 grams, Carbohydrates: 43 grams, Cholesterol: 150 milligrams, Fiber: 4.8 grams

 Serve with a slice of cornbread (page 64) or Dilly Bread (page 63) on the side for a complete autumn meal.

Chicken Florentine Soup

2 whole boneless, skinless chicken breasts (4 halves)
5 cups chicken stock
10 ounces frozen spinach, thawed
1/2 teaspoon nutmeg
1/2 cup butter
1/2 cup flour
3 cups milk
salt and pepper to taste

In a large saucepan cook chicken in stock for 20 minutes or until the chicken is cooked through. Remove the chicken from broth and cut into 1-inch cubes; set aside. Add the thawed spinach and nutmeg to the broth, cook 10 minutes over medium heat.

In a separate small pan over medium heat, whisk the butter and the flour for 3 minutes, add the milk and stir until thickened and smooth. Transfer to the soup pot.

Add the chicken cubes to the soup. Heat for five minutes and serve.

Serves: 6

Nutritional Information per Serving
Calories: 380, Fat: 22 grams, Protein: 29 grams, Carbohydrates: 17 grams, Cholesterol: 90 milligrams, Fiber: 1.5 grams

ICE FISHING - A WINTER PASTIME

There must be something in the water to make thousands of Wisconsin residents want to sit out on a frozen body of water in sometimes sub-arctic temperatures. Yes, there is something in the water; they are called fish.

Fishing is not just a warm weather sport. In fact, many Wisconsinites choose to spend their spare time waiting for a hungry fish to latch onto their baited hooks – summer or not!

The ice fishermen and women who brave the elements can be seen on all of Wisconsin's beautiful lakes waiting to catch a tasty meal. Some of the fishermen have shanties to protect themselves from the brutal elements. Others find their comfort from heavy clothing and a well-padded bucket on which to sit.

Passing the time, waiting for the tip-up flag to announce the catch of a fish, many engage in conversation, cribbage, or a nice nap.

Asian Ginger Chicken Soup

64 ounces Asian ginger chicken stock
1 whole boneless, skinless chicken breast
1 zucchini, peeled and chopped
2 large carrots, peeled and chopped
2 medium red potatoes, peeled and chopped
1 large onion, diced
2 tablespoons olive oil
6 cloves garlic, minced
1 1/2 cups cut green beans
1 tablespoon grated gingerroot
1/3 cup chutney
1 teaspoon herbs de Provence
1 teaspoon lavender (optional)
1 1/2 cups frozen peas or halved fresh pea pods
salt and pepper to taste

HERBS DE PROVENCE:

Herbs de Provence is a dried herb mixture available at specialty foods stores and some supermarkets. A combination of dried thyme, basil, savory and fennel seeds can be used.

In a large stock pot cook chicken in stock for 20 minutes on medium heat. Remove the chicken, cool slightly and cut into 1-inch cubes.

Add the zucchini, carrots and potatoes to the stock; continue to cook over medium heat.

Meanwhile, sauté the onion in the olive oil in a medium skillet until translucent; add to the stock.

Add the garlic, green beans, ginger, chutney and herbs to the stock. Cook 15 minutes. Add the lavender and peas and cook an additional 5 minutes. Add salt and pepper, as desired.

Serves: 8

Nutritional Information per Serving
Calories: 165, Fat: 5 grams, Protein: 13 grams, Carbohydrates: 18 grams, Cholesterol: 15 milligrams, Fiber: 3.5 grams

 If you cannot find Asian chicken soup stock (which has garlic and ginger in it), you may add an additional tablespoon of grated ginger root to the soup.

Turkey Wild Rice Soup

3 cups water
2/3 cup wild rice, uncooked
2 tablespoons butter
1 medium onion, chopped
2 celery ribs, diced
2 carrots, diced
1/4 cup all purpose flour
4 cups chicken or turkey broth
2 tablespoons dry sherry (optional)
2 cups half and half
2 cups diced cooked turkey breast, diced
1/2 teaspoon salt
1/4 teaspoon pepper
2 teaspoons chopped parsley

Wash wild rice and put in a large saucepan. Add 3 cups water and bring to a boil for a full minute. Reduce heat to simmer; cook 45 minutes. Drain.

Melt butter in a large stockpot over medium heat. Sauté the onion, celery and carrots on medium high heat until tender. Reduce heat and blend in the flour; cook until bubbly. Gradually add the sherry and the broth, stirring constantly. Bring to a boil and hold boil for 1 minute. Add the wild rice, half and half, turkey, parsley and seasonings. Simmer for 20 minutes.

Garnish with reserved parsley.

Serves: 8

Nutritional Information per Serving
Calories: 280, Fat: 13 grams, Protein: 21 grams, Carbohydrates: 19 grams, Cholesterol: 60 milligrams, Fiber: 1.7grams

Ask your butcher to cut deli turkey in thick slices so you can easily cube it.

HOOFERS WINTER CARNIVAL

Every year Hoofers, a student outing club at the University of Wisconsin, organizes a Winter Carnival to make the most of Wisconsin winters and the frozen waters of nearby lakes.

Participants can watch ice diving demonstrations, participate in ice sculpting and compete in broomball, ice bowling and ice sailing.

Of course, no carnival would be complete without gathering to enjoy bratwursts, Wisconsin's favorite sausage, while warming toes at the bonfire.

Hoofers, organized in 1931, gives University students, faculty and staff an opportunity to get involved in outdoor activities including sailing, horseback riding, skiing and snowboarding, mountaineering, biking, kayaking and SCUBA diving. Hoofers takes advantage of local recreational facilities and also plans cross country trips to some of the most popular outdoor excursion sites.

 Firehouse Chili

3 pounds cubed (or coarsely ground) sirloin tip roast
2 tablespoons oil
2 tablespoons salt
8 tablespoons chili powder
2 tablespoons dark red chili powder
2 tablespoons hot chili powder
1/2 tablespoon dark red chili powder
1/2 teaspoon hot chili powder
2 tablespoon cumin
white pepper to taste
1 cup celery chopped fine
1/2 teaspoon coriander (optional)
1 1/4 ounces tomato sauce
2 cups chicken broth
3/4 cup Bloody Mary mix
3 jalapeño peppers, chopped fine
1 serrano pepper, chopped fine
1/4 teaspoon cayenne pepper (optional)
1 can minced Ortega peppers
6 ounces beer

Notes:

Brown meat over medium heat, about a pound at a time. Add salt and pepper to taste. Drain liquid and set meat aside to cool. Add onion, garlic and oil to pot and sauté for about 3 minutes. Add chili powders and approximately 2 ounces of chicken stock (to prevent sticking) and mix well. Add meat and remaining spices, tomato sauce, Bloody Mary mix, beer, chicken stock and peppers. Simmer for approximately 1 hour, adding more liquid if too thick. Add cayenne pepper during last 30 minutes of cooking if needed.

Serves: 8

Nutritional Information per Serving
Calories: 500, Fat: 34 grams, Protein: 35 grams, Carbohydrates: 13 grams, Cholesterol: 100 milligrams, Fiber: 4.6 grams

 Chopping the meat very fine helps it to absorb the full flavor of the spices and peppers.

One Pot Sausage Soup

This is a wonderful soup on a chilly night and it's even better the next day.

1/2 pound ground Italian sausage
3 medium zucchinis, sliced
2 (14.5 ounce) cans chopped tomatoes
1 medium onion, sliced
1 1/2 cups sliced cabbage
1 (14.5 ounce) can Great Northern beans, drained
1 (10.5 ounce) can beef broth
1 teaspoon basil
1/2 teaspoon oregano
salt and pepper to taste

Brown sausage in a large frying pan or stockpot. Remove the sausage with a slotted spoon, keeping the fat in the pot. Add the onion and zucchini to the pot and sauté for 5 minutes or until the onion is translucent. Add remaining ingredients and sausage to the onion-zucchini mixture. Simmer, covered, 45 minutes.

Serves: 8

Nutritional Information per Serving
Calories: 190, Fat: 9 grams, Protein: 10 grams, Carbohydrates: 15 grams,
Cholesterol: 20 milligrams, Fiber: 4.9 grams

MERRIMAC "FERRY TALE"

The continued existence of the Colsac Ferry in Merrimac, Wisconsin, can only be attributed to one thing: nostalgia. Though an interstate system bridge is nearby, tourists flock by the thousands to take the mile-long boat trip across the Wisconsin River.

The Colsac Ferry has shuttled people and cars between Columbia and Sauk counties for more than 100 years and is the only remaining ferry on the state highway network. Travelers can take the ferry any day of the week at any hour, as long as the Wisconsin River isn't frozen. The ferry doesn't cost any money, but users should be willing to spend some time aboard the ferry.

According to the Wisconsin Department of Transportation, August, the peak of the season, brings up to 1,200 vehicles a day, creating a line of up to 50 or more vehicles per trip. So, bring some spare change to buy treats from the small ice cream and beverage stands along the approaching roads to help pass the time with a smile.

Beef Burgundy Stew

1 cup Burgundy wine
1/2 cup beef broth
2 bay leaves
1 1/2 teaspoons fresh thyme or 1/2 teaspoon dried
1/4 cup chopped parsley
1 tablespoon tomato paste
salt and pepper to taste
2 cups pearl onions, blanched and peeled
1 pound beef stew meat
1/4 pound mushrooms, sliced and sauteed

In a Dutch oven combine wine, broth, bay leaves, parsley, thyme, tomato paste, salt and pepper. Bring to a boil; add onions. Reduce heat, cover and cook until onions are almost tender, about 20-25 minutes.

Add stew meat to broth. Cook 10-15 minutes stirring occasionally. Add mushrooms; cook 10 minutes. Add more Burgundy, broth or water if needed. Remove the bay leaves before serving.

Serves: 4

Notes:

Nutritional Information per Serving
Calories: 400, Fat: 24 grams, Protein: 35 grams, Carbohydrates: 11 grams, Cholesterol: 115 milligrams, Fiber: 2.5 grams

Lamb & Pasta Stew

Even those who claim to dislike lamb love this stew!

1 1/2 pounds lamb (leg or shoulder steaks), cubed
1 well-washed leek (white part only), chopped
3 cups chicken stock
1 (14.5 ounce) can diced tomatoes
1 onion, chopped
2 cups orzo
2 tablespoons olive oil
1 teaspoon nutmeg
1 teaspoon cinnamon
1 tablespoon fresh mint, chopped
salt and pepper to taste

In a large saucepan over medium-high heat, brown the lamb on all sides. Add leek and chicken stock. Cover and simmer 1 1/2 hours. Remove the meat and trim away the fat and bones. Return meat to pot and continue to simmer over low heat.

In a large frying pan, sauté the chopped onion and orzo in olive oil until it begins to brown. Add to lamb.

Add remaining ingredients and stir well. Cover and simmer until pasta is cooked, about 30 minutes. (If necessary, add more water for cooking the pasta.)

Serves: 6

Nutritional Information per Serving
Calories: 435, Fat: 25 grams, Protein: 25 grams, Carbohydrates: 27 grams, Cholesterol: 60 milligrams, Fiber: 2.2 grams

KITES ON ICE

February can be a cold and dreary time of year. But not in Madison where the Kites on Ice Festival lights up the cold, clear skies with brilliant colors. Every year, families and busloads of children gather on the frozen waters of Lake Monona or Lake Mendota to watch a mystical, magical world of kites come to life.

Nearly 50,000 spectators come to this two-day, one-of-a-kind event to watch world-class kiters from all over demonstrate their skill, exhibit synchronized flying shows and teach the art and science of kites.

Festival spectators gather inside to sip hot chocolate and to learn how artists create the exotic kites displayed outside. Outside, children dressed like miniature Michelin men, watch brilliantly colored kites do loop-de-loops across the crystalline sky. On Saturday night the crowd is treated to a spectacular fireworks display.

The Kites on Ice Festival is just one way that Madisonians celebrate and enjoy the winter months. The cold weather brings a whole new world of outdoor fun that makes the icy days of winter seem much warmer.

Lentil Stew

A stew you can make in less than an hour.

2 cups uncooked lentils
6 cups vegetable broth
1 tablespoon olive oil
2 large onions, chopped
3 large carrots, peeled and chopped
2 stalks celery, chopped
3 cloves garlic, minced
1 (15 ounces) can Italian-style diced tomatoes
1 teaspoon oregano
1/2 teaspoon thyme
1/2 teaspoon marjoram
1/2 cup fresh parsley, minced
1/4 cup dry sherry
salt to taste
fresh pepper to taste
1/2 cup grated Parmesan cheese

LENTILS:

Compared to other types of dried beans, lentils are relatively quick and easy to prepare. They readily absorb a variety of wonderful flavors from other foods and seasonings, are high in nutritional value and are available throughout the year.

Wash lentils in a colander under running water. In a large stock pot, combine lentils with broth. Bring to a boil over high heat, reduce heat, cover and simmer for 30 minutes or until lentils are soft.

Meanwhile, heat olive oil in a medium skillet. Cook onions, carrots, celery, and garlic over medium heat until onions are translucent. Add tomatoes, oregano, thyme, marjoram and parsley. Bring to a slow boil and cook until vegetables are tender and soup reaches desired consistency. Thin soup with extra broth, as desired. Add salt and pepper to taste.

Add sherry just before serving.. Top each serving with Parmesan cheese.

Serves: 8

Nutritional Information per Serving
Calories: 380, Fat: 7 grams, Protein: 22 grams, Carbohydrates: 58 grams, Cholesterol: 5 milligrams, Fiber: 19.3 grams

White Chicken Chili

Chili

3 cups chicken broth
2 whole boneless, skinless chicken breasts (4 halves)
1 tablespoon vegetable oil
2 large onions, sliced
1 clove garlic, minced
1 cup dry white wine
2 (15 ounce) cans cannelloni beans, rinsed and drained
1 (14.5 ounce) can white corn
1/4 cup lime juice
1 (4 ounce) can diced green chilies
1 small jalapeno chili, stemmed, seeded and minced (optional)
1/4 cup minced fresh cilantro
1 teaspoon dried oregano
3/4 teaspoon ground cumin
1/4 teaspoon ground cinnamon
1 cup shredded Monterey Jack cheese

Condiments

diced (peeled) plum tomatoes
shredded jack cheese
sliced ripe olives
cilantro sprigs

In a large stock pot, bring broth to boil over high heat. Add the chicken breasts, reduce heat and cover. Simmer 15–20 minutes, until the breast is cooked through. Remove the chicken from the broth, and tear into bite-sized pieces.

Continue boiling the broth on high until reduced to 2 cups, about 7 minutes. Transfer to a bowl.

In cleaned stock pot, heat vegetable oil over medium-high heat. Add the onions and garlic, sautéing until the onions are golden and sweet, about 15 minutes. Add the chilies, cilantro, oregano, cumin and cinnamon and sauté an additional 5 minutes. Add the broth, wine, beans, and lime juice. Bring to a boil over high heat, reduce heat to simmer, covered, for 15 minutes.

Stir in the reserved chicken and cheese. Heat until hot and ladle into bowls, adding condiments to taste.

Serves: 6

Nutritional Information per Serving
Calories: 360, Fat: 13 grams, Protein: 26 grams, Carbohydrates: 32 grams, Cholesterol: 40 milligrams, Fiber: 6.8 grams

Vegetarian Chili

Bulgur wheat makes this vegetarian chili taste just like the real thing!

1 tablespoon vegetable oil
1 medium onion, chopped
1 medium green pepper, seeded and chopped
1 stalk celery, diced
2 cloves garlic, minced
2 large carrots, peeled and chopped
2 (15 ounce) can kidney beans, undrained
1 (15 ounce) can crushed tomatoes, undrained
1 (15 ounce) can tomato sauce
1 (15 ounce) can Italian-flavored diced tomatoes
8 ounces green chilies
3/4 cup bulgur wheat
1 1/2 teaspoons chili powder
1/2 teaspoon cumin
dash of Tabasco sauce
salt and pepper
1 cup low fat shredded cheddar cheese

Notes:

In a large stockpot heat oil. Add onions and sauté until translucent. Add peppers, celery, and garlic, cook until tender. Add carrots, kidney beans, tomatoes, tomato sauce, chilies, bulgur wheat, chili powder and cumin. Bring to a boil. Reduce heat and boil gently for 30-40 minutes or until bulgur wheat is tender and chili is reduced to the desired consistency. Stir occasionally.

Add Tabasco, salt and pepper to taste. Ladle into bowls and top each serving with cheddar cheese.

Serves: 6

Nutritional Information per Serving
Calories: 350, Fat: 7 grams, Protein: 19 grams, Carbohydrates: 53 grams,
Cholesterol: 10 milligrams, Fiber: 17.5 grams

Peanutty Chicken Stew

A recipe that gets rave reviews.

3 tablespoons butter
2 onions, diced
1 tablespoon minced garlic
1 red pepper, diced
6 cups chicken stock
1 (15 ounce) can tomato puree
2 teaspoon black pepper
1 teaspoon crushed red pepper
3/4 cup rice
1/2 cup peanut butter
1 pound cooked, diced chicken
salt to taste

Melt the butter in a heavy large pot over low heat. Increase heat and sauté the onions until they start to become translucent. Add garlic and sauté for 2 minutes. Add the red pepper and sauté an additional 5 minutes. Add the chicken stock, tomato puree, black pepper and crushed red pepper.

Bring to a boil and add the rice, stirring often. When the rice is cooked, about 20 minutes, add the peanut butter to the soup and mix thoroughly. Add the diced chicken and salt to taste. Serve piping hot.

Serves: 6

Nutritional Information per Serving
Calories: 510, Fat: 22 grams, Protein: 43 grams, Carbohydrates: 35 grams,
Cholesterol: 80 milligrams, Fiber: 4.3 grams

SKATES AND STICKS

Madison's numerous lakes, ponds and creeks, coupled with the freezing cold temperatures of winter, make the city an ideal destination for fun winter activities like ice skating and hockey.

On the weekends, several area parks with frozen ponds are populated with recreational skaters testing their figure skating or hockey skills. With the sea of colorful scarves, hats and mittens, the scene resembles something from a Norman Rockwell painting.

For those more serious about their skating, indoor and outdoor ice venues offer athletes trying to hone their skating and hockey skills the opportunity to do so year round. Some area athletes have even gone beyond the recreational love of the sport and have brought recognition and pride to Madison via their participation in statewide, national, and even Olympic competitions. Madison-area native Casey Fitzrandolph, for example, brought home a gold medal in speed skating in the 2002 Olympics and Madisonian Eric Heiden captured the gold in 1980.

Whether for fun or for serious competition, ice-related activities help make Wisconsin winters enjoyable.

❦ Summertime Avocado and Tomato Soup

This 2-soup dish adds great visual appeal to your meal.

3/4 cup milk
1 tablespoon fresh lemon juice
2 ripe avocados, halved and peeled
1 large cucumber, peeled, seeded and cut into pieces
2 large green onions (including tops), chopped
1/3 cup canned chicken broth
1 pound ripe tomatoes, seeded and quartered
1 cup packed roasted red bell peppers (from a jar)
1 tablespoon sugar
1 tablespoon fresh tarragon leaves
Sour cream
Fresh tarragon sprigs

AVOCADO:

High protein content makes avocados a good meat substitute, and unlike animal fat, the fat is not saturated. The big surprise in avocados is how high they are in dietary fiber—they have one of the highest fiber contents of any fruit or vegetable. They are also packed with vitamins A, C, and E - primary vitamins in the antioxidant group that protect the cells in human tissue.

Mix the milk and lemon juice together and let sit for 5 minutes until thickened. Place the thickened milk, avocados, cucumber and green onions in a food processor. Blend until smooth. Add 1/3 cup chicken broth. Season to taste with salt and pepper. Blend to mix. Transfer soup to bowl. Cover and refrigerate.

Place tomatoes, bell peppers and sugar in a clean processor. Blend until smooth. Add tarragon leaves. Season with salt and pepper. Blend 30 seconds. Transfer to bowl. Cover and chill.

Ladle both soups simultaneously into each soup bowl, so you have half a bowl of red and half green. Garnish each with a dollop of sour cream and a tarragon sprig.

Serves: 4

Nutritional Information per Serving
Calories: 250, Fat: 14 grams, Protein: 7 grams, Carbohydrates: 25 grams, Cholesterol: 5 milligrams, Fiber: 8.7 grams

 Both soups can be made 4 hours ahead. If the avocado soup is very thick, thin slightly with more broth.

Gazpacho

4 cups tomato juice
1 small Vidalia (or other sweet) onion, finely chopped
2 cups diced tomatoes, peeled and seeded
1/2 cup minced green pepper
1/2 cup minced red pepper
1 teaspoon honey
1 clove garlic, minced
1 medium cucumber, peeled, seeded and diced
2 tablespoons fresh lemon juice
2 tablespoons fresh lime juice
1 tablespoons red wine vinegar
1 teaspoon minced fresh tarragon
1 teaspoon minced fresh basil
1/4 cup finely chopped parsley
dash Tabasco sauce
2 tablespoons olive oil
salt and pepper to taste

Combine all ingredients in a large bowl. For a creamier consistency, blend slightly in a food processor or blender. Chill two hours or overnight.

Serves: 4

Nutritional Information per Serving
Calories: 175, Fat: 7 grams, Protein: 4 grams, Carbohydrates: 24 grams,
Cholesterol: 0 milligrams, Fiber: 4.0 grams

HATS, SCARVES AND MITTENS

"The Junior League meets a great need for our students here at Mendota Elementary School. The hats, scarves and mittens that we receive contribute to the quality of life for our students."

-Pat Smith,
Mendota Elementary,
Madison, Wisconsin

Cold Cucumber Soup

A refreshing cool soup for a hot day!

3 medium cucumbers, peeled and seeded
2 tablespoons butter
1 leek (white part only), chopped
1 bay leaf
1 tablespoon flour
3 cups chicken broth
1 teaspoon salt
1 cup half and half
2 tablespoons lemon juice
salt and pepper to taste
2 teaspoons fresh dill, chopped, plus sprigs for garnish

Notes:

Chop 2 of the cucumbers. Melt butter in a heavy large saucepan over medium heat. Sauté the cucumbers with the white part of the well-washed leek. Add the bay leaf and simmer for 20 minutes until the cucumbers are tender. Add the flour and stir. Add the chicken broth and salt and simmer 30 minutes. Remove from heat; cool slightly. Remove the bay leaf.

Blend well in a food processor until smooth. Remove to a bowl and chill 1 hour.

Finely grate the remaining cucumber. Add to the chilled soup. Add the half and half and lemon juice. Stir in the dill. Add salt and pepper to taste. Chill at least 30 minutes.

Serve in chilled soup cups with a sprig of fresh dill.

Serves: 6

Nutritional Information per Serving
Calories: 160, Fat: 10 grams, Protein: 8 grams, Carbohydrates: 10 grams, Cholesterol: 2.5 milligrams, Fiber: 1.4 grams

garden
of eatin'

Salads that tempt your taste buds

salads

Artichoke and
Rice Salad **132**

Autumn Abundance
Fruit Medley **111**

Caesar Salad **120**

Chilled Asparagus Vinaigrette **131**

Cucumber Pasta Salad **128**

Curry Chicken Salad **124**

Door County Cherry, Turkey and Pasta
Salad **129**

French Beef Salad **127**

Greek Pasta Salad **126**

Mixed Baby Greens
with Asparagus
and Oranges **114**

Pear, Arugula and
Endive Salad with
Candied Walnuts **112/113**

Red and White Salad **118**

Red Poppy Salad with
Goat Cheese **115**

Romaine Spinach
Salad **123**

Sparkling Fruit
Compote **110**

Spinach Salad with Hot Bacon
Dressing **122**

Sunshine Salad with
Toasted Almonds **116**

Symphony Salad **121**

Tangy Asian
Chicken Salad **125**

Tomato Gorgonzola
Salad **119**

Tuscan Tuna and
Bean Salad **130**

Wild Rice Salad **133**

Winter Salad **117**

photo by Zane Williams

Dane County Farmers' Market

The Dane County Farmers' Market is one of Madison's most popular traditions. Every Saturday morning from April to November, the capitol grounds swell with thousands of locals and visitors shopping the outdoor, European-style market. Madisonians show their enthusiasm for the rich harvests of the region by crowding sidewalks in search of brilliant cut and potted flowers as well as fresh produce and baked goods.

Hundreds of vendors in canopied booths sell Wisconsin's bounty of seasonal fruits and vegetables such as sweet strawberries, ruby-red tomatoes, crispy snap peas, juicy watermelon and tasty sweet corn – all summertime favorites. True to our dairyland roots, vendors also boast varieties of Wisconsin's award-winning, regional cheeses including cheddar, Baby Swiss and Colby Jack. Potted herbs, honey and maple syrup round out the culinary offerings at this top-rated market.

The Dane County Farmers' Market supplies any chef with an abundance of fresh ingredients to put together a spectacular summer feast for friends and family.

garden fresh lunch menu

Cold Cucumber Soup
page 106

Mixed Baby Greens with Asparagus and Oranges
page 114

Leek Tart
page 74

Dilly Bread
page 63

White Chocolate Fruit Tart
page 251

Pink Punch
page 44

109

Sparkling Fruit Compote

1/2 cup sugar
1 cup water
1 teaspoon lemon zest
1/2 cup lemon juice
4 oranges, peeled and sectioned
2 cups seedless grapes, halved
2 cups fresh pineapple, cut into chunks
1 cup fresh strawberries, sliced
1 cup fresh blueberries
2 kiwis, peeled and sliced
2 cups dry champagne, or sparkling cider, chilled

HOW TO DO A ZEST:

Use a paring knife, or grater. Scrape only the colored part of the skin away from the fruit. Use the grater and rub peel back and forth. The zest holds the most highly concentrated and flavorful oils of a fruit.

Combine sugar and water in saucepan; bring to a boil. Cover, cook 5 minutes. Uncover and cool. Stir in lemon zest and juice.

In a large bowl place oranges, grapes and pineapple. Pour sugar mixture over and toss to coat. Cover and chill.

Just before serving, add berries and kiwi to fruit mixture. Pour champagne on top.

Serves: 8

Nutritional Information per Serving
Calories: 200, Fat: 0 grams, Protein: 2 grams, Carbohydrates: 47 grams, Cholesterol: 0 milligrams, Fiber: 4.3 grams

Autumn Abundance Fruit Medley

3 bananas, sliced
2 red apple, cored and cut in chunks
2 pears, cored and cut in chunks
1/2 cup pecans, chopped
1/2 cup golden raisins
1/3 cup flaked coconut

Dressing
1 cup low fat vanilla yogurt
1 tablespoon honey
1/2 teaspoon cinnamon

Combine fruit with coconut in a large bowl.

Combine dressing ingredients and mix with fruit. Toss lightly. Chill no more than 3 hours before serving.

Serves: 6

Nutritional Information per Serving
Calories: 225, Fat: 5 grams, Protein: 3 grams, Carbohydrates: 42 grams,
Cholesterol: 2 milligrams, Fiber: 4.4 grams

Pear, Arugula and Endive Salad with Candied Walnuts

2 tablespoons red wine vinegar
2 tablespoons fresh lemon juice
1 tablespoon chopped fresh parsley
2 teaspoons Dijon mustard
6 tablespoons walnut oil (or olive oil)
6 tablespoons extra-virgin olive oil
12 cups, about 12 ounces, arugula, torn into pieces
4 heads Belgian endive, trimmed, leaves separated
2 firm but ripe pears, halved, cored, thinly sliced lengthwise
1 cup feta cheese
Candied Walnuts

Notes:

In medium bowl whisk together vinegar, lemon juice, parsley and mustard. Add walnut oil and olive oil; whisk until well blended. Season dressing to taste with salt and pepper. (Can be made 1 day ahead. Cover and chill. Let stand at room temperature 1 hour and re-whisk before continuing.)

Toss arugula in large bowl with enough dressing to coat. Divide dressed arugula among 10 plates. Arrange endive leaves and pear slices atop arugula on each plate. Drizzle with more dressing. Sprinkle with Candied Walnuts and serve.

Serves: 10

Nutritional Information per Serving
Calories: 275, Fat: 21 grams, Protein: 5 grams, Carbohydrates: 17 grams, Cholesterol: 10 milligrams, Fiber: 6.7 grams

Candied Walnuts

nonstick vegetable oil spray
1 cup walnuts
2 tablespoons light corn syrup
1 tablespoon sugar
1/2 teaspoon salt
1/4 teaspoon ground black pepper
1 tablespoon brown sugar
1/8 teaspoon cayenne pepper

Preheat oven to 325 degrees. Spray baking sheet with nonstick spray.

Combine walnuts and all remaining ingredients in medium bowl; toss to coat. Spread nut mixture on prepared baking sheet, some nuts may clump together.

Bake 15 minutes, stirring occasionally to break up clumps, until nuts are deep golden and sugar mixture is bubbling. Cool completely on baking sheet. (Can be made 3 days ahead. Store in airtight container.)

Makes 1 cup.

Serves: 10

Nutritional Information per Serving
Calories: 40, Fat: 2 grams, Protein: 1 gram, Carbohydrates: 5 grams
Cholesterol: 0 milligrams, Fiber: 0.2 grams

 These candied walnuts can be made ahead and frozen.

OLBRICH BOTANICAL GARDENS

In 1916 a 20 acre stretch of stagnant backwater along the shores of Lake Monona began its transformation into Olbrich Botanical Gardens. Today, thousands of visitors stroll through the gardens to enjoy the serenity of the Thai Pavilion, the glow of the rose garden and the fragrance of the herb garden.

The centerpiece of the Thai Garden is the graceful sala, one of only three Thai pavilions outside of Thailand.

Olbrich Botanical Garden's award-winning Rose Garden is home to more than 700 species including hybrid tea roses, floribundas, grandifloras and shrub roses.

Recent expansions include a Sunken Garden, with an elegant 80-foot reflecting pool and formal plantings.

Olbrich Botanical Gardens is tended by a loyal army of hard-working volunteers. The results provide a spectacular backdrop for hundreds of weddings and other celebrations and inspiration to gardeners young and old.

Mixed Baby Greens with Asparagus and Oranges

This beautifully presented salad is perfect for the first spring crop of fresh asparagus.

Dressing
- 2/3 cup regular or low-fat mayonnaise
- 1/2 cup buttermilk
- 2 tablespoons chopped fresh basil
- 2 tablespoons olive oil (preferably extra-virgin)
- 2 tablespoons white wine vinegar
- 2 tablespoons chopped fresh tarragon

Salad
- 24 spears fresh asparagus
- 4 oranges
- 8 cups (20 ounces) mixed baby greens
- 1 tablespoon chopped fresh basil
- 1 tablespoon chopped fresh tarragon
- 1/2 cup thinly sliced red onion

HOW TO SNAP
ASPARAGUS:

Asparagus has a natural
breaking point. Hold each
piece with one hand on each
end half way up the stalk and
bend. Discard bitter,
woody ends.

To make dressing, whisk all ingredients in medium bowl to blend. Then chill until cold.

Cook asparagus in large pot of boiling salted water until crisp-tender, about 2 minutes. Transfer asparagus to bowl of ice water to cool. Drain.

Cut peel and white pith from oranges. Using a small sharp knife, cut between membranes to release segments.

Arrange asparagus spears in sunburst pattern on a large platter. Place orange segments between asparagus spears. Mound greens in center of platter. Sprinkle salad with basil and tarragon. Top with red onion slices. Drizzle some dressing over the salad. Pass the remaining dressing separately.

Serves: 8

Nutritional Information per Serving
Calories: 230, Fat: 18 grams, Protein: 3 grams, Carbohydrates: 15 grams, Cholesterol: 10 milligrams, Fiber: 3.4 grams

Red Poppy Salad with Goat Cheese

This is a great way to enjoy fresh strawberries!

Dressing
- 1/4 cup sugar
- 2 tablespoons red wine vinegar
- 1 1/2 teaspoons sesame seeds, toasted
- 1 1/2 teaspoons olive oil
- 1 teaspoon minced onion
- 3/4 teaspoon poppy seeds
- 1/4 teaspoon paprika
- 1/8 teaspoon salt

Salad
- 6 cups, about 1 pound, baby spinach or torn spinach
- 2 cups sliced strawberries
- 2 tablespoons slivered almonds, toasted
- 2 1/2 ounces crumbled goat cheese

Combine all of the dressing ingredients in a jar with a tight-fitting lid. Cover dressing tightly and shake vigorously.

Combine the spinach and strawberry slices in a large bowl and mix gently. Pour the dressing over the spinach mixture, tossing gently to coat.

Spoon 1 cup of salad onto each of 6 plates; sprinkle each serving with some toasted almonds, and 1 tablespoon of goat cheese.

Serves: 6

Nutritional Information per Serving
Calories: 130, Fat: 6 grams, Protein: 4 grams, Carbohydrates: 15 grams, Cholesterol: 0 milligrams, Fiber: 2.8 grams

To toast almonds, spread in a single layer in a shallow pan. Stir and carefully and watch for 2-3 minutes. If sesame or poppy seeds are not available, substitute pine nuts.

GEORGIA O'KEEFFE

Georgia O'Keeffe was an American artist who found her inspiration through nature and the landscapes around her. Her floral paintings, which she created throughout her long career, are world famous. She painted in her own personal style, using strong vibrant colors and sensual lines.

O'Keeffe was born on November 15, 1887 in Sun Prairie, Wisconsin, which is ten miles north of Madison. She was the second of seven children and grew up on the family dairy farm. O'Keeffe attended school in Madison and received art lessons throughout high school. In 1905, she attended the School of Art Institute of Chicago and over the next ten years, she continued to teach and study art. American photographer Alfred Stieglitz first showed O'Keeffe's paintings in his gallery in New York City. Stieglitz and O'Keeffe were married in 1924. They split their time between New York and New Mexico. O'Keeffe moved to New Mexico in the 1940's, where the stunning vistas and stark landscapes inspired her work until her eyesight started to fail in the 1970's. She continued her art as she produced ceramics and pottery until her death on March 6, 1987.

Sunshine Salad
with Toasted Almonds

Dressing
> 4 tablespoons vegetable oil
> 2 tablespoons sugar
> 2 tablespoons white wine vinegar
> 1 tablespoon fresh parsley, chopped

Toasted Almonds
> 2 tablespoons sugar
> 1 tablespoon butter
> 2 ounces slivered almonds

Salad
> 4 cups mixed greens
> 3 green onions, thinly sliced
> 1 (11 ounce) can mandarin oranges, drained
> 1 cup sliced strawberries
> 2 stalks celery, chopped

HOW TO TREAT
LETTUCE:

After rinsing, remove core.
Lettuce leaves should be torn
by hand or cut with a plastic
knife to avoid brown edges.

To make dressing, whisk oil, 2 tablespoons sugar, vinegar and parsley in medium bowl to blend. Chill until ready to use.

Melt 2 tablespoons sugar and butter over low heat, add almonds; stir until they are lightly brown being careful not to burn them. Cool on wax paper and break apart.

Place salad ingredients in a large bowl, add dressing, toss and top with almonds.

Serves: 6

Nutritional Information per Serving
Calories: 215, Fat: 13 grams, Protein: 3 grams, Carbohydrates: 23 grams, Cholesterol: 5 milligrams, Fiber: 4.9 grams

 If in a hurry, use one 10 ounce bag of lettuce.

Winter Salad

Dressing
- 1/3 cup sugar
- 1/3 cup lemon juice
- 2 tablespoons onion, finely chopped
- 1 teaspoon Dijon mustard
- 1/2 teaspoon salt
- 2/3 cup canola oil
- 1 tablespoon poppy seeds

Salad
- 1 head Romaine lettuce, torn into pieces
- 1 cup Swiss cheese, shredded
- 1 cup cashews or cashew pieces
- 1/4 cup dried cranberries
- 1 cup apple, chopped with skin
- 1 cup pear, chopped with skin

Whisk all dressing ingredients together; set aside.

Combine salad ingredients in large salad bowl. Toss with dressing.

Serves: 6

Nutritional Information per Serving
Calories: 525, Fat: 40 grams, Protein: 10 grams, Carbohydrates: 32 grams, Cholesterol: 15 milligrams, Fiber: 3.7 grams

WISCONSIN - A SEA OF RED

One would think that satellite photos of the state of Wisconsin would come back red. Not because of the number of Badger fans, but for seas of bright red cranberries scattered throughout the state. The cranberry is native to North America and Wisconsin produces more than 300 million pounds of the fruit annually, that's more than half of the 575 million pounds Americans consume each year!

In fact, these glowing berries contribute such a large amount of money to the state economy, that in 2004, the cranberry became the Wisconsin State fruit.

The popularity of the cranberry is increasing in our health-conscious society. It is a low calorie, high vitamin and mineral fruit with great fiber content. And, as chefs discover how this versatile, tart, red, native fruit can be used in many different dishes like Cranberry Upside Down Sour Cream Cake (page 259) and Mediterranean Rice with Pine Nuts and Dried Cranberries (pg 159), its growth will continue to provide additional jobs and income for the state.

Red and White Salad

A wonderful recipe for any holiday that brings out the child in you!

1 (6 ounce) package raspberry gelatin
2 cups boiling water
1 cup cold water
1 (12 ounce) package frozen raspberries

Topping
8 ounces cream cheese, softened
8 ounces prepared whipped topping
1 cup plus 2 tablespoons sugar
3/4 cup crushed pretzels
1/2 cup melted butter

Mix raspberry gelatin with hot and cold water according to package directions. Stir in raspberries. Let the gelatin set for about 3 hours.

Preheat oven to 350 degrees.

In a medium bowl, combine melted butter and 2 tablespoons sugar. Add pretzels to butter-sugar mixture and mix well. Spread crushed pretzels evenly on a baking sheet. Bake for 10 minutes. Cool completely.

In a medium bowl, combine cream cheese and 1 cup sugar. Blend in whipped topping. Spread over set gelatin.

Spread cooled pretzel mixture on top of the cream cheese layer. Keep refrigerated until ready to serve.

Serves: 10

Nutritional Information per Serving
Calories: 500, Fat: 26 grams, Protein: 5 grams, Carbohydrates: 62 grams, Cholesterol: 80 milligrams, Fiber: 2.1 grams

Low fat cream cheese may be substituted without changing the taste of this recipe.

Notes:

Tomato Gorgonzola Salad

Dressing
1/3 cup olive oil
3 tablespoons balsamic vinegar
2 teaspoons Dijon mustard
1/4 cup chopped basil
salt and pepper to taste

Salad
16 ounces mixed baby greens
4 ounces Gorgonzola cheese
1 red onion, sliced very thin
2 tablespoons pine nuts
3 large tomatoes, sliced

Dressing: Whisk all ingredients together; set aside or refrigerate.

In a salad bowl toss lettuce with cheese, red onion and pine nuts. Drizzle dressing over the salad mixture; toss gently.

Arrange sliced tomatoes on a large platter. Spoon salad over the top.

Serves: 8

Nutritional Information per Serving
Calories: 175, Fat: 14 grams, Protein: 5 grams, Carbohydrates: 7 grams, Cholesterol: 10 milligrams, Fiber: 1.9 grams

FARM TO FEAST
A CULINARY ADVENTURE

Monroe, Wisconsin, located just 45 miles south of Madison, is proudly known as the Swiss Cheese Capital of the United States.

Swiss immigrants arrived in Monroe in the 1800s importing their knowledge of dairying and cheesemaking. Swiss cheese grew in popularity by the end of the 1800s and by 1900, Monroe earned its "Swiss Cheese Capital" title.

Monroe and the surrounding countryside is also home to the oldest brewery in Wisconsin and second oldest brewery in the nation, the Joseph Huber Brewing Company. Huber is still in operation today making many of its award-winning Berghoff beers.

The neighboring town of New Glarus also has a strong Swiss heritage and laid claim to the title of "Little Switzerland." It also boasts a number of cheesemakers and is home to famous beers such as "Spotted Cow" and "Fat Squirrel" from the New Glarus Brewery.

These two towns play host to "Farm to Feast Culinary Getaways" which include cooking classes, several food sampling sessions, a beer tasting and a personalized, behind-the-scenes tour of the history and cultural influence of the small towns.

Caesar Salad

Dressing

    2 cloves garlic, minced
    1/2 cup vegetable oil
    1/4 cup lemon juice
    2 tablespoons white wine Worcestershire sauce
    1/2 teaspoon pepper
    1/4 teaspoon salt
    1 egg, blended

Salad

    3 heads Romaine lettuce, torn into pieces
    1 head Bibb lettuce
    1/2 cup Parmesan cheese, grated
    1/2 cup crumbled blue cheese
    2 cups croutons

HOW TO MAKE FRESH CROUTONS:

Take 2 cups of Italian or French bread and cut into 1-inch cubes. Mix with 3 tablespoons olive oil, 1 teaspoon seasoned salt and 1 teaspoon dried parsley. Toss and spread on a cookie sheet. Bake at 325 degrees for 2 minutes or until light brown.

Mix garlic and oil in a small bowl. Set aside for several hours.

Prepare the dressing just before serving. To the garlic-oil mixture add lemon juice, Worcestershire, salt and pepper and egg; blend well.

In a salad bowl mix both kinds of lettuce with cheeses and croutons. Add dressing and toss gently. Serve immediately.

Serves: 8

Nutritional Information per Serving
Calories: 215, Fat: 18 grams, Protein: 5 grams, Carbohydrates: 9 grams, Cholesterol: 30 milligrams, Fiber: 1.2 grams

Symphony Salad

Dressing

 1/4 small onion, chopped
 1/4 cup cider vinegar
 2 teaspoons spicy brown mustard
 1/2 teaspoon sugar
 1/2 teaspoon salt
 1/4 teaspoon fresh ground pepper
 3/4 cup vegetable oil

Salad

 2 heads Romaine lettuce
 1 (14 ounce) can hearts of palm, drained and quartered
 1 (14 ounce) can artichoke hearts, drained and quartered
 4 ounces crumbled blue cheese
 1/2 pound bacon, cooked, drained and crumbled

Dressing: In a blender, purée onion with vinegar. Transfer to medium bowl. Using an electric mixer, blend in mustard, sugar, salt and pepper. Gradually add oil in steady stream and continue beating until thick. Set aside or refrigerate.

Mix lettuce, hearts of palm, artichoke hearts, blue cheese and bacon in large salad bowl. Toss with dressing.

Serves: 8

Nutritional Information per Serving
Calories: 550, Fat: 45 grams, Protein: 15 grams, Carbohydrates: 21 grams, Cholesterol: 35 milligrams, Fiber: 4.2 grams

Spinach Salad with Hot Bacon Dressing

Dressing
- 1 1/2 cups bacon, cooked and crumbled (about 8 slices)
- 1 1/2 cups chopped onion
- 2 1/2 cups cold water
- 3/4 cup cider vinegar
- 1/4 cup lemon juice
- 3 tablespoons cornstarch
- 1/2 cup sugar
- 3/4 teaspoon salt
- 1/4 teaspoon pepper
- 10 ounces fresh spinach leaves

HOT BACON
DRESSING:

Hot bacon dressing is also
wonderful served over warm
cooked sliced red potatoes for
German Potato Salad. Garnish
with chopped fresh parsley.

Fry bacon until almost crisp. Add onion and fry until tender and translucent. Add remaining dressing ingredients and cook until slightly thickened.

Serve warm over raw spinach leaves.

Serves: 10

Nutritional Information per Serving
Calories: 180, Fat: 11 grams, Protein: 7 grams, Carbohydrates: 13 grams, Cholesterol: 19 milligrams, Fiber: .5 grams

 You can use 1 full cup of cider vinegar instead of the vinegar and lemon juice combination.

Romaine Spinach Salad

Dressing
- 3/4 cup sugar
- 1/2 vegetable oil
- 1/2 olive oil
- 1/3 cup red wine vinegar
- 1 teaspoon dry mustard
- 1 teaspoon salt
- 1 1/2 tablespoons poppy seeds

Salad
- 1 head romaine lettuce
- 2 (10 ounce) bags of spinach
- 1 pint strawberries, sliced
- 4 ounces Swiss cheese, shredded
- 8 ounces whole cashews

In a blender, combine all dressing ingredients and blend for 3 minutes; set aside.

In a large salad bowl place greens, strawberries, cheese and cashews.
Add dressing and toss gently.

Serves: 10

Nutritional Information per Serving
Calories: 440, Fat: 34 grams, Protein: 7 grams, Carbohydrates: 27 grams, Cholesterol: 10 milligrams, Fiber: 3.3 grams

Curry Chicken Salad

Dressing

> 2/3 cup mayonnaise
> 1 tablespoon mustard
> 1 teaspoon curry powder
> 1/8 teaspoon salt

Salad

> 4 cups cooked chicken cut into chunks (about 3 breasts)
> 1 (8 ounce can) pineapple chunks, drained or 1 cup fresh pineapple
> 1/3 cup raisins
> 1/3 cup thinly sliced celery
> 3 tablespoons thinly sliced green onion
> 1/3 cup slivered almonds, toasted
> 6-8 large lettuce leaves (such as Boston, Bibb or Romaine)
> 1 pound red grapes

Notes:

Dressing: In a small bowl combine all dressing ingredients, mix well and set aside.

Salad: In a large bowl mix chicken, pineapple, raisins, celery and green onion. Pour dressing over and mix until well coated. Refrigerate for 1 hour.

Arrange lettuce leaves on plates. Spoon chicken salad over the lettuce and sprinkle with slivered almonds. Garnish with red grapes.

Serves: 4

Nutritional Information per Serving
Calories: 490, Fat: 33 grams, Protein: 18 grams, Carbohydrates: 30 grams, Cholesterol: 60 milligrams, Fiber: 3.1 grams

Low-fat mayonnaise is a tasty substitute.

Tangy Asian Chicken Salad

This is a wonderful main dish salad to bring to a pot-luck or serve at a luncheon. It never fails to elicit requests for the recipe!

3/4 cup vegetable oil
6 tablespoons rice vinegar
1/4 cup sugar
1/2 teaspoon cracked pepper
2 (3 ounce) packages of chicken-flavored ramen noodles
4 cups cooked chicken (about 3 breasts), finely chopped
4 cups cabbage, shredded
3/4 cup lightly toasted sliced almonds
1/3 cup chopped onion
1/4 cup lightly toasted sesame seeds
1 (11 ounce) can mandarin oranges, drained

In a small bowl, whisk together oil, vinegar, sugar, pepper and the contents of the 2 seasoning packets from noodles. Set aside.

Boil noodles according to directions, for 2-3 minutes or until tender. Drain and transfer to a large bowl.

Pour 1/4 cup of the oil-vinegar mixture over noodles and toss to coat. Add chicken, cabbage, almonds, onion, sesame seeds and oranges to noodle mixture. Pour remaining oil-vinegar mixture over salad and toss to combine. Cover and chill for 2-24 hours.

Serves: 8

Nutritional Information per Serving
Calories: 450, Fat: 31 grams, Protein: 15 grams, Carbohydrates: 28 grams,
Cholesterol: 40 milligrams, Fiber: 2.6 grams

Make a full day ahead for the best flavor.

THE PROUD TRADITION OF WORLD-FAMOUS WISCONSIN CHEESE

For over 150 years, Wisconsin cheesemakers have been making some of the World's best cheeses. It is a rich and proud tradition that has made Wisconsin known as America's Dairyland.

Wisconsin cheesemaking is rooted in the traditions of European cheesemaking, proudly nurtured by every generation since the early pioneers. Wisconsin began and continues to advance the country's highest cheesemaking standards. Years ago, Wisconsin was the first state to grade its cheese for quality. Then, Wisconsin was first to insist that a licensed cheesemaker oversee every pound of cheese made in the state. Now, Wisconsin has more licensed cheesemakers than any other state and is home to some of the finest craftsmen in the world.

Wisconsin produces more award-winning cheeses than any other state or country and accounts for 26% of the nation's cheese supply.

Greek Pasta Salad

Dressing
>2/3 cup extra virgin olive oil
>6 tablespoons fresh lemon juice
>1/4 cup red wine vinegar
>4 cloves garlic, minced
>3 tablespoons minced fresh oregano
>1 teaspoon salt
>1 teaspoon freshly ground pepper

Salad
>12 ounces spiral, rotini, or shell pasta, cooked al dente
>2 regular or 4 Roma tomatoes, chopped
>3 ribs celery, chopped
>1 cucumber, peeled, seeded and chopped
>5 green onions, chopped
>2 small green bell peppers, seeded and chopped
>1 1/2 cup chopped fresh parsley
>12 ounces feta cheese, crumbled
>20 kalamata olives, pitted
>12 pepperoncini (pickled green mild chili peppers), minced

HOW TO PIT AN OLIVE:

Using the flat side of a chef's knife, place over the olive. Use the other hand to strike the knife with the palm of your hand.

Dressing: Whisk oil, lemon juice, vinegar, garlic, oregano, salt and pepper until combined. Set aside.

Salad: Combine pasta, tomatoes, celery, cucumber, green onions, bell peppers, parsley, feta, olives and pepperoncini in a large serving bowl. Pour dressing over salad and toss gently to coat. Cover and refrigerate 2-3 hours to allow flavors to blend.

Serves: 10

Nutritional Information per Serving
Calories: 395, Fat: 24 grams, Protein: 10 grams, Carbohydrates: 35 grams, Cholesterol: 30 milligrams, Fiber: 2.6 grams

French Beef Salad

This is a delicious way to use your leftover beef!

Dressing
  4 tablespoons olive oil
  4 teaspoons red wine vinegar
  1/4 teaspoon dry mustard
  pinch each of chervil, thyme and basil

Salad
  3 tablespoons olive oil
  1 pound mushrooms, sliced
  1/2 tablespoon lemon juice
  salt and pepper to taste
  1/4 pound Swiss cheese, cut into strips
  1 (14 ounce) can hearts of palm, sliced
  20 cherry tomatoes, halved
  1 (2.25 ounce) can sliced black olives
  4 cups, (about one pound) leftover or pre-cooked roast beef or
  tenderloin, sliced

Whisk all dressing ingredients together; set aside.

Sauté mushrooms in oil with lemon, salt and pepper. Cool slightly.

In a large salad bowl combine cheese, hearts of palm, tomatoes, black olives and beef. Add mushrooms. Drizzle dressing over the salad and toss gently.

Serves: 4-6

Nutritional Information per Serving (based on 4 servings)
Calories: 820, Fat: 60 grams, Protein: 33 grams, Carbohydrates: 37 grams, Cholesterol: 100 milligrams, Fiber: 3.4 grams

 You may substitute fresh parsley for the chervil.

Cucumber Pasta Salad

16 ounce package garden rotini, cooked
1 cup canola oil
1 cup white vinegar
3/4 cup white sugar
4 tablespoons parsley flakes
1 Vidalia onion, chopped
1 tablespoon garlic powder
1 tablespoon Accent
1 1/2 tablespoons salt
1/2 tablespoon pepper
1 cucumber seeded, peeled and cubed
1 carrot shredded
1 small can (2.25 ounces) sliced black olives

Combine all ingredients, refrigerate at least one hour or overnight and enjoy!

Serves: 8

Nutritional Information per Serving
Calories: 575, Fat: 30 grams, Protein: 8 grams, Carbohydrates: 68 grams, Cholesterol: 0 milligrams, Fiber: 2.5 grams

 You can substitute 16 ounces of linguine for the rotini pasta. You may also substitute 1 large zucchini for the cucumber.

Notes:

Door County Cherry, Turkey and Pasta Salad

Dressing
- 2 cups mayonnaise
- 2 tablespoons Dijon mustard
- 1/4 cup confectioner's sugar
- 2 tablespoons champagne or other white wine vinegar
- 2 tablespoons water
- 1/2 teaspoon poppy seeds
- 2 teaspoon salt

Salad
- 1 pound rotelle or rotini pasta
- 1 tablespoon. olive oil
- 6 ounces turkey breast, cooked and diced
- 3 ounces dried cherries
- 1/2 cup diced yellow onion
- 1/2 cup diced celery
- 1/2 cup almonds, sliced and toasted

In a small bowl combine all dressing ingredients, mix well and set aside.

Cook pasta; drain well. Toss pasta in olive oil. Cool completely.

In large bowl, combine pasta, turkey, cherries, onions, celery and 1/4 cup almonds. Mix in dressing to desired consistency. Add salt and pepper to taste.

Transfer to a serving dish. Top with remaining almonds before serving.

Serves: 6

Nutritional Information per Serving
Calories: 980, Fat: 66 grams, Protein: 20 grams, Carbohydrates: 77 grams, Cholesterol: 65 milligrams, Fiber: 3.6 grams

 Substitute low-fat mayonnaise for a lower calorie salad.

Tuscan Tuna and Bean Salad

Dressing

- 3 tablespoons lemon juice
- 2 tablespoons olive oil
- 2 tablespoons chopped fresh basil or 2 t. dried basil
- 1/4 teaspoon salt
- 1/8 teaspoon pepper
- 1 garlic clove, minced

Salad

- 1 cup uncooked orzo
- 1 1/2 cups frozen cut green beans
- 1 (16 ounce) can great northern or cannellini beans, rinsed and drained
- 1 (6 ounce) can water-packed white tuna, drained and broken into chunks
- 1/3 cup pitted kalamata olives, drained and halved
- 3 tablespoons chopped red onion

DID YOU KNOW?

According to the Wisconsin Farm Bureau Federation, Wisconsin leads the nation in production of cranberries, snap beans and cabbage for kraut.

Whisk all dressing ingredients together; refrigerate until serving time.

Cook orzo as directed on package, adding green beans during last 5-7 minutes. Cook until orzo and green beans are tender. Drain, rinse with cold water. Drain again.

In large bowl, combine cooked orzo and green beans with all remaining salad ingredients; stir gently. Cover; refrigerate at least 1 hour or until chilled.

To serve, drizzle dressing over salad and toss gently.

Serves: 4

Nutritional Information per Serving
Calories: 345, Fat: 9 grams, Protein: 22 grams, Carbohydrates: 44 grams, Cholesterol: 15 milligrams, Fiber: 7.6 grams

 When in season, you may substitute fresh beans for frozen.

Chilled Asparagus Vinaigrette

This can be served as an individual salad or on a platter as a buffet dish.

3 tablespoons pine nuts
1/4 cup extra virgin olive oil
1/2 cup lemon juice
1 clove garlic, minced
1/2 teaspoon dried oregano
1/2 teaspoon dried basil
salt and pepper
1 pound fresh asparagus

Blanch asparagus in boiling water. Chill.

In a heavy skillet over medium heat, toast pine nuts. Stir constantly and remove from heat immediately when they are toasted or they will burn. Set aside.

Combine oil, lemon juice, garlic, oregano and basil in a small bowl and whisk together. Add salt and pepper to taste. Add the pine nuts. Pour over the chilled asparagus and let stand covered in the refrigerator a couple of hours before serving.

Arrange asparagus on a platter with tongs or on salad plates for individual servings.

Serves: 4

Nutritional Information per Serving
Calories: 175, Fat: 16 grams, Protein: 3 grams, Carbohydrates: 5 grams, Cholesterol: 0 milligrams, Fiber: 1.7 grams

 Artichoke and Rice Salad

Excellent for a buffet or luncheon.

2 (4.4 ounce) packages chicken flavored rice mix
8 green onions, thinly sliced
1 pepper, seeded and chopped
3 (6 ounce) jars marinated artichoke hearts, drained
24 pimiento-stuffed olives, drained and sliced
1 teaspoon curry powder
2/3 cup mayonnaise

HOW TO SEED A PEPPER:

Wash pepper and slice from the stem to the base. Scoop out seeds. Rinse well.

Prepare rice according to directions on packages, omitting the butter. Cool in a large bowl. Add onions, bell pepper and olives.

Drain artichoke hearts, reserving the marinade of one jar plus the spices in the bottom of another jar. Discard remaining marinade. Combine the marinade, reserved spices and curry powder with the mayonnaise.

Cut the artichokes in half; add to the rice mixture. Toss with marinade mayonnaise dressing. Chill.

Serves: 6

Nutritional Information per Serving
Calories: 490, Fat: 25 grams, Protein: 10 grams, Carbohydrates: 57 grams, Cholesterol: 15 milligrams, Fiber: 10 grams

Wild Rice Salad

2 cups wild rice
6 1/2 cups chicken stock
1 cup pecan pieces, toasted
1 cup dried cranberries
zest of 2 oranges
1/2 cup fresh orange juice
1/4 cup fresh mint, chopped
6 green onions, chopped
1/3 cup olive oil
1 1/2 teaspoon salt (optional)
2 tablespoons lemon juice

Rinse wild rice and put into a large saucepan. Add stock and bring to a boil. Reduce heat to a simmer and cook uncovered 40-45 minutes, or until rice is done. Drain into a strainer and then transfer to a large bowl. (Rice may be cooked one day ahead. Cover and refrigerate.)

Add rest of ingredients, except for pecans, and toss well. Let stand for 2-4 hours.

Add pecans, toss, serve at room temperature or chilled. Garnish with parsley.

Serves: 8-10

Nutritional Information per Serving
Calories: 500, Fat: 19 grams, Protein: 12 grams, Carbohydrates: 71 grams, Cholesterol: 0 milligrams, Fiber: 9 grams

MADISON AREA SAFE KIDS

"The Junior League of Madison has worked in partnership with the MADISON AREA SAFE KIDS Coalition to prevent unintentional injuries to children 14 and under in the Madison and surrounding areas. Unintentional injury remains the leading cause of death among children as a result of motor vehicle crashes, including pedestrians and bicyclists, drowning, fire and burns, choking, firearms, falls and poisoning. The Junior League has been instrumental in assisting at car safety seat checks to help improve the safe transportation of children in our community. We look forward to expanding our partnership with the Junior League of Madison in the coming years."

-Nan Peterson
MADISON AREA SAFE KIDS,
(MASK) Coordinator
U.W. Children's Hospital

substitutions

If you find yourself missing an ingredient, try these substitution ideas.

- ☙ Substitute 3 tablespoons semisweet chocolate pieces or 1 ounce unsweetened chocolate plus 1 tablespoon sugar for 1 ounce semisweet.

- ☙ Substitute 1/4 cut unsweetened cocoa powder plus 1/3 cup sugar and 3 tablespoons shortening for 4 ounces sweet baking chocolate.

- ☙ Substitute 3 tablespoons unsweetened cocoa powder plus 1 tablespoon cooking oil or shortening, melted for 1 ounce unsweetened.

- ☙ Substitute 8 ounces regular cream cheese for 8 ounces mascarpone cheese.

- ☙ Substitute 1 tablespoon melted butter plus enough whole milk to make 1 cup for 1 cup half-and-half or light cream.

- ☙ Substitute 1 cup plain yogurt for 1 cup dairy sour cream.

- ☙ Substitute 1 bouillon cube or 1 tsp granules mixed with 1 cup boiling water for 1 cup of broth.

- ☙ Substitute 1/8 teaspoon garlic powder for one small clove of garlic.

winning
sides

Vegetables & side dishes that score big points

vegetables & side dishes

Asparagus with Roasted Red Peppers in Dijon Vinaigrette 138

Badger State Beans 155

Beans with Basil 142

Carrot Soufflé 141

Cinnamon Glazed Carrots 140

Citrus Sweet Potatoes 156

Corn Casserole 147

Creamy Red Potatoes 158

Door County Wild Rice 157

French Risotto 152

Garlic Mashed Potatoes 154

Gratin Dauphinoise 161

Green Bay Beans 143

Green Rice 150

Honey Roasted Onions 145

Jalapeño Corn Pudding 148

Mediterranean Rice with Pine Nuts and Dried Cranberries 159

Mushroom Gratin 146

Potluck Potatoes 160

Raspberry Asparagus 139

Sideline Beans 151

Spiced Cranberries 162

Squash Apple Bake 149

Sweet Potato Casserole 153

Tomato-Stuffed Peppers 144

photo by Lynn Wood

The Fans Make The Difference

Madison residents and alumni are avid sports fans - and with good reason. The University of Wisconsin-Madison perennially has strong athletes in a variety of sports, such as basketball, football and volleyball. Trips to the NCAA Final Four and the Rose Bowl are common expectations for Badgers and their supporters, who always make the cross-country trips to back the team. The attention that UW sports bring to the city of Madison is invaluable to store owners and community members; during sporting events the downtown area is populated with local and out-of-town fans. Madison's student fans have also gained a reputation as being extremely loyal, with a never-ending supply of school spirit that surely impacts opposing teams.

Madison also has a non-university athletic team that provides entertainment for the local sports fan. The Madison Mallards, a Summer Collegiate team designed to hone the talents of college baseball players from around the country, is a popular team for families and friends to support during the summer months. With plenty of home games and events like Oldies Night, the Mallards promote the sport of baseball in a fun environment suitable for all ages. Families, college students and alumni can all find a team to support in the city of Madison.

fall tailgate menu

137

Asparagus with Roasted Red Peppers in Dijon Vinaigrette

2 pounds asparagus, ends removed
2 red bell peppers
2 tablespoons white wine vinegar
2 tablespoons capers, rinsed, drained and coarsely chopped
1 tablespoon Dijon mustard
2 cloves garlic, minced
1 large shallot, finely chopped
salt and freshly ground black pepper
1/4 cup extra virgin olive oil
3 ounces soft, mild goat cheese
1/3 cup grated Parmesan cheese

Notes:

Cook asparagus in large pot of boiling salted water until bright green and tender, about 3-4 minutes. Transfer asparagus to bowl of ice water to cool. Drain.

Roast the red peppers directly over a gas flame on your range, or grill, or under the broiler, turning until charred and blackened all over. Place in a small brown paper bag and let sit for at least 10 minutes. Remove skin and seeds from peppers. Cut into 1/4-inch strips.

In a medium bowl, stir together the vinegar, capers, mustard, garlic and shallot. Season with salt and pepper. Whisk in the olive oil.

On a large serving platter arrange asparagus side by side, with all tips pointing in the same direction. Lay the pepper strips over the asparagus and drizzle with half of the vinaigrette. Crumble the goat cheese over and top with Parmesan cheese.

Serves: 8

Nutritional Information per Serving
Calories: 140, Fat: 11 grams, Protein: 6 grams, Carbohydrates: 5 grams, Cholesterol: 15 milligrams, Fiber: 1.8 grams

Raspberry Asparagus

Great summer side dish or buffet item.

2 bundles asparagus, about 2 pounds
1 cup frozen raspberries
1 tablespoon honey
1/2 cup shredded Swiss cheese

Cook asparagus in large pot of boiling salted water until crisp-tender, about 2 minutes. Transfer asparagus to bowl of ice water to cool. Drain.

In a blender, puree the raspberries with the honey. Serve over the chilled asparagus. Sprinkle with grated Swiss cheese.

Serves: 8

Nutritional Information per Serving
Calories: 60, Fat: 2 grams, Protein: 3 grams, Carbohydrates: 7 grams,
Cholesterol: 5 milligrams, Fiber: 2.3 grams

 Serve over lettuce for a great salad.

CAMP RANDALL STADIUM
HOME OF THE BADGERS

Camp Randall Stadium, built in 1917, is the home to Wisconsin's football team and Badger fans. The current capacity ranks it among the nation's largest school-owned stadiums.

Camp Randall was not always home to just athletics. The site was originally owned by the Wisconsin Agricultural Society, which held its annual state fair on the grounds. For a short duration, the Agricultural Society allowed the government to train over 70,000 troops at the Camp Randall complex.

After peace was restored, the land was returned to state fair property. The fair later moved to Milwaukee, and in 1893, the state presented the site to the university as a memorial athletic field.

Intercollegiate athletics began on campus in 1881, and football joined the scene in 1889. The stadium was built at its present site in 1913. A tragic collapse of the wooden bleachers in 1915 prompted the UW to make plans for concrete stands.

Two years later, a 10,000-seat concrete stadium was built with a grant of $15,000 from the state legislature. The first game played in Camp Randall Stadium was a thrilling 10-7 homecoming victory over Minnesota in 1917.

Cinnamon Glazed Carrots

1 (16 ounce) bag baby carrots
1/2 cup water
2 tablespoons butter, melted
3 tablespoons brown sugar
1/2 teaspoon cinnamon
salt to taste

Steam carrots in 1/2 cup water until tender; drain. Combine warm melted butter, brown sugar and cinnamon in saucepan and cook just until brown sugar dissolves and mixture starts to thicken.

Pour sauce over carrots. Add salt to taste.

Serves: 6

Nutritional Information per Serving
Calories: 80, Fat: 6 grams, Protein: 1 grams, Carbohydrates: 16 grams, Cholesterol: 15 milligrams, Fiber: 0.2 grams

 For a little extra color add some dried cranberries or halved walnuts.

Notes:

Carrot Soufflé

A colorful side dish!

6 large carrots, cooked and mashed
4 tablespoons flour
1 teaspoon vanilla
3 teaspoons sugar
4 eggs
4 tablespoons butter, softened

Preheat oven to 350 degrees. Grease round soufflé dish.

Combine all ingredients in a mixer and blend well.

Bake for 30-35 minutes.

Serves: 6

Nutritional Information per Serving
Calories: 160, Fat: 10 grams, Protein: 4 grams, Carbohydrates: 13 grams, Cholesterol: 140
milligrams, Fiber: 1.9 grams

Beans with Basil

1 pound slender string beans, cleaned, ends snipped
4 tablespoons rice vinegar
6 tablespoons cider vinegar
2 tablespoons water
pinch of sugar
2 tablespoons chopped fresh basil
2 tablespoons minced garlic
2 tablespoons extra virgin olive oil

USING KITCHEN SHEARS:

One of the handiest utensils may be your kitchen shears. Use it for everything from cutting butchers' twine to herbs. When in a hurry, use shears to snip basil, cut beans or harvest chives.

In a large pot of boiling water, cook beans until tender, about 3-5 minutes. Drain beans in a colander and transfer to a bowl of ice water to cool; drain well.

Combine vinegars, water, salt, sugar, basil, garlic and olive oil. Pour over beans. Marinate in refrigerator 1-2 hours.

Serves: 4

Nutritional Information per Serving
Calories: 110, Fat: 7 grams, Protein: 2 grams, Carbohydrates: 10 grams, Cholesterol: 0 milligrams, Fiber: 3.5 grams

Green Bay Beans

2 pounds whole green beans, trimmed
1 red pepper, cut into 1/4 inch strips
1/3 cup butter
1 clove garlic, minced
1/2 teaspoon crushed thyme
1/4 teaspoon ground white pepper

Preheat oven to 375 degrees. Grease an oval baking dish.

Cook beans in salted water for 3 minutes. Plunge into ice water. Drain. Place beans in a buttered oval baking dish.

In a small saucepan, melt butter and sauté the garlic for 3 minutes. Add thyme and pepper and pour mixture over beans. Toss to coat. Arrange red pepper strips over the green beans decoratively or toss with beans. (Can be made up to 1 day ahead. Cover and refrigerate; bring back to room temperature before baking.)

Bake for 7-10 minutes, until heated through.

Serves: 8

Nutritional Information per Serving
Calories: 100, Fat: 7 grams, Protein: 2 grams, Carbohydrates: 8 grams, Cholesterol: 20 milligrams, Fiber: 3.6 grams

FROZEN TUNDRA TAILGATING

There is nothing quite like the experience of tailgating in the parking lot of historic Lambeau Field in Green Bay, Wisconsin, prior to watching America's Football Team, the Green Bay Packers. It is a time-honored tradition that young and old carry out every home game, sometimes braving the worst of Wisconsin's freezing winter weather.

As seasoned Packer tailgaters know, there are countless ways to enjoy a tailgate - regardless of whether you have made the trek to Lambeau Field or you're "tailgating" in your own backyard. However, it would truly be an injustice not to mention some of the food that fills the air with wonderful pre-game aromas as thousands of Packer fans relish in their favorite team's "soon-to-be" victory.

Appetizers usually include cheese, summer sausage, crackers, chips and dips. Sides will include potato and pasta salads, baked beans and cole slaw. The main course will typically include the oh-so-famous bratwurst, burgers, chili, steaks, pork chops or grilled chicken.

Lambeau Field has been sold out on a season-ticket basis for over 40 years. The current waiting list is more than 57,000 and averages a three year wait!

 Tomato-Stuffed Peppers

3 large red or orange peppers
9 small or plum tomatoes, peeled and quartered
3 large garlic cloves, sliced
6 tablespoons olive oil
fresh minced basil, for garnish
salt and pepper to taste

HOW TO PEEL TOMATOES:

Score a small cross on the top of each tomato. Plunge tomatoes into boiling water 1-2 minutes. Peel skin down from the cross.

Preheat oven to 350 degrees.

Wash the peppers thoroughly. Slice each pepper down the center, including the stems. Be careful to cut through the entire length of the stem as evenly as possible. (Leaving the stem helps maintain the shape of the pepper during cooking.) Remove the seeds and any green or white parts from the inside of the pepper halves. Place the peppers open-side up in a glass tray or other high-sided pan or dish.

Stuff the pepper halves with the tomato pieces. It should take about 1 1/2 tomatoes per pepper half. Sprinkle the garlic cloves evenly over the peppers. Pour one tablespoon of olive oil over each pepper half and sprinkle with salt and pepper. For increased flavor, you may choose to increase oil to two tablespoons per pepper half.

Bake for 30 minutes or until pepper edges begin to brown and juices around pepper are bubbling.

Serves: 6

Nutritional Information per Serving
Calories: 175, Fat: 14 grams, Protein: 2 grams, Carbohydrates: 10 grams, Cholesterol: 0 milligrams, Fiber: 2.4 grams

Honey Roasted Onions

2 large Vidalia onions, about 1 1/4 pounds
1 tablespoon water
1/4 cup honey
1 tablespoon butter, melted
1 teaspoon paprika
1/2 teaspoon salt
1/2 teaspoon curry powder
1/4 teaspoon ground red pepper

Preheat oven to 350 degrees.

Peel onions, cut in half crosswise. Place onions cut sides down in an 8-inch square baking dish; drizzle with water. Cover with foil; bake for 30 minutes.

In a small bowl, combine honey, butter, paprika, salt, curry powder and red pepper. Turn onions over; brush half of honey mixture over onions.

Bake uncovered an additional 30 minutes or until tender, basting with remaining honey mixture after 15 minutes

Serves: 4

Nutritional Information per Serving
Calories: 110, Fat: 3 grams, Protein: 1 grams, Carbohydrates: 20 grams, Cholesterol: 10 milligrams, Fiber: 1.0 grams

 This recipe is an excellent garnish for steak or a roast and can also be served over other vegetables such as carrots or squash.

Mushroom Gratin

This is a wonderful accompaniment to any steak dinner.

1 pound small whole mushrooms
5 tablespoons butter
2 beef bouillon cubs
1/2 cup hot water
1/2 cup half and half
1/2 teaspoon salt
1/4 teaspoon pepper
1 cup grated Parmesan cheese
1/2 cup bread crumbs

HOW TO WASH MUSHROOMS:

When cleaning mushrooms, use a damp paper towel and rub gently. Do not run under water because mushrooms will absorb the water.

Preheat over to 350 degrees. Grease an 8-or 9-inch baking dish.

In a medium saucepan, melt butter. Add mushrooms and sauté until mushrooms are tender, about 8 minutes. Transfer mushrooms to greased baking dish.

Dissolve the bouillon cubes in hot water, set aside.

In a small saucepan, melt remaining 3 tablespoons of butter; blend in flour. Cook slowly and then add the half and half, salt, pepper and bouillon. Cook until smooth, mixing often. Pour over mushrooms.

In a small bowl combine cheese and bread crumbs. Sprinkle over mushrooms.

Bake for 30 minutes, until top becomes light golden brown.

Serves: 6

Nutritional Information per Serving
Calories: 225, Fat: 16 grams, Protein: 9 grams, Carbohydrates: 11 grams, Cholesterol: 45 milligrams, Fiber: 1.4 grams

Corn Casserole

2 (15 ounce) cans corn, drained (liquid from 1 can reserved)
1 (14 3/4 ounce) can creamed corn
1 (15 ounce) box cornbread mix
1/2 cup butter
2 eggs
8 ounces sour cream

Preheat oven to 350 degrees.

Combine corn, reserved liquid, creamed corn, corn bread mix, butter, eggs and sour cream in a large bowl. Pour into a 9x13-inch baking pan.

Bake for 1 hour.

Serves: 8

Nutritional Information per Serving
Calories: 630, Fat: 26 grams, Protein: 13 grams, Carbohydrates: 86 grams, Cholesterol: 90 milligrams, Fiber: 8.5 grams

GO BUCKY!

The badger has been the mascot for the University of Wisconsin since the turn of the century, but he wasn't always called "Bucky."

At sporting events, schools nationwide historically employed real animals as mascots. At the UW, the tradition was to bring a badger on a leash to every football game.

Badgers, however, love to dig. By half-time, the fellow responsible for our mighty mascot would be holding a leash that disappeared into a hole on the sideline. Worse, a badger is known to have a nasty disposition when disturbed. No one had any interest in getting the badger out of the hole at the end of the game.

It was clearly time to recruit a cheerleader, wearing a paper maché mask, to take over as mascot for the University of Wisconsin. The UW mascot has had many names - from Bernie to Bouncy. Ultimately, a contest determined our mascot's moniker once and for all. The winning entry was "Buckingham U. Badger'"— "Bucky" for short.

The rest is UW history.

 # Jalapeño Corn Pudding

2 slices bread
1 medium onion, sliced
1 green pepper, stem and seeds removed, coarsely chopped
1 jalapeño pepper, seeds and veins removed, coarsely chopped
1 cup water
3 tablespoons butter
1 teaspoon salt
1/8 teaspoon pepper
2 tablespoons flour
1 cup milk
1/4 teaspoon cayenne
1/4 teaspoon dry mustard
1 (10 ounce) package frozen corn, thawed
1 egg

Preheat oven to 375 degrees.

Tear 1 slice of bread into pieces and place in blender; blend 5 seconds. Set aside to use as topping. Combine onion, green pepper and water in blender. Blend 5 seconds. Pour into sieve to drain.

In a heavy skillet, melt 2 tablespoons of the butter over medium heat. Add onion mixture and sauté until soft.

Place salt, pepper, flour, milk, remaining butter, cayenne, mustard, corn, egg and remaining slice of bread into blender. Blend 5 seconds.

Combine green pepper mix and corn mix together and pour into a deep casserole dish. Sprinkle with bread that was set aside for topping. Dot topping with butter.

Bake for 1 hour.

Serves: 4

Nutritional Information per Serving
Calories: 255, Fat: 12 grams, Protein: 7 grams, Carbohydrates: 30 grams, Cholesterol: 75 milligrams, Fiber: 2.9 grams

You can make this recipe "child-mild" by leaving out the jalapeno and cayenne.

Notes:

Squash Apple Bake

1 large butternut squash
1 Jonagold, Golden Delicious or other baking apple
1 cup brown sugar
1/2 cup butter
1 tablespoon flour
1 teaspoon mace

Preheat oven to 350 degrees.

Peel the squash and cut into pieces of approximately one inch square. Peel the apple and cut into pieces that are smaller than the squash. (For a more gourmet presentation thinly slice the squash and apples, lay them in a tartlet pan and pour the brown sugar mixture over. Bake time would be shorter.)

Place the squash in a 9x13-inch oven proof pan and top with the apple pieces.

In a small saucepan melt together brown sugar, butter, flour and mace.

Drizzle the brown sugar mixture over the squash and apples. Cover with aluminum foil.

Bake for 1 hour.

Serves: 8

Nutritional Information per Serving
Calories: 220, Fat: 11 grams, Protein: 1 grams, Carbohydrates: 29 grams, Cholesterol: 30 milligrams, Fiber: .5 grams

 You can substitute 1 1/2 teaspoons nutmeg for the mace.

Green Rice

2 1/2 cups chicken stock
1 cup dry white wine or Vermouth
1 1/2 teaspoons salt
1/4 teaspoon freshly ground black pepper
1 tablespoon olive oil
2 tablespoons butter
1 cup green onions, finely chopped
1 1/2 cups finely chopped spinach
1 cup Italian (flat leaf) parsley, minced
2 cups short grain rice

SHORT GRAIN RICE:

Use short-grain rice when you prefer a stickier texture and a softer grain after cooking. It pairs well with many Asian dishes and is used in dishes such as paella and risotto.

Combine chicken stock and wine or Vermouth with salt and pepper in a saucepan and heat to almost boiling.

Heat a 2-quart heavy saucepan with a tight-fitting lid. Add oil and butter. Add the onions, parsley and spinach. Stir to coat with oil. Cover and cook over low heat for 5 minutes. Mix in the rice and stir until rice turns translucent. Add 2 cups of the hot stock mixture. Cover and cook over low heat 7-10 minutes. Add the remaining broth, cover and cook another 10 minutes, or until the rice is tender and light. Fluff rice and serve.

Serves: 6

Nutritional Information per Serving
Calories: 360, Fat: 8 grams, Protein: 12 grams, Carbohydrates: 59 grams, Cholesterol: 10 milligrams, Fiber: 2.5 grams

 # Sideline Beans

3 (15 ounce) cans Great Northern beans, drained
and rinsed
1 1/2 pounds lean pork, cut into 1 inch cubes
1 (14 ounce) bottle ketchup
1/2 cup molasses
2 tablespoons prepared mustard
1 1/2 cups packed brown sugar
1/4 large sweet onion, chopped
1/2 teaspoon salt

Preheat the oven to 350 degrees.

Combine all the ingredients, mixing gently but well. Place in a bean pot, casserole or slow cooker.

Bake, uncovered, for 5-6 hours; cover during the last hour.

Serves: 12

Nutritional Information per Serving
Calories: 320, Fat: 6 grams, Protein: 15 grams, Carbohydrates: 51 grams, Cholesterol: 50 milligrams, Fiber: 6.3 grams

 This is a wonderful dish to prepare in a slow cooker and bake overnight on low.

French Risotto

This is a delicate dish that is best paired with chicken and fish.

Bouquet Garni
>   2 parsley sprigs
>   1 sprig thyme
>   1/2 bay leaf
>   cheese cloth

Risotto
>   2 cups low-sodium chicken broth
>   1 cup dry white wine or Vermouth
>   1/4 cup onion, minced
>   4 tablespoons butter
>   1 1/2 cups Arborio rice
>   1/4 teaspoon thyme
>   1/4 cup grated Parmesan cheese
>   salt and freshly ground pepper, to taste

BOUQUET GARNI:

"Bouquet garni" is a small bunch of herbs, usually parsley, thyme and bay leaf that are either tied together or placed in a cheesecloth bag and used to flavor soups, stews and broths.

Preheat oven to 375 degrees.

Place parsley, thyme and bay leaf on a square of 2 layers of moistened cheesecloth. Gather cheesecloth and tie securely.

Combine broth and wine in a saucepan and heat to boiling.

In an ovenproof casserole with tight fitting lid, melt butter over medium to low heat. Add onion and sauté until tender but not browned, about 5 minutes. Add rice and stir over moderate heat until rice turns translucent, then milky, 2-3 minutes, stirring constantly.

Pour boiling broth and wine into casserole with rice. Add thyme and season with salt and pepper. Add bouquet garni and bring to simmer, stirring once. Cover casserole and place in lower third of preheated oven. In approximately 4 minutes, check to see that liquid is maintaining a slow boil. Replace lid and reduce heat to 350 degrees. All liquid should be absorbed in about 15 minutes. If there is still liquid in the bottom of casserole, return to oven for an additional 2-3 minutes.

Discard bouquet garni, add Parmesan and stir.

Serves: 6

Nutritional Information per Serving
Calories: 275, Fat: 9 grams, Protein: 8 grams, Carbohydrates: 40 grams, Cholesterol: 25 milligrams, Fiber: 0.1 grams

Sweet Potato Casserole

2 cans sweet potatoes (2 pounds)
1 teaspoon salt
1/2 teaspoon cinnamon
1/2 teaspoon nutmeg
1/2 cup butter
4 eggs
2 teaspoons vanilla
1 cup sugar

Topping
1/4 cup soft butter
3/4 cup brown sugar
3 tablespoons four
1/2 cup pecans, chopped

Preheat oven to 350 degrees. Grease a 9x13-inch casserole.

In a large mixing bowl, whip sweet potatoes, spices, butter, eggs and sugar. Pour into prepared pan.

Topping: In a small bowl mix all topping ingredients by hand forming a crumble. Sprinkle on top of the casserole.

Bake uncovered for 35-40 minutes, until casserole is bubbly and golden.

Serves: 16

Nutritional Information per Serving
Calories: 225, Fat: 11 grams, Protein: 2 grams, Carbohydrates: 30 grams, Cholesterol:7 0 milligrams, Fiber: 1.4 grams

THE 5TH QUARTER

The fifth quarter is not a piece of extra currency needed for a bottle of soda from a vending machine. It's a time-honored tradition observed at the conclusion of all UW-Madison home football games.

The fifth quarter began in 1977 when the University of Wisconsin Marching Band decided to play for a short time after a Badger football game. The after game concert initially included a 10 minute rendition of "You've Said It All" for the student section. Over the years, the tradition has increased in popularity.

Now, win or lose, the Wisconsin Marching Band will play for 40-50 minutes at the end of home football games with nearly 40,000 spectators staying to watch and dance with the band. The music selection consists of "On Wisconsin," "You've Said It All," "Varsity," "The Beer Barrel Polka," "Chicken Dance," "Space Badgers" and other fan favorites that motivate students, alumni and fans of all ages.

So, don't leave right after a football game. Stick around, avoid traffic and dance with the UW Marching Band!

Garlic Mashed Potatoes

3 cloves garlic
5 large red potatoes, quartered
2 tablespoons olive oil
3/4 cup cream
2 tablespoons butter, melted
1/4 teaspoon salt
1/2 cup grated Parmesan cheese

Preheat oven to 350 degrees.

Place peeled garlic cloves in aluminum foil and pour olive oil over garlic. Seal edges of foil packet and bake for 30 minutes. Remove from packet, drain off oil. Snip end of clove and squeeze paste into a small dish. Mash with a fork.

Cover potatoes with salted cold water in a large pot; simmer, uncovered, until tender, about 18 minutes. Cool slightly and mash.

Combine cooked potatoes with garlic, cream, butter and salt. Top with Parmesan cheese and return to oven until cheese melts. Serve immediately or keep warm in a low oven until ready to serve.

Serves: 6

Nutritional Information per Serving
Calories: 230, Fat: 17 grams, Protein: 5 grams, Carbohydrates: 14 grams, Cholesterol: 40 milligrams, Fiber: 1.1 grams

Notes:

Badger State Beans

This dish is great for a tailgate Super Bowl party. A hearty fall or winter side dish that can be a main dish if more meat is added.

1/2 pound ground beef or 1 pound ground turkey
1/2 pound bacon
1 small onion, chopped
1 (16 ounce) can pork and beans
1 (16 ounce) can kidney beans, drained
1 (16 ounce) can yellow butter beans, drained
1 (16 ounce) can black beans, drained
1/2 cup ketchup
1/2 cup brown sugar
1/4 cup white sugar
2 tablespoons molasses
1/2 teaspoon dry mustard

Preheat oven to 350 degrees.

In a large frying pan brown ground beef, bacon and onion. Drain off the excess fat.

In a 2-quart casserole dish combine the rest of the ingredients. Add meat mixture.

Bake uncovered for 1 hour and 15 minutes.

Serves: 12

Nutritional Information per Serving
Calories: 430, Fat: 15 grams, Protein: 22 grams, Carbohydrates: 22 grams,
Cholesterol: 35 milligrams, Fiber: 12.6 grams

ELROY "CRAZY LEGS" HIRSCH

After a long touchdown run for Wisconsin in 1942, Elroy Hirsch was described as looking like a "demented duck," whose "crazy legs were gyrating in six different directions all at the same time."

From that day on he was known as "Crazy Legs" and went on to become one of the NFL's most exciting players and earn a place in the Pro Football Hall of Fame.

Best known for his unorthodox running style, Hirsch starred at Wisconsin for one season before moving to Michigan. He played nine years in the NFL and led the Los Angeles Rams to the league title in 1951. He enjoyed a brief movie career, and eventually returned to Madison as the Badgers' athletic director from 1969-1987.

Otto Hirsch, his father and a Wausau ironworker, once said: "We lived two miles from school. Elroy ran to school and back, skipping and crisscrossing his legs in the cement blocks of the sidewalks. He said it would make him shiftier."

Every year thousands of people gather in Madison for an annual run called the Crazylegs Classic to raise money for athletic scholarships. Since its inception in 1982, it has raised $4.2 million with more than 116,000 runners and walkers.

Citrus Sweet Potatoes

2 tablespoons unsalted butter
3/4 cup fresh squeezed orange juice (approximately 2 large oranges)
1/3 cup brown sugar
1 tablespoon cornstarch
1/2 teaspoon salt
1/2 teaspoon orange zest
2 pounds sweet potatoes, peeled and quartered or thickly sliced
parsley for garnish (optional)
pecans or hickory nuts, chopped, for garnish (optional)

SWEET POTATOES:

Not just for Thanksgiving anymore… They're among the most nutritious of vegetables. Their bright color is a key to their high beta-carotene content, and they also contain the carotenoids lutein and zeaxanthin. Eaten with the skin, a baked sweet potato is an excellent fiber source. These naturally sweet treats supply substantial amounts of vitamins C and B6, and manganese, as well as a small amount of potassium.

Preheat oven to 400 degrees.

Over medium heat, melt the butter in a medium saucepan. Add the orange juice, brown sugar, cornstarch, salt and zest. Cook until thickened.

Spread the sweet potatoes in a 9x13-inch casserole dish and pour the orange sauce over them.

Cover and bake for 40 minutes, basting the yams once or twice. Garnish with chopped parsley and nuts.

Serves: 6

Nutritional Information per Serving
Calories: 235, Fat: 4 grams, Protein: 2 grams, Carbohydrates: 48 grams, Cholesterol: 10 milligrams, Fiber: 5.4 grams

Door County Wild Rice

3/4 cup wild rice
24 ounces chicken broth
1/2 cup pearl barley
1/4 cup dried cherries, chopped
1/4 cup currants
1 tablespoon unsalted butter
1/2 cup sliced toasted almonds

Preheat oven to 350 degrees.

Combine the broth and the wild rice in a large saucepan and bring to a boil.
Reduce heat and simmer, covered, for 10 minutes.

In a 2-quart casserole dish combine the barley, cherries, currants and butter.
Add the rice and stir.

Cover and bake for 1 hour, or until the liquid has been absorbed.

Stir in toasted almonds and serve.

Serves: 8

Nutritional Information per Serving
Calories: 185, Fat: 4 grams, Protein: 8 grams, Carbohydrates: 29 grams, Cholesterol: 5 milligrams,
Fiber: 3.8 grams

Creamy Red Potatoes

As delicious as they are simple.

12-14 medium red potatoes, washed and cubed
1 1/2 tablespoons seasoned salt
1/2 cup butter, cut into pieces
1 1/2 cups heavy cream

Preheat oven to 350 degrees. Grease a 9x13-inch pan.

Cover potatoes with salted cold water in a large pot; simmer, uncovered, until tender, about 15 minutes. Drain.

Arrange potatoes in prepared pan. Sprinkle seasoned salt liberally over potatoes and dot with butter pieces. Pour cream over the top.

Bake, uncovered, 45-60 minutes until cream is absorbed. Stir once, after about 40 minutes.

Serves: 8

Nutritional Information per Serving
Calories: 520, Fat: 27 grams, Protein: 10 grams, Carbohydrates: 60 grams,
Cholesterol: 85 milligrams, Fiber: 7.0 grams

 This can be made ahead and popped into the oven when ready to bake. Adding 1/2 cup blue or Swiss cheese, or green onion to the top adds variety.

Notes:

Mediterranean Rice with Pine Nuts and Dried Cranberries

An unusual blend of spices makes this dish exotic.

1 tablespoon olive oil
1 large onion, finely chopped
1 cup long grain white rice
1/2 teaspoon ground sage
1/4 teaspoon coriander
1/8 teaspoon cinnamon
1/2 teaspoon salt
2 cups fat-free chicken broth
1/4 cup pine nuts, toasted
1/2 cup dried cranberries
1/4 cup chives, chopped

Heat oil in a large saucepan over medium heat. Add onions and cook until translucent. Add rice, sage, coriander, cinnamon and salt. Stir over medium-high heat until rice is lightly browned. Remove from heat and carefully add broth.

Return to heat and bring to a boil. Reduce heat and cover pan. Boil gently for 20 minutes or until rice is tender and liquid has been absorbed. Remove from heat. Stir in pine nuts, dried cranberries and chives.

Serves: 6

Nutritional Information per Serving
Calories: 200, Fat: 5 grams, Protein: 4 grams, Carbohydrates: 35 grams, Cholesterol: 0 milligrams, Fiber: 1.6 grams

Potluck Potatoes

32 ounce package frozen hash browns, thawed
1 (10 3/4 ounce) can cream of chicken or cream of mushroom soup
8 ounces cheddar cheese, grated
2 cups sour cream
1 tablespoon salt
1/2 cup onion, diced
3 tablespoons butter, melted
3 cups cornflake cereal, crushed

Preheat oven to 350 degrees.

In a large bowl mix hash browns, soup, cheese, sour cream, salt and onion.
Transfer to a 9 x 13-inch baking dish. (Can be made ahead and frozen. To serve,
thaw potatoes, add topping and bake as directed.)

In a small bowl combine cereal and butter and spread over potatoes.

Bake for 1 hour.

Serves: 12

Nutritional Information per Serving
Calories: 285, Fat: 18 grams, Protein: 9 grams, Carbohydrates: 22 grams, Cholesterol: 45
milligrams, Fiber: 1.3 grams

Notes:

Gratin Dauphinoise

5 tablespoons butter
1/4 teaspoon minced garlic (about 1 small clove)
2 1/2 pounds Yukon Gold potatoes, peeled and sliced thin
1 teaspoons salt
1/2 teaspoon pepper
1 cup Gruyère cheese, shredded
1 1/2 cups whipping cream
1 tablespoon flour

Preheat oven to 400 degrees.

Combine 1 tablespoon butter and garlic and use to grease a 2 1/2-quart casserole dish. Layer half of the sliced potatoes in casserole; sprinkle with 1/2 teaspoon of salt and 1/4 teaspoon pepper. Cut 2 tablespoons butter into small pieces and dot over potato slices. Sprinkle 1/2 cup cheese over all. Create another layer with the remaining potato slices, salt, pepper, butter and cheese.

Combine whipping cream with flour in a small saucepan, stirring until smooth. Heat over medium heat until hot, but do not allow to boil. Pour over potato slices.

Cover and bake for 20 minutes. Uncover and bake for an additional 30-40 minutes or until potatoes are tender.

Serves: 8

Nutritional Information per Serving
Calories: 365, Fat: 28 grams, Protein: 7 grams, Carbohydrates: 21 grams,
Cholesterol: 95 milligrams, Fiber: 1.7 grams

UW COMMUNICATIVE DISORDERS

"Through the course of the Books And Me (BAM) Project, more than a hundred speech and language students in the Department of Communicative Disorders at the University of Wisconsin-Madison have engaged children in Head Start classes with books and materials supplied by the Junior League of Madison. Children learn to love books, to tell stories, to name letters, to rhyme and play with sounds and to begin to figure out the code...all leading to reading!

The Junior League's financial support of this project allowed the purchase of equipment to test the hearing of the over 700 children from Head Start in Dane County. These screenings help to ensure that hearing problems aren't holding kids back from listening & learning.

Thank you Junior League!"

-Peggy Rosin, University of Wisconsin Department of Communicative Disorders

Spiced Cranberries

The perfect Thanksgiving side and topping.

24 ounces cranberries
3 cups sugar
1 1/2 cups water
7 whole cloves
3 whole allspice
3 (3-inch) cinnamon sticks

CRAZY FOR
CRANBERRIES:

Did you know that cranberries
were once a symbol of peace?
This North American berry,
once considered an important
food and medicine for native
Americans, is a rich source
of antioxidants.

Combine sugar and water in a saucepan and bring to a boil over medium heat. Stir constantly until sugar dissolves. Add the spices and reduce heat. Simmer for 5 minutes and add the cranberries. Stir once or twice and wait for the cranberries to begin to pop, about 3-4 minutes. Remove from the heat and cool. Pour into jars and refrigerate, covered, for several days. May be refrigerated for a month.

Serves: 6

Nutritional Information per Serving
Calories: 525, Fat: 2 grams, Protein: 1 grams, Carbohydrates: 126 grams, Cholesterol: 0 milligrams, Fiber: 11.7 grams

under the
dome

Capital ideas for the main course

main course

POULTRY

Cha Cha Chicken 171
Chicken Caesar Wrap 180
Chicken Crepes 172
Chicken Marsala 175
Chicken Pot Pie 169
Chicken Roll-Ups 174
Chicken Tetrazzini 167
Hawaiian Chicken Sandwich 179
Jamaican Jerk Chicken 178
Lemon Chicken 170
Lemony Chicken Kabobs 176
Mediterranean Stuffed
Chicken Breast 168
Seasoned Tomato Sauce 166
Stuffed Chicken Parmesan 166
Tequila Lime Chicken 177

GAME

Bacon Wrapped Duck Kabobs 183
Honey-Chili Roasted Duck 181
Pheasant with Mushroom Sauce 182
Venison with Nouveau-
Cherry Sauce 184

MEAT

All Day Barbecued Pork 207
Apricot Stuffed Crown Roast 198
Asian Beef with Fresh Pea Pods 192
Beef Tenderloin with Wisconsin
Blue Cheese Sauce 186
Bo Go Gy 190
Champagne Ham Sandwiches 208
Coffee Glazed Oven Brisket 193
Everyday Rub 199

German Pot Roast 194
Ginger and Mint Lamb Chops 211
Grilled Crusted Pork Tenderloin
with Tomatillo Sauce 200
Herb Crusted Lamb with
Roasted Potatoes 209
Honey-Lime Pork Chops 201
Individual Beef Wellingtons 185
Lamb Burgers 210
Olive Paste with Blue Cheese 189
Peppered Steaks with
Whiskey Sauce 188
Phoenix Barbecue Sauce 203
Pilgrim Pork Chops 204
Pork Roast with Sautéed Pears 205
Pork Tenderloin with Herbed
Breadcrumb Crust 197
Pork Tenderloin with Lime
Cilantro Pesto 196
Presidential Beef Burgundy 195
Steak Fajitas 191
Sumptuous Sweet and
Sour Pork 202
Tenderloin Fillets with
Port Sauce 187
Wisconsin Brats 206

SEAFOOD

Baked Feta Shrimp 212
Baked Tilapia in
Tomato-Fennel Sauce 216
Beurre Blanc 227
Cod in Court Bouillon 229
Confetti Crab Cakes 214

Easy Stuffed Halibut Fillets 222
Marinated Grilled Shrimp 225
New Orleans Style BBQ Shrimp 213
Orange Roughy with Shallots
and Capers 219
Rèmoulade Sauce 215
Roasted Monkfish 221
Salmon Burgers 218
Salmon with Chili Mango Salsa 217
Savory Swordfish 223
Spicy Salmon with Cilantro Salsa 228
Szechwan BBQ Shrimp 224
Tangy Lemon Snapper 220
Tartar Sauce 218
Walleye with Beurre Blanc 226

PASTA & GRAINS

Bean Enchilada Casserole 240
Blue cheese, walnut, and
pear pizza 243
Chicken Marengo 235
Feta Shrimp with Farfalle 230
Garlicky Crab Linguine 231
Great Lakes Pizza 244
Jambalaya with Scallops 233
Lamb Ragu with Pasta 234
Light Fettuccine Alfredo 237
Mayor Dave's Chicken on Pasta 236
Mexican Rice Casserole 241
Pasta Primavera 239
Shrimp and Linguine in
Tomato Cream 232
Spinach Manicotti 238
Tangy Thai Chicken Pizza 242

photo courtesy of Wisconsin Dept. of Tourism

Madison - A Capitol City

The most-recognizable building in the Madison skyline is the domed structure of the State Capitol, located in the heart of downtown Madison. Reaching to a height of over 200 feet, the Capitol dome is the second-highest in the U.S., just 17 inches shorter than the building it is modeled after, the nation's capitol in Washington, D.C.

Madison's first master plan was created in 1909 by urban planner, John Nolen, the namesake of the picturesque drive, which called for a series of government buildings connecting the State Capitol with Lake Monona and a lakeside park.

That lakeside park on Monona became the site of the Monona Terrace Community and Convention Center. This architectural landmark brought to life one of the final creative visions of world-renowned architect, Frank Lloyd Wright. Wright, a Richland Center, Wisconsin native, first proposed the convention center in 1938. However, it wasn't until July of 1997, 59 years after the inception of the project, that the Monona Terrace Community and Convention Center opened to the public.

Madison's skyline accurately reflects the city as a political, educational and social center, as many university and state government buildings fill out the skyline along the waterfront of both Lake Mendota and Monona.

delightful dinner menu

Blue Cheese and
Pecan Spread
page 15

Chestnut Soup
page 86

Individual Beef
Wellington
page 185

Cinnamon
Glazed Carrots
page 140

Gratin Dauphinois
page 161

Bavarian Apple Torte
page 252

Irish Cream Coffee
page 46

165

Stuffed Chicken Parmesan

8 ounces ricotta cheese
1 cup shredded mozzarella cheese
1/4 cup grated Parmesan cheese
1 tablespoon chopped parsley
4 boneless, skinless chicken breast halves
1/2 cup flour
2 eggs, beaten
3/4 cup Italian bread crumbs
3/4 teaspoon Italian seasoning
1/4 teaspoon garlic powder
1/4 teaspoon ground black pepper
1/4-1/2 cup olive oil
2 cups Seasoned Tomato Sauce (see recipe below or use your own favorite)
1 1/2 cups shredded mozzarella cheese
1/2 cup grated Parmesan cheese

SEASONED TOMATO SAUCE:

1 (14-16 ounce) jar of chunky, meatless pasta sauce; 1/2 cup dry red wine; 2 tablespoons dried Italian or spaghetti seasoning; 3 tablespoons grated Parmesan cheese.

In a small saucepan over medium-low heat, combine all sauce ingredients. Warm thoroughly.

In a medium mixing bowl, stir together ricotta, mozzarella, Parmesan and parsley; set aside.

Flatten chicken breast with kitchen mallet, place filling on half of chicken breast, fold over and secure with toothpicks.

Place flour in shallow bowl or pie tin. Place eggs in another shallow bowl or pie tin. Mix breadcrumbs and Italian seasoning, garlic powder and pepper in a third shallow bowl or pie tin. Carefully dip each chicken breast in flour, then egg, then seasoned crumbs and set on a plate lined with waxed paper. Allow chicken to rest in the refrigerator for at least 30 minutes, up to overnight.

Preheat oven to 350 degrees.

Heat oil in large skillet. When oil is hot, add chicken and cook over medium low heat until coating is golden brown. Carefully turn chicken and cook on second side. Transfer chicken to baking dish. Spoon tomato sauce over chicken and sprinkle with cheeses.

Bake, covered, for 35-40 minutes. Remove cover and bake another 15-20 minutes, until cheese is bubbly.

Serves: 4

Nutritional Information per Serving
Calories: 940, Fat: 55 grams, Protein: 59 grams, Carbohydrates: 52grams, Cholesterol: 250 milligrams, Fiber: 5.5 grams

Chicken Tetrazzini

This recipe freezes well and kids love it!

8 ounces thin spaghetti
1/4 cup butter, softened
2 cups canned mushrooms, drained
1 (12 ounce) can Cream of Mushroom soup
1 (12 ounce) can Cream of Chicken Soup
1 pint sour cream
1 pint French onion dip
4 cups cooked, diced chicken or turkey
1/2 cup grated Parmesan cheese

Preheat oven at 350 degrees.

Cook spaghetti according to package directions. Drain and toss with butter. Add remaining ingredients, except Parmesan cheese, and mix well. Pour into 9x13-inch baking dish and sprinkle with desired amount of Parmesan. Bake for 1 hour.

Serves: 10

Nutritional Information per Serving
Calories: 455, Fat: 30 grams, Protein: 25 grams, Carbohydrates: 21 grams, Cholesterol: 100 milligrams, Fiber: 1.3 grams

UNIVERSITY OF WISCONSIN - MADISON

Located in the heart of a city and a state with a deserved reputation for a high quality of life, UW-Madison is a pillar of the community.

As one of the leading public research universities in the world, UW-Madison has a longstanding commitment to and history of making a broad range of resources and intellectual assets available around the world.

The University boasts a strong model for technology transfer through the Wisconsin Alumni Research Foundation and the University Research Park, which is internationally known for its expertise in getting emerging, research-based businesses into the marketplace.

UW-Madison is proud to hold the same core value that it articulated 100 years ago – *The Wisconsin Idea* that the borders of the university are the borders of the state and today the borders of the world.

Mediterranean Stuffed Chicken Breast

6 boneless, skinless chicken breast halves
1 (10 ounce) package frozen, chopped spinach, thawed and drained
salt and pepper, to taste
8 ounces feta cheese, crumbled
1/2 cup mayonnaise
1 clove garlic, minced
1/4 cup flour
1/2 teaspoon paprika
12 strips of bacon
toothpicks

Preheat oven to 325 degrees.

Notes:

Cut a pocket into chicken breasts. Salt and pepper chicken breasts; set aside.

In a medium bowl combine spinach, feta, mayonnaise and garlic. (Can be made 1 day in advance. Cover and chill.) Stuff mixture into chicken breast pockets.

In a shallow bowl or pie tin, combine flour and paprika. Dip chicken into flour mixture to lightly coat. Wrap bacon around each breast and secure with toothpicks. Place chicken breasts on a broiler pan.

Bake, uncovered, for 1 hour.

Serve with garlic mash potatoes and asparagus.

Serves: 6

Nutritional Information per Serving
Calories: 680 , Fat: 52 grams, Protein: 45 grams, Carbohydrates: 8 grams,
Cholesterol: 145 milligrams, Fiber: 1.4 grams

Chicken Pot Pie

A tasty surprise on a cold Wisconsin winter day.

2 tablespoons butter
2 tablespoons vegetable oil
1 medium yellow onion, chopped
2 carrots, peeled, diced
2 stalks celery, diced
1 teaspoon minced garlic
1/2 teaspoon seasoning salt
1/4 teaspoon salt
1/4 teaspoon fresh cracked pepper
8 ounces mushrooms, sliced
1 (14.5 ounce) can Irish potatoes, diced
1/2 teaspoon fresh thyme, chopped
2 tablespoons dry sherry
1/4 cup flour
2 cups chicken stock or broth
1 cup half and half
3 cups cubed cooked chicken (or 2 (13 ounce) cans chicken breasts in water)
1/2 cup fresh or frozen peas
1 tablespoon chopped fresh parsley leaves
1 (15 ounce) prepared refrigerator piecrust

Preheat oven to 375 degrees. Grease a 2-quart casserole dish.

In a large stockpot, melt butter and heat the oil over medium-high heat. Add the onion, carrots and celery; sauté until soft, 5 minutes. Add the garlic, seasoning salt, salt and pepper, cook for 30 seconds. Add the mushrooms, potatoes and thyme and cook, stirring until the mushrooms are soft and have given all their liquid, about 3 minutes. Add the sherry and cook until moisture is absorbed. Mix in flour and cook, stirring, for 2 minutes. Stirring constantly, slowly add the chicken stock and half and half and cook until the mixture is smooth and thickened, about 5 minutes. Add the chicken, peas and parsley, stir well, and cook until chicken is heated through.

Pour mixture into casserole dish and place pie crust over dish. Tuck and crimp edges to seal completely. Cut 4–6 small vent slats into the top.

Bake for 20-30 minutes, until crust is golden brown. Let stand 10 minutes and serve warm.

Serves: 4

Nutritional Information per Serving
Calories: 850 , Fat: 48 grams, Protein: 55 grams, Carbohydrates: 50 grams, Cholesterol: 150 milligrams, Fiber: 5.0 grams

 For individual servings, place mixture into bowls and cut crust for each bowl. Bake for 15-20 minutes or until crust is golden brown.

Lemon Chicken

1 cup chicken broth
1/3 cup sugar
1/3 cup lemon juice
2 tablespoons water
1 tablespoon dry sherry
1 1/2 teaspoons soy sauce
1/4cup plus 2 tablespoons corn starch
1/2 cup vegetable oil
6 medium boneless, skinless chicken breast halves
1 teaspoon salt
1 teaspoon pepper
1/2 (10 ounce) bag spinach

In a small saucepan combine chicken broth, sugar, lemon juice, water, sherry and soy sauce. Whisk in the 2 tablespoons cornstarch. Cook over medium heat until sauce is thickened, stirring constantly. Keep warm over low heat.

Heat oil in a large heavy skillet. Sprinkle chicken with salt and pepper. Coat chicken with corn starch. When oil is hot, cook chicken until lightly browned and cooked through, about 10 minutes.

Shred spinach coarsely and arrange on platter. Arrange chicken on spinach and pour lemon sauce over the top.

Serves: 6

Nutritional Information per Serving
Calories: 275 , Fat: 11 grams, Protein: 23 grams, Carbohydrates: 21 grams, Cholesterol: 50 milligrams, Fiber: 1.1 grams

 To complete the presentation, place cooked rice on the platter and place spinach and chicken on top!

Notes:

Cha Cha Chicken with Sherry Mushroom Sauce

1/3 cup fresh grated Parmesan cheese
1/2 cup dry bread crumbs
2 tablespoons minced fresh parsley
salt and freshly ground pepper, to taste
1/2 teaspoon garlic powder
4 chicken breasts skinless, boneless
1/2 cup butter, melted
3 tablespoons lemon juice
paprika

Sauce

2 shallots, minced
2 tablespoons butter
4 ounces fresh mushrooms, sliced
1/4 cup dry sherry
1 teaspoon flour
1/2 cup chicken broth
1 cup half and half
2 tablespoons minced fresh parsley
1/8 teaspoon ground nutmeg
1/2 teaspoon salt
freshly ground pepper, to taste

Preheat oven to 350 degrees. Grease a 9x9-inch baking dish.

Chicken: In a small bowl combine cheese, bread crumbs, 2 tablespoons parsley, salt, pepper and garlic powder. In a shallow bowl or dish put the melted butter. Dip chicken in butter and coat with crumb mixture. Roll chicken up and secure with a toothpick. Place seam side down in prepared baking dish. Moisten top of chicken with lemon juice and sprinkle with paprika. Bake for 45 minutes. When chicken becomes golden brown, cover with foil to prevent over browning. Remove toothpicks and spoon sauce over chicken.

Sauce: Sauté shallots in butter over medium low heat until tender. Increase heat to medium high, add mushrooms and sauté for 3-5 minutes. Add wine and boil until liquid is completely evaporated. Sprinkle mushrooms with flour and cook for 1 minute. Stir in broth and half and half. Boil until sauce thickens, stirring constantly. Add parsley, nutmeg, salt and pepper.

Serves: 4

Nutritional Information per Serving
Calories:540 , Fat: 40 grams, Protein: 33 grams, Carbohydrates: 11 grams, Cholesterol: 170 milligrams, Fiber: 0.8 grams

 Chicken Crepes

A wonderful brunch dish that you can make in advance.

Crepes
  1 1/4 cups beer
  1 cup sifted flour
  1/4 cup water
  3 eggs
  2 tablespoons melted butter
  1/2 teaspoon salt

Filling
  5 tablespoons of butter
  5 tablespoons of flour
  3/4 cup dry white wine
  1 cup of whipping cream
  1 cup of Swiss cheese grated
  1 cup of chicken stock
  1/2 teaspoon of Worcestershire sauce
  salt and pepper to taste
  2 tablespoons of fresh parsley
  2 cups of chicken cooked and quarter size pieces
  1/2 cup of rope sliced olives
  paprika to sprinkle
  1 avocado, sliced

Notes:

Crepes: Combine all ingredients in a medium sized mixing bowl and beat until batter is smooth. Cover bowl and let stand at room temperature for one hour.

Lightly oil bottom of a non-stick frying pan or crepe pan and place over medium heat. Ladle approximately 1/4 cup batter into pan and swirl to coat the bottom. Bubbles will form quickly, in about 30 seconds, and when crepe begins to pull away from the side of pan, quickly turn it over. This is enough crepe batter to make 14 crepes, so there will be extra. (Crepes can be made ahead and frozen. Just place a sheet of waxed paper between each layer and then place in a freezer safe container or wrap in plastic wrap.)

Preheat oven to 375 degrees. Grease a 9x13-inch baking dish.

Filling: In a non-stick skillet melt butter flour to make a roux. Add broth wine and cream; thicken until smooth.

Add 3/4 of the cheese stir until melted. Add Worcestershire sauce and salt and pepper. Simmer for 2 minutes.

In a large bowl combine cooked chicken and olives. Add cooked sauce and mix well. Pour 1 cup of chicken mixture onto each crepe and roll up. Place each crepe side by side in prepared pan. Cover the top of the rolled crepes with the warm sauce. (Can be prepared 1 day in advance. Cover and refrigerate until ready to bake.)

Bake for 15 minutes. Add avocado slices and sprinkle with paprika. Cook for 5 minutes more. Remove from oven and let stand for 5 minutes before serving.

Serves: 8

Nutritional Information per Serving
Calories: 400 , Fat: 22 grams, Protein: 19 grams, Carbohydrates: 20 grams, Cholesterol: 135 milligrams, Fiber: 1.3 grams

Chicken Roll-Ups

For guests or for bringing to a friend in need. Freezes well and reheats nicely.

4 boneless, skinless, chicken breast halves
4 deli ham slices
4 slices Monterey Jack cheese
1 egg; beaten
3 tablespoons water
1/3 cup breadcrumbs
1/3 cup grated Parmesan cheese
1/2 cup white wine
1/4 cup butter
5 tablespoons flour
1/2 cup shredded mozzarella cheese

Preheat oven to 350 degrees.

Wash chicken, pat dry with paper towels. Pound chicken breast between two pieces of wax paper until very thin. Place one slice of ham, one slice of cheese in the middle of the chicken breast. Roll up, tucking sides in, and secure with toothpicks skewers.

Place beaten egg and water together in shallow bowl. Mix breadcrumbs and Parmesan cheese together in a separate shallow bowl. Dip chicken roll ups in egg-water mixture then the bread-cheese mixture.

Heat large sauté pan on medium heat. Melt butter watching closely not to burn. Brown chicken on all sides. Remove and place in 11x7-inch baking dish. Add wine to sauté pan and cook 5 minutes scraping to loosen browned bits. Add flour and stir until thickened. Pour sauce over chicken and cover with foil.

Bake, covered, for 30 minutes or until cooked through. Sprinkle cheese over top and bake an additional 10 minutes, uncovered, or until cheese is bubbly.

Serves: 4

Nutritional Information per Serving
Calories: 500, Fat: 30 grams, Protein: 42 grams, Carbohydrates: 15 grams, Cholesterol: 180 milligrams, Fiber: 0.5 grams

Notes:

Chicken Marsala

1/2 cup flour
1 teaspoon salt
1/2 teaspoon fresh ground black pepper
1/2 teaspoon dried thyme
1/2 teaspoon dried rosemary
1 teaspoon dried basil
1/2 teaspoon dried sage
1/2 teaspoon dried oregano
4 boneless, skinless chicken breast halves
2 tablespoons olive oil
2 tablespoons butter
2 cloves crushed garlic
1/2 pound fresh mushrooms, sliced
2/3 cup Marsala wine
1/4 cup heavy cream

Mix together flour with salt, pepper and dried herbs in a small bowl; set aside.
Pound chicken breast between two pieces of wax paper until 1/2-inch thick.
Dredge chicken in the flour mixture.

Heat oil and butter in a large skillet until hot; add garlic and sauté two minutes.
Add the chicken and brown for 2-3 minutes per side. Transfer meat to a warm
serving platter and cover to keep warm.

Add mushrooms to the skillet and cook 5 minutes. Add the wine and heat to
boiling scraping up browned bits. Continue to boil, stirring occasionally for 3
minutes; add cream and bring to a boil. Reduce heat and simmer for 2 minutes.

Pour sauce over warmed chicken on platter and serve with rice, pasta, or
roasted red potatoes.

Makes 4 servings

Nutritional Information per Serving
Calories: 345, Fat: 19 grams, Protein: 23 grams, Carbohydrates: 15 grams, Cholesterol: 85
milligrams, Fiber: 0.7 grams

Lemony Chicken Kabobs

1/2 cup fresh lemon juice
1/4 cup oil
1 tablespoon sugar
1 tablespoon vinegar
2 teaspoons salt
1 teaspoon pepper
1/4 teaspoon cayenne pepper
2 garlic cloves, minced
2 whole chicken breasts (4 halves)
3 small zucchini
1/2 pound mushrooms

8 wooden skewers, soaked in water 30 minutes

Mix lemon juice, oil, sugar, vinegar, salt, pepper, cayenne pepper and garlic
Whisk together until incorporated.

Cut chicken into 1x1-inch cubes. Cut zucchini into rounds or 1-inch chunks.
Wash and cut stems off mushrooms. Add vegetables and chicken to marinade,
toss and let marinate in the refrigerator for at least 4 hours.

Thread chicken and vegetables, alternately, on skewers.

Broil or grill for 15-20 minutes or until chicken is cooked through.

Serves: 4

Nutritional Information per Serving
Calories: 265, Fat: 15 grams, Protein: 22 grams, Carbohydrates: 11 grams, Cholesterol: 50
milligrams, Fiber: 1.9 grams

 Serve these kebobs with our French Risotto for light summer dinner.

Notes:

Tequila Lime Chicken

1/2 cup gold tequila
1 cup fresh squeezed lime juice (5-6 limes)
1/2 cup fresh squeezed orange juice (2 oranges)
1 tablespoon chili powder
1 jalapeno pepper, seeded and minced
2 tablespoons fresh, chopped cilantro (optional)
1 tablespoon minced fresh garlic (3 cloves)
2 teaspoons kosher salt
1 teaspoon black pepper
3 whole chicken breasts, skin on (6 split breasts)

Combine tequila, lime juice, orange juice, chili powder, jalapeño, cilantro, garlic, salt and pepper in a large 9x13-glass pan or large airtight bag. Add the chicken and refrigerate overnight.

Prepare grill and brush the rack with oil to prevent sticking.

Remove the chicken breasts from marinade; discard marinade. Sprinkle chicken with salt and pepper.

Grill chicken, skin down, for 5 minutes, until nicely browned. Turn the chicken and cook for 10 minutes more, until just cooked through. Remove from grill to a plate. Cover tightly and allow to rest for 5 minutes. Serve hot or at room temperature.

Serves: 6

Nutritional Information per Serving
Calories: 180, Fat: 2 grams, Protein: 21 grams, Carbohydrates: 8 grams, Cholesterol: 50 milligrams, Fiber: 0.8 grams

Jamaican Jerk Chicken

1/4 cup hot peppers, stemmed, seeded and chopped
1 teaspoon ground allspice
6 garlic cloves, minced
2 tablespoons peeled and chopped fresh ginger
2 tablespoons brown sugar
1/4 cup yellow mustard
1 teaspoon ground cinnamon
hot pepper sauce, to taste
1/2 cup olive oil
2 green onions, sliced
1/4 cup cider vinegar
2 tablespoons lime juice
salt and fresh ground pepper
4 whole chicken breasts (8 halves)

Notes:

Puree hot peppers in blender or food processor. Add allspice, garlic, ginger, sugar, mustard, cinnamon, hot pepper sauce, olive oil, green onions, vinegar and lime juice, and blend until mixture is a smooth paste. Add salt and pepper to taste and blend again.

Gently lift the skin away from the chicken exposing the meat. Rub spice mixture onto the outside of the chicken breast. Cover with plastic wrap and refrigerate for 2 hours.

Prepare grill. On an oiled rack set 4-6 inches over glowing coals grill the chicken, covered if possible, for 10-15 minutes on each side, or until it is cooked through.

Serves: 8

Nutritional Information per Serving
Calories: 240, Fat: 15 grams, Protein: 21 grams, Carbohydrates: 5 grams, Cholesterol: 50 milligrams, Fiber: 0.8 grams

 If you can't grill, you can roast chicken in 2 large shallow (1-inch-deep) baking pans in upper and lower thirds of a 400 degree oven, switching position of pans halfway through roasting, 40-45 minutes total.

Hawaiian Chicken Sandwich

1/2 cup soy sauce
1/2 cup dry sherry, sake, or bourbon
2 tablespoons sugar
5 cloves garlic, minced
1/2 teaspoon ground ginger
4 boneless, skinless chicken breast halves
8 slices pepper-jack cheese
1 (8 ounce) can pineapple rings, drained
4 kaiser rolls or hard rolls

In a small bowl, combine soy sauce, sherry, sugar, garlic and ginger. Whisk together.

In a shallow bowl or large airtight bag, place chicken in marinade and refrigerate for at least 4 hours, up to 8 hours.

Prepare charcoal grill to a medium temperature.

Grill the chicken for 15 minutes, turning often. About half way through cooking the chicken, place the pineapple on the grill. Turn once.

When chicken and pineapple are cooked, place one pineapple ring on each breast half. Place two slices cheese over the pineapple. Close the grill lid and cook for 5 minutes or until cheese is melted.

Serve on toasted kaiser rolls as a sandwich. Serve with mayonnaise or teriyaki sauce, lettuce, onion and tomato.

Serves: 4

Nutritional Information per Serving
Calories: 510, Fat: 21 grams, Protein: 39 grams, Carbohydrates: 34 grams, Cholesterol: 100 milligrams, Fiber: 0.6 grams

 Chicken Caesar Wrap

4 chicken breast halves, cooked
salt and pepper to taste
1/2 cup mayonnaise
1/2 cup sour cream, plus more for garnish
2 cloves garlic, minced
2 tablespoons lemon juice
1 cup shredded Parmesan cheese
salt and pepper to taste
3 cups chopped Romaine lettuce
1/2 cup chopped cherry or grape tomatoes
4 (10-inch) flour tortillas
1 avocado, sliced

Prepare barbecue (medium-high heat) or preheat broiler. Season chicken with salt and pepper.

Notes:

Grill or broil chicken until cooked through, about 4 minutes per side. Transfer chicken to plate. Cool; chop into 1/2-inch cubes.

In a small bowl, combine mayonnaise, sour cream, garlic, lemon juice, 1/2 cup cheese, salt and pepper in a mixing bowl.

Wrap tortillas in paper towels and heat in microwave on high 1 minute. (Or heat each tortilla in dry skillet over medium heat 1 minute per side.)

To assemble, spread 2–3 tablespoons of the dressing onto on half of the tortilla. Place 1/4 of the chopped chicken on the dressing. Add lettuce, tomatoes and cheese. Drizzle another tablespoon of dressing over the top.

Roll the tortilla burrito style and secure with a toothpick. Garnish each wrap with a dollop of sour cream and 3 slices of avocado.

Serves: 4

Nutritional Information per Serving
Calories: 740, Fat: 45 grams, Protein: 36 grams, Carbohydrates: 48 grams, Cholesterol: 90 milligrams, Fiber: 5.1 grams

Honey-Chili Roasted Duck

For families with hunters or people who just love duck!

1 (4 pound) whole duck
1/2 tablespoon chopped fresh thyme
3 cloves chopped garlic
1 tablespoon sea salt
1/2 teaspoon fresh ground black pepper
3 tablespoon olive oil
4 tablespoon honey
1/2 teaspoon ground chili powder
1 1/2 tablespoon soy sauce
1 tablespoon lemon juice
2 tablespoon Dijon mustard
1/2 cup dark rum

Place roasting pan in oven. Preheat oven to 425 degrees.

Wash duck well inside and out. Pat dry. In a small bowl, combine thyme, garlic, salt, pepper and olive oil. Rub duck inside and out with the mixture. Place duck in the preheated pan.

Bake for 20 minutes, lower oven temperature to 350 degrees and roast 45 minutes more.

In a small bowl, combine honey, chili powder, soy sauce, lemon juice, mustard and rum.

Remove duck from oven, keeping oven on, and let rest 10 minutes. Pour off hot duck fat. Baste duck with honey mixture and return to oven.

Roast 15 minutes, brushing with honey mixture every five minutes. Remove from oven and let rest five minutes.

Serves: 4

Nutritional Information per Serving
Calories: 640, Fat: 50 grams, Protein: 14 grams, Carbohydrates: 18 grams, Cholesterol: 90 milligrams, Fiber: 0.3 grams

 Using fresh or organic duck yields a much lower fat content.

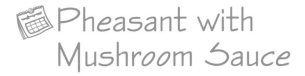

Pheasant with Mushroom Sauce

6 pheasant breasts
1 quart milk
1/2 teaspoons salt
1/2 teaspoons pepper
1/2 teaspoon onion powder
3 tablespoons butter
1 12 ounce package fresh sliced mushrooms
3 12 ounce cans reduced fat cream of mushroom soup
1 1/2 cup dry sherry
4 teaspoons paprika
1 1/2 cup low fat sour cream
1 pound angel hair pasta
1 red pepper, thinly sliced (for garnish)

Notes:

Reserve 3/4 cup milk. Soak the pheasant in remaining milk for 4-6 hours, refrigerated.

Drain the pheasant, and pat dry. Discard the milk. Sprinkle pheasant with salt pepper and onion powder.

In a large sauté pan over medium-high heat, melt the butter and sauté the pheasant for 2 minutes. Add the soup and 3/4 cup sherry, stirring to coat the pheasant. Sprinkle the paprika over the breasts, cover and simmer on low for 1 hour.

Cook pasta according to directions. Drain; set aside.

When the pheasant is done, add the remaining sherry. Remove the breasts and keep warm on a separate plate.

Add 3/4 cup milk and sour cream to the sauté pan. Mix well and warm slightly. Pour sauce over the pheasant.

Serve on pasta and garnish with a thin strips of pepper.

Serves: 6

Nutritional Information per Serving
Calories: 880, Fat: 33 grams, Protein: 52 grams, Carbohydrates: 77 grams, Cholesterol: 150 milligrams, Fiber: 3.1 grams

 Bacon Wrapped Duck Kabobs

Marinate 1 day in advance.

2 pounds wild or farm raised duck breast meat, skin removed
32 ounces Italian dressing
2 pounds bacon
2 medium zucchini
3 large Vidalia onions
16 ounces mushrooms

Cut duck into 1 1/2-2 inch cubes. Place meat in a non-metallic container. Pour dressing over duck, enough to cover meat. Cover and refrigerate at least 24 hours.

Cut bacon strips in half lengthwise and in half widthwise, so one slice yields 4 pieces. Slice zucchini into rings. Cut onion into quarters and then cut each quarter in half. Wash mushroom and trim stems.

Prepare the grill with a large bed of coals and medium–high heat is desirable.

To assemble: skewer a ring of zucchini, followed by a mushroom, and then onion. To skewer the duck, wrap a piece of the bacon around the duck, then run the skewer through the bacon to secure. Starting with zucchini again, repeat until skewer is full. Repeat entire process until all ingredients are used.

Grill for about 15 minutes or until duck is cooked, being careful not to overcook.

Serves: 8

Nutritional Information per Serving
Calories: 900, Fat: 70 grams, Protein: 57 grams, Carbohydrates: 9 grams,
Cholesterol: 180 milligrams, Fiber: 2.4 grams

Venison with Nouveau-Cherry Sauce

A rich, post-harvest meal to celebrate the release of the "nouveau" wines.

Dry Brine

3 tablespoons dark brown sugar
1 tablespoon kosher salt
1/2 teaspoon fresh cracked white pepper
1/4 teaspoon dried sage
1/4 teaspoon dried thyme

Venison

3-4 pound venison roast
1 teaspoon fresh ground black pepper
3 tablespoons vegetable oil
1 cup diced red onion
3 tablespoons chopped fresh sage
1 1/2 cups low sodium beef stock
1 1/4 cups Beaujolais Nouveau wine
1 (8.75 ounce) can pitted dark sweet cherries
salt and pepper to taste

WINE SUGGESTION:

Beaujolais Nouveau is a special category of 7-9-week-old wine that's released annually on the third Thursday of November. This "new" wine is made from the better grapes of the basic Beaujolais appellation and is meant to be drunk very young.

Combine the five ingredients for the brine in a small bowl. Rub entire roast with brine mixture. Cover venison with plastic wrap and refrigerate 1-2 hours.

Preheat oven to 300 degrees.

Rinse brine from roast with cold water. Season roast with black pepper. In a large oven-proof skillet heat oil over high heat and sear the outside of the roast, approximately 3 minutes per side.

Remove roast from skillet, leaving skillet on the stove. Sauté onions until tender but not browned. Add sage and sauté for 1 minute. Return venison to pan along with stock and wine. Transfer skillet to oven and roast for approximately 1 hour, or until internal temperature is 135 degrees for medium-rare.

Remove skillet from oven; transfer roast to platter and cover with aluminum foil. Strain liquid from skillet and then return strained liquid to skillet. Heat to boiling and reduce liquid by 1/3. Add cherries and heat through. Salt and pepper to taste.

Thinly slice roast and serve with Nouveau-Cherry sauce. Garnish with fresh sage.

Serves: 6

Nutritional Information per Serving
Calories: 530, Fat: 21 grams, Protein: 70 grams, Carbohydrates: 9 grams, Cholesterol: 185 milligrams, Fiber: 0.8 grams

Individual Beef Wellingtons

Your guests will feel like royalty when you serve this elegant meal.

4 tablespoons corn oil
4 (6 ounce) filet mignons, about 2 inches thick
salt and pepper to taste
1 tablespoon butter
1 pound fresh mushrooms, finely chopped
1 shallot, finely chopped
1 tablespoon minced garlic
1/4 cup Burgundy wine
6 puff pastry shells, thawed
1 egg white
1 teaspoon water

Preheat oven to 425 degrees.

Heat oil in heavy frying pan. Over high heat, quickly sear the edges of each piece of beef tenderloin. Do not allow the meat to cook in the oil. Remove from the pan; drain on paper towels; salt and pepper very lightly. Chill in the refrigerator.

Melt butter in a large frying pan. Sauté mushrooms and shallot. Season with 1/2 teaspoon salt and 1/4 teaspoon pepper. Stir occasionally over medium heat until the liquid from the mushrooms has evaporated. Add the wine and continue cooking until it has reduced. Cool mixture in the refrigerator. Pour off any accumulated liquid.

Cut 2 of the puff pastry shells in half. Combine each half with a whole pastry shell so that you have 4 dough balls. Lightly flour a work surface and rolling pin. Place one of the dough balls on a lightly floured work surface; using a rolling pin, flatten into a 10-inch circle. (Reserve any extra pastry for making leaves or other decorative pastry for the top of the Wellingtons.) In the middle of the circle, put 2 tablespoons of the cooled, drained mushroom mixture. Place one of the beef tenderloin pieces on top of the mushrooms and pat 4 tablespoons of the mushroom mixture around and on top of the meat. Wrap up the meat with the pastry shell and place seam-side down on a cookie sheet. Repeat with the remaining pastry and meat.

In a small bowl beat egg white and water. Brush each pastry with egg glaze. Bake for 20-25 minutes, until the pastry is a light golden color.

Serves: 4

Nutritional Information per Serving
Calories: 915, Fat: 60 grams, Protein: 56 grams, Carbohydrates: 38 grams,
Cholesterol: 150 milligrams, Fiber: 1.4 grams

Beef Tenderloin with Wisconsin Blue Cheese Sauce

Marinate the beef 1 day in advance.

2 pounds center cut beef tenderloin
2 tablespoons olive oil
salt and pepper to taste
1 tablespoon minced shallots (about 2 small shallots)
3 tablespoons dry Madeira or ruby port wine
2 cups beef stock
1/3 cup heavy cream
2 ounce Wisconsin Blue Cheese
4 tablespoons unsalted butter, softened
6 tablespoons chopped toasted walnuts, for garnish
1 tablespoon minced fresh parsley, for garnish

WINE SUGGESTION:

Botham Vineyards Uplands Reserve
The strong fruit essences of this earthy and spicy dry, red wine capture and soften the blue cheese and walnut flavors of this entrée's sauce component creating a smooth, round goodness for the palate.
A delightful companion to most red meats, Uplands Reserve is a willing and ardent companion for tenderloin. Its medium body enhances, rather than overpowers the meat and leaves room for the beef's true flavors to emerge.
Grown, produced and bottled by Botham Vineyards, Inc. of Barneveld, Wisconsin, Uplands Reserve has earned national and international acclaim for its regionally distinctive blend of substantial fruit character and spicy heat. Drinks well young, ages beautifully. Serve at room temperature.

Rub tenderloin all over with 1 tablespoon of oil. Lightly sprinkle meat with salt and pepper. Loosely cover with plastic wrap, and marinate for 24 hours. One hour before cooking, remove meat from refrigerator and pat dry.

Heat a non-stick skillet over high heat and rub 1 tablespoon oil all over the tenderloin. When pan is hot, sear meat on all sides, about 4 minutes total. Transfer to a wire rack and let rest at least 20 minutes. Transfer tenderloin to a baking dish.

Preheat oven to 450 degrees.

Discard any fat in the pan, add shallots and Madeira and reduce to a glaze over medium-high heat, about 5 minutes. Add the beef stock and reduce to 1/2 cup, about 10 minutes. Add cream and simmer for 5 minutes.

In a small bowl mix blue cheese and 4 tablespoons of butter until smooth and creamy.

Bake tenderloin fillets 18-20 minutes, for medium rare, up to 25 minutes for medium.

Over medium-low heat gently warm the sauce in the skillet; whisk in the cheese-butter mixture by adding 1/4 of the mixture at a time. When the sauce is well blended, reduce the heat to low and keep warm.

Slice meat and arrange in overlapping slices on the sauce. Garnish with nuts and parsley.

Serves: 4

Nutritional Information per Serving
Calories: 790, Fat: 53 grams, Protein: 74 grams, Carbohydrates: 3 grams, Cholesterol: 260 milligrams, Fiber: 0 grams

Tenderloin Fillets with Port Sauce

1 tablespoon butter
1/2 cup minced shallots
1 cup dry red wine
3/4 cup port
1 cup beef broth
1 teaspoon chopped plus 2 sprigs fresh rosemary
1 tablespoon olive oil
4 (6 ounce) beef tenderloin steaks, about 1-inch thick
3 tablespoons unsalted butter, chilled, cut into 3 pieces
Salt and pepper to taste

Melt butter in heavy large saucepan over medium-high heat. Add shallots and sauté until tender, about 3 minutes. Stir in wine and port. Boil 5 minutes. Add beef broth and 2 sprigs rosemary and boil until liquid is reduced to 1/3 cup, about 12 minutes. Strain sauce and set aside. (Can be prepared 1 day ahead. Cover and refrigerate.)

Heat oil in heavy large skillet over medium-high heat. Season steaks with salt and pepper. Add steaks to skillet and cook to desired doneness, about 4 minutes per side for medium-rare. Transfer steaks to platter. Tent with foil to keep warm.

Add port sauce to skillet and bring to boil. Remove from heat. Gradually add unsalted butter, whisking just until melted. It may be necessary to turn heat on low if butter is not melting. Stir in chopped rosemary. Season to taste with salt and pepper.

Spoon sauce over steaks and serve.

Serves: 4

Nutritional Information per Serving
Calories: 600, Fat: 31 grams, Protein: 51 grams, Carbohydrates: 9 grams, Cholesterol: 170 milligrams, Fiber: 0 grams

Peppered Steaks with Whiskey Sauce

2 tablespoons minced shallots
1 tablespoon red wine vinegar
3 1/2 teaspoons cracked black pepper
2 cups beef stock
1 cup chicken stock
2 (8 ounce) beef tenderloin steaks
1/2 teaspoon dried rosemary
1/2 teaspoon dried thyme
1/2 teaspoon dried marjoram
1/4 cup olive oil
1 tablespoon whiskey

Notes:

In heavy medium saucepan, boil shallots in vinegar and 1 1/2 teaspoons pepper until almost no liquid remains in the pan, about 2 minutes. Add both stocks and boil until liquid is reduced to 1/2 cup, about 20 minutes. (Sauce can be prepared 1 day in advance. Cover and refrigerate)

Place steaks in baking dish. In a small bowl mix 2 teaspoons cracked pepper, rosemary, thyme and marjoram. Rub mixture on both sides of steaks. Pour oil over steaks, turning to coat. Cover and let stand 1 hour. Remove meat from marinade.

Heat heavy large skillet over medium high heat. Add steaks and sear on both sides. Reduce heat to medium and cook meat to desired doneness, about 3 minutes per side for rare.

Transfer steaks to plates. Add sauce to skillet and bring to boil. Mix in whiskey and remove from heat. Spoon sauce over steaks and serve.

Serves: 2

Nutritional Information per Serving
Calories: 650, Fat: 32 grams, Protein: 80 grams, Carbohydrates: 4 grams,
Cholesterol: 190 milligrams, Fiber: 0 grams

 Use Olive Paste with Blue Cheese (page 189) as an alternative to the Whiskey Sauce in this recipe.

Olive Paste with Blue Cheese

1/4 pound pitted black olives
1 garlic clove, minced
3 tablespoons olive oil
2 tablespoons pine nuts
1 sourdough or French baguette, cut into 1/4-inch slices
8 ounces blue cheese

Combine olives, garlic, olive oil and pine nuts in blender. Blend until mixture resembles a smooth paste.

Spread olive mixture on bread. Cover with blue cheese.

Serves: 6

Nutritional Information per Serving
Calories: 225, Fat: 20 grams, Protein: 9 grams, Carbohydrates: 2 grams, Cholesterol: 30 milligrams, Fiber: 0.1 grams

 # Bo Go Gy

This Asian shish kabob is excellent with rice pilaf.

1/2 cup soy sauce (we recommend Kikkoman's)
1 teaspoon garlic powder
6 tablespoons sugar
1 teaspoon minced ginger
1 1/2 teaspoons black pepper
1/4 cup green onions, chopped
1/4 sesame seeds, toasted
3 tablespoons bourbon
2-3 pounds sirloin or tenderloin steak, cubed
1 pint cherry tomatoes
8 ounces mushrooms
4 medium onions, quartered
2 tablespoons olive oil
8 wooden skewers, soaked in water 30 minutes

Notes:

In a small bowl combine soy sauce, garlic powder, sugar, ginger, pepper, green onions, sesame seeds and bourbon. Whisk together until combined well. Reserve 1/4 cup of marinade for basting.

In a shallow 9x13-inch glass pan place cubed meat so it is evenly spread out. Pour marinade over meat and stir until all pieces have been coated. Cover and refrigerate over night.

Prepare grill to a medium heat.

Remove meat from marinade; discard marinade. Skewer meat leaving a small amount of space between cubes for even browning. Skewer vegetables separately, as cooking time varies from meat.

In a small bowl whisk 1/4 reserved marinade with 2 tablespoons of olive oil.

Grill the meat first, basting with marinade. When meat is almost done, begin grilling the vegetables, cook until done.

Serve skewers on a platter or remove meat and vegetables from skewers and serve in a large bowl.

Serves: 6

Nutritional Information per Serving
Calories: 420, Fat: 19 grams, Protein: 49 grams, Carbohydrates: 10 grams, Cholesterol: 135 milligrams, Fiber: 2.6 grams

Steak Fajitas

1/2 cup lime juice
2 scallions, sliced
3 cloves garlic, minced
1/4 cup cilantro, chopped
2 tablespoons vegetable oil
1/2-1 teaspoon red pepper flakes
1/4 teaspoon coriander seed
1/4 teaspoon cumin
1/8 teaspoon anise seed (optional)
1 1/2-2 pounds flank or skirt steak

Place all ingredients, except steak, in blender or food processor. Blend until well combined. Place steak in a large glass dish or airtight bag. Pour marinade over meat; refrigerate in marinade for 12-24 hours. Turn occasionally to be certain sides are coated.

Prepare a medium-hot charcoal fire or gas grill.

Remove steak from marinade; discard the marinade. Grill steak 2-4 minutes a side for rare to medium-rare steak. Let stand 5 minutes and slice thinly.

Serve with warmed flour tortillas, salsa, guacamole, sautéed onions and peppers and sour cream.

Serves: 8

Nutritional Information per Serving (without tortillas)
Calories: 180, Fat: 12 grams, Protein: 16 grams, Carbohydrates: 2 grams, Cholesterol: 40 milligrams, Fiber: 0.3 grams

 You can substitute chicken or shrimp in place of beef for an equally delicious fajita. For chicken, marinate 4-8 hours; for shrimp, marinate 45 minutes-2 hours.

Asian Beef with Fresh Pea Pods

Marinade
- 2 tablespoons water
- 1 tablespoon sake or white wine
- 1 tablespoon soy sauce
- 1 tablespoon vegetable oil
- 1 tablespoon fresh ginger, minced
- 1 teaspoon cornstarch
- 1/2 teaspoon sesame oil
- 1/2 teaspoon baking soda
- 1/2 teaspoon salt
- 1/2 teaspoon sugar
- 1/2 teaspoon black pepper
- 1/2 pound flank steak, thinly cut diagonally

Stir Fry
- 1 teaspoon cornstarch
- 1/4 cup plus 3 tablespoons water
- 1/2 pound fresh pea pods
- 3 tablespoons vegetable oil
- 1/2 teaspoon salt
- 1 tablespoon oyster sauce

Notes:

Marinade: Combine all ingredients for marinade. Place steak in a large glass dish or airtight bag. Pour marinade over meat; and let rest at least 6 hours. (Can be prepared and stored in refrigerator overnight. Bring to room temperature before cooking.)

In a small bowl combine cornstarch with 3 tablespoons of water; set aside. Heat 2 tablespoons of oil in wok or deep saucepan over medium high heat. Add the beef, discard the marinade, and quickly stir fry to rare, about 2 minutes. Stir continuously. Remove from wok and reserve on a plate.

Add remaining 1 tablespoon of oil to wok. Add pea pods, salt and 1/4 cup water. Cover and let come to a boil. Add the cornstarch-water mixture and oyster sauce. Stir for 1 minute. Return the beef to the wok and let come to boil again.

Remove from wok and serve with rice.

Serves: 4

Nutritional Information per Serving
Calories: 210, Fat: 16 grams, Protein: 12 grams, Carbohydrates: 5 grams, Cholesterol: 30 milligrams, Fiber: 1.4 grams

 Coffee Glazed Oven Brisket

A great recipe for a family meal.

3 pounds beef brisket
kosher salt
fresh cracked pepper
2 tablespoons vegetable oil
1/2 cup freshly brewed strong black coffee
1/2 cup ketchup
1/2 cup chili sauce
1/2 cup honey
1/3 cup Worcestershire sauce
1 garlic clove, minced
1 tablespoon soy sauce

Preheat oven to 325 degrees.

Season surface of beef with salt and pepper. In a large Dutch oven, over medium-high heat, warm 2 tablespoons vegetable oil. Add brisket, fat side down, and cook until well browned, about 4-5 minutes per side. Remove from heat.

In a small bowl, combine coffee, ketchup, chili sauce, honey, Worcestershire sauce, garlic and soy sauce. Whisk together until well combined.

Place brisket in oven-safe pan and pour sauce over brisket. Cover with lid or foil.

Bake, covered, for 3 hours turning brisket after 1 1/2 hours.

Remove from oven; slice on the bias against the grain. Transfer remaining sauce from Dutch oven to gravy boat, and serve with brisket.

Serves: 6

Nutritional Information per Serving
Calories: 860, Fat: 64 grams, Protein: 39 grams, Carbohydrates: 32 grams, Cholesterol: 165 milligrams, Fiber: 0.5 grams

German Pot Roast

An easy slow cooker recipe for a special week-night meal.

1 (4-pound) beef chuck roast
salt and pepper to taste
1 cup water
1 (8 ounce) can tomato sauce
2 garlic cloves, minced
1/4 cup ketchup
1 tablespoons Worcestershire sauce
dash hot sauce
2 tablespoons brown sugar
1/2 teaspoon dry mustard
1/4 cup lemon juice
1/4 cup red wine vinegar
3 medium onions, sliced

Notes:

Salt and pepper entire roast.

In a small bowl, combine water, tomato sauce, garlic, ketchup, Worcestershire sauce, hot sauce, brown sugar, dry mustard, lemon juice and red wine vinegar. (Can be prepared 1 day in advance.)

Place roast in slow cooker and layer onion around roast. Pour sauce over. Turn on low and cook for 8 hours.

Serves: 8

Nutritional Information per Serving
Calories: 500, Fat: 35 grams, Protein: 36 grams, Carbohydrates: 10 grams, Cholesterol: 130 milligrams, Fiber: 1.3 grams

Serve with Cinnamon Glazed Carrots (page 140) and Garlic Mashed Potatoes (page 154).

Presidential Beef Burgundy

8 ounces thick sliced bacon
3 pounds beef chuck, cut into 1-inch cubes
salt and pepper to taste
3 tablespoons flour
3 cups Burgundy wine
3 cups beef stock or broth
2 tablespoons tomato paste
1 tablespoon chopped fresh rosemary leaves
2 cups carrots, peeled and chopped
8 ounces chanterelle mushrooms (dried or fresh)
12 ounces egg noodles
2 tablespoons butter
2 tablespoons parsley, chopped

In a large heavy skillet cook the bacon to desired doneness. Remove bacon; drain and coarsely chop. Remove 1/2 of the drippings from the skillet.

Heat the remaining drippings on medium heat. Add the beef cubes and salt and pepper to taste. After beef has begun to brown, about 5 minutes, sprinkle in the flour. Stir constantly over medium heat for 5 more minutes. Add wine, beef broth, tomato paste, reserved bacon and rosemary. Bring to a boil. Cover and reduce to a simmer for 2 hours, stirring often.

About 45 minutes before serving, add diced carrots and mushrooms.

Prepare egg noodles according to package instructions. Drain and toss with butter and parsley.

Serve beef over noodles on a large platter or individual plates.

Serves: 8

Nutritional Information per Serving
Calories: 800, Fat: 43 grams, Protein: 47 grams, Carbohydrates: 40 grams, Cholesterol: 160 milligrams, Fiber: 2.5 gram

This recipe comes from Laurel Rice, one of the founding members and a two-time President of the Junior League of Madison. In 1993 Laurel hosted a holiday party to thank all of the members who worked so hard on the Kitchen Tour, our signature fundraiser. Laurel served this recipe with croissants, broccoli florets and dessert cookies. The party was such a success that the group decided to hold the party every year, on the same day, with the same menu and, unfortunately for many, with the same guest list. The entree, the party and Laurel are Madison Junior League legends!

 Pork Tenderloin with Lime Cilantro Pesto

This dish needs to marinate overnight.

Marinade
- 1/2 cup white wine
- 2 cloves garlic, minced
- 1 tablespoon olive oil
- 2 pounds pork tenderloin

Pesto
- 3 cloves of garlic
- 2 tablespoons minced fresh ginger
- 1 cup chopped green onions, tops included
- 1/4 cup cilantro, packed
- 1 jalapeno pepper, seeded
- 5 tablespoons fresh lime juice
- 6 tablespoons olive oil
- 1/2 cup grated jalapeno cheese
- 1/4 cups toasted pine nuts, to garnish

Combine all marinade ingredients; set aside. Cut tenderloin lengthwise almost in half and lay out flat in a large glass baking dish. Top with marinade; cover and refrigerate overnight.

Pesto: In a food processor combine garlic, ginger, green onions, cilantro, jalapeño and lime juice. Slowly add olive oil until mixture thickens.

Remove pork from marinade, discard marinade. Spread half of pesto mixture over tenderloin. Sprinkle grated cheese over pesto. Fold tenderloin halves back together and tie with kitchen string to secure, about every inch. Spread remaining pesto over tenderloin and chill for at least 2 hours.

Preheat oven to 400 degrees.

Place tenderloin on rack and bake until firm about 25 minutes. Remove from oven and cover to keep warm. Reserve all juices. Remove string and cut tenderloin into slices.

Fan slices on a platter. Top with warm juices and sprinkle with toasted pine nuts.

Serves: 8

Nutritional Information per Serving
Calories: 340, Fat: 19 grams, Protein: 38 grams, Carbohydrates: 4 grams, Cholesterol: 80 milligrams, Fiber: 0.8 grams

BREW SUGGESTION:

German Beer
Spaten Oktoberfest - Brewery: Spaten - Munich, Germany Description: Spaten's Ur-Märzen Oktoberfest has an excellent, medium-bodied aroma. It is an amber, sweet, all-malt bier, lagered for 14 weeks. Additionally, it is the most popular bier at the Oktoberfest celebration in Munich, and the world's number one Oktoberfest bier. 5.76% ABV

Micro Brew
Capital Blonde Doppelbock - Brewery: Capital Brewery - Middleton, WI Description: A deep golden color leads one to an extremely flavorful, yet very drinkable beer of great character. Treat this malt monster with respect! Unfortunately, this is a limited-release beer, and is available only in March and April. 6.9% ABV

Pork Tenderloin with Herbed Breadcrumb Crust

3 cups fresh breadcrumbs made from French bread
2/3 cup chopped fresh parsley
2/3 cup grated Parmesan cheese
2 tablespoons chopped fresh rosemary
1 3/4 teaspoons crumbled bay leaves
salt and pepper to taste
3 pounds pork tenderloin, trimmed
4 tablespoons Dijon mustard
2 large eggs, beaten
4 tablespoons butter
2 tablespoons olive oil

Preheat oven to 375 degrees.

In large bowl, mix breadcrumbs, parsley, cheese, rosemary and bay leaves. Season to taste with salt and pepper.

Rub tenderloins with mustard. Sprinkle pork with salt and pepper. Dip tenderloin into eggs, then into breadcrumb mixture, coating completely.

In heavy large skillet over medium-high heat, heat 2 tablespoons butter and 1 tablespoon oil. Add half of pork; cook until golden on all sides, about 5 minutes. Place on rack set in large roasting pan. Wipe out skillet. Repeat with remaining 2 tablespoons butter, 1 tablespoon oil and pork.

Roast pork 20 minutes, until crust is golden and thermometer insert into center reads 145 degrees. Transfer pork to cutting board. Let stand 5 minutes. Slice pork and serve.

Serves: 8

Nutritional Information per Serving
Calories: 590, Fat: 23 grams, Protein: 62 grams, Carbohydrates: 33 grams, Cholesterol: 175 milligrams, Fiber: 2.8 grams

Apricot Stuffed Crown Roast

1 (6-pound) crown roast of pork, 12-16 ribs
salt and pepper to taste
tin foil

Stuffing
 1 tablespoon sugar
 1 teaspoon instant chicken bouillon
 3/4 cup hot water
 1/4 cup dried apricots, snipped
 4 cups dry whole wheat bread cubes (about 5 1/2 slices of bread)
 1 large apple, peeled, cored and chopped
 1/2 teaspoon finely shredded orange peel
 1/2 teaspoon salt
 1/2 teaspoon ground sage
 1/4 teaspoon ground cinnamon
 1/8 teaspoon pepper
 1/2 cup chopped celery
 1/4 cup chopped onion
 4 tablespoons butter

Basting Sauce
 1/4 cup orange juice
 1 tablespoon light corn syrup
 1/2 teaspoon soy sauce

Garnish
 1 (16 ounce) can apricots, drained

Preheat oven to 325 degrees.

Place roast, bone tips up, on rack in shallow roasting pan. Sprinkle roast inside and out with salt and pepper. Make a ball of tin foil and press into cavity to hold open. Wrap tips of rib bones with foil to prevent burning.

Roast on middle rack for 2 1/2 hours.

Stuffing: Dissolve sugar and bouillon in hot water. Place apricots in a small bowl. Pour bouillon and sugar mixture over apricots and let stand for 5 minutes. In a large bowl combine bread cubes, apple, orange peel, salt, sage, cinnamon and pepper.

RUBS:

There are two types of rubs used to flavor meat, wet and dry. A wet rub is made with a combination of dried or fresh herbs and spices, salt, pepper and sometimes sugar. Rubs when combined with small amounts of oil, mustards or other wet ingredients create a paste know as the wet rub. Rubs are quick and easy and are a wonderful way to flavor food, especially when left to marinate for an hour or more.

In a small pan, sauté celery and onion in butter until tender, 5 minutes. Add to bread mixture. Add apricot mixture and toss lightly to moisten. If necessary, add 1/4 cup more water.

Remove all foil from roast and pack stuffing lightly into center of roast, mounding high. In a small bowl, combine orange juice, corn syrup and soy sauce. Spoon some over meat, reserve some for basting.

Return roast to oven, uncovered for 45-60 minutes more, or until meat thermometer reads 170 degrees. Baste occasionally with orange juice mixture.

Carefully transfer to warm platter. Garnish with canned apricot halves. Slice between ribs to serve.

Serves: 12

Nutritional Information per Serving
Calories: 450, Fat: 26 grams, Protein: 37 grams, Carbohydrates: 15 grams, Cholesterol: 120 milligrams, Fiber: 1.0 grams

Everyday Rub

This rub is tasty on virtually everything. It can be made in large quantities and stored in the refrigerator until needed.

  1 teaspoon dry mustard
  1 teaspoon granulated onion
  1 teaspoon paprika
  1 teaspoon kosher salt
  1/2 teaspoon granulated garlic
  1/2 teaspoon coriander
  1/2 teaspoon black pepper

Combine ingredients in a bowl. Press the rub into all sides of the meat, fish or poultry. Put in an airtight bag and refrigerate for one hour prior to grilling or baking.

Makes 2 tablespoons.

Grilled Crusted Pork Tenderloin with Tomatillo Sauce

1 1/2 tablespoons ground coriander
1 1/2 tablespoons ground cumin
1 1/2 tablespoons ground pepper
3/4 tablespoon salt
2 (1-pound) pork tenderloins
1 pound tomatillos
1/2 yellow onion
2 fresh jalapeño, serrano or habañero chilies
2 cloves garlic
1 tablespoon olive oil
1/2 bunch cilantro, coarsely chopped
salt and pepper to taste

In a shallow bowl or pie plate, mix coriander, cumin, pepper and salt. Roll the pork tenderloins in the spices. (Can be made 4 hours ahead. Cover and chill.)

Preheat oven to 450 degrees.

Remove outer, papery covering of tomatillos. In a large pot of boiling water, boil tomatillos for 8 minutes or until tender. Drain and set aside to cool.

Brush the onion, chilies and garlic with oil.

Roast on a foil-lined baking sheet or in a roasting pan for 15-20 minutes, until the onion starts to brown and is tender and the chilies are brown, approximately 15-20 minutes. The garlic may need to be removed earlier, at around 10 minutes: remove when it starts to brown. Peel outer skin from chilies and seed them. (Wear rubber gloves to do this.)

Place tomatillos, onion, chilies, garlic and cilantro in a blender. Blend until smooth. Season to taste with salt and pepper. Serve hot or at room temperature. (Can be made up to 5 days in advance. Cover and refrigerate.)

Prepare barbecue to medium-high heat. Grill until cooked through, about 4 minutes per side. Let stand 5 minutes; slice and serve with Tomatillo Sauce.

Serves: 6

Nutritional Information per Serving
Calories: 315, Fat: 10 grams, Protein: 48 grams, Carbohydrates: 8 grams, Cholesterol: 100 milligrams, Fiber: 2.3 grams

Notes:

Honey-Lime Pork Chops

1/2 cup lime juice
1/2 cup reduced sodium soy sauce
2 tablespoons honey
2 cloves garlic, minced
6 (4 ounce) boneless pork loin chops

Sauce
3/4 cup reduced sodium chicken broth
1 clove garlic, minced
1 1/2 teaspoons honey
1/2 teaspoon lime juice
1/4 teaspoon browning sauce
dash pepper
2 teaspoons cornstarch
2 tablespoons water

In a large airtight bag, combine the first five ingredients. Seal bag and turn to coat. Refrigerate for 8 hours or overnight. Remove chops; discard marinade.

Preheat oven to broil.

Broil chops 4 inches from heat for 6-7 minutes on each side.

Sauce: In a small bowl, combine cornstarch and water; set aside. In a small saucepan, combine the broth, garlic, honey, lime juice, browning sauce and pepper. Bring to a boil. Slowly add cornstarch-water mixture into the broth. Return sauce to a simmer. Cook for 1-2 minutes until thickened. Serve sauce over pork chops.

Serves: 6

Nutritional Information per Serving
Calories: 190, Fat: 12 grams, Protein: 19 grams, Carbohydrates: 2 grams, Cholesterol: 60 milligrams, Fiber: 0 grams

Sumptuous Sweet and Sour Pork

This dish goes well over your favorite rice.

Sauce
- 1/2 cup carrots, peeled and sliced
- 1 small pepper (any color), seeded, cut into 1-inch pieces
- 1 onion, chopped in 1/2 inch chunks
- 1/2 cup pineapple chunks
- 3/4 cup sugar
- 1/3 cup ketchup
- 1 tablespoon light soy sauce
- 1/4 teaspoon salt
- 1 cup water
- 1/4 cup cider vinegar
- 3 1/2 tablespoons cornstarch

Pork
- 1/2 cup flour
- 1/4 cup cornstarch
- 1/2 teaspoon baking powder
- 1 tablespoon beaten egg plus enough water to total 1/2 cup
- 1 teaspoon canola, corn, or peanut oil
- 1 1/2 pounds boneless pork chops, cut into 1-inch cubes
- 1 teaspoon dry sherry
- 1/4 teaspoon salt
- dash of pepper
- vegetable oil for frying

Notes:

Sauce: In a small saucepan of boiling water, parboil the carrots, peppers and onion for two minutes. Remove vegetables and rinse in cold water to stop cooking. Set aside.

In a 2-quart saucepan, combine sugar, ketchup, soy sauce, salt and 2/3 cup water. Bring mixture to a boil and add vinegar. In a small bowl combine cornstarch with 1/3 cup water and mix well. When liquid comes back to a boil stir in cornstarch solution. Cook until sauce thickens. Add parboiled vegetables and pineapple to sauce. Keep warm.

Pork: In a large mixing bowl, combine flour, 1/4 cup cornstarch, baking powder, egg mixture and oil and beat with a wooden spoon until mixture becomes a smooth paste which is slightly more viscous than pancake batter. Use water to thin if necessary, adding one teaspoon of water at a time. Set aside.
In another bowl combine the pork, sherry, salt and pepper together. Set aside.

In a wok or deep fryer heat 2 inches of oil to a temperature of 375-400 degrees. Dip pork cubes into batter and coat completely. Carefully place pork into hot oil one piece at a time. Do not overcrowd the pan or fryer with the pork. (It will take 2-3 batches to complete the frying.) Deep fry until golden brown, about 5-7 minutes. Remove with wire skimmer and drain on paper towels while frying the remaining pork.

Place pork pieces on white rice and pour sweet and sour sauce over the top.

Serves: 4

Nutritional Information per Serving
Calories: 700, Fat: 30 grams, Protein: 29 grams, Carbohydrates: 78 grams, Cholesterol: 85 milligrams, Fiber: 1.9 grams

 For really crispy pork, place the pork back in the oil for a second frying. The second frying will really crisp-up the coating.

Phoenix Barbeque Sauce

    1/2 large onion, minced
    4 cloves garlic, minced
    3/4 cup whiskey
    2 cups ketchup
    1/3 cup vinegar
    1/4 cup Worcestershire sauce
    1/2 cup brown sugar, packed
    3/4 cup molasses
    1/2 teaspoon pepper
    1/2 teaspoon salt
    1/4 cup tomato paste
    2 tablespoons liquid smoke
    1/2 teaspoon hot sauce

In medium saucepan, melt butter. Add onions and garlic and cook until golden. Add whiskey and turn off burner. Light a match and ignite sauce. Allow sauce to burn for 30 seconds, covered. Add remaining ingredients and simmer for 20 minutes.

Serves: 10

Nutritional Information per Serving
Calories: 200, Fat: 0 grams, Protein: 1 grams, Carbohydrates: 46 grams, Cholesterol: 0 milligrams, Fiber: 1.0 grams

 Liquid smoke is a smoke-flavored liquid seasoning available at specialty foods stores and many supermarkets.

Pilgrim Pork Chops

6 pork loin chops, 3/4 inch thick
salt and pepper
1 tablespoon butter
1 teaspoon salt
1/4 teaspoon pepper
1 (16 ounce) can whole berry cranberry sauce
2 tablespoons chili sauce
1 tablespoon minced onion
2 teaspoons mustard
1/2 teaspoon ground ginger
1 (6 ounce package) stuffing mix

MARINADES:

Marinades improve the texture and flavor of foods that are soaked in it. Wine, vinegar, and fruit juices are some of the more common marinades. When combined with oil, it leaves a moisturizing coating for cooking. Garlic, spices, herbs and salt are common ingredients for flavor. Never marinate food in aluminum, which will leave a metallic taste.

Sprinkle pork chops with salt and pepper.

In a large frying pan, over medium high heat, melt butter and lightly brown pork chops, add 2 tablespoons of water, cover tightly, reduce heat and cook for 45 minutes or until pork chops are tender.

In a medium bowl, combine cranberries, chili sauce, onions, mustard and ginger; pour into pan with chops.

Prepare stuffing mix to package directions. Place 1/3 cup stuffing mix on each chop. Cover and cook on medium-low for 12-15 minutes. Remove chops to warm platter.

Drizzle chops with cranberry sauce; serve remaining sauce on the side to pass.

Serves: 6

Nutritional Information per Serving
Calories: 450, Fat: 16 grams, Protein: 26 grams, Carbohydrates: 50 grams, Cholesterol: 75 milligrams, Fiber: 0.8 grams

Pork Roast with Sautéed Pears

1 (3-4 pound) pork loin roast
3 cloves garlic
freshly ground pepper
3 sprigs rosemary
3 tablespoons butter
4 pears, peeled and diced
1/4 cup dry red wine
4 tablespoons red currant jelly
2 tablespoons Worcestershire sauce
2 teaspoons of red wine vinegar
Pinch of cayenne

Preheat oven to 400 degrees

Thinly slice 2 cloves of garlic. Using a paring knife, pierce slits into the roast and insert the garlic slices.

Pepper the roast generously and rub the rosemary onto the roast. Leave rosemary on top of the roast. Place on a roasting pan.

Roast, uncovered for 2 hours, or until at thermometer reads 140 degrees. Remove the roast from the roasting pan, leaving the liquids in the pan, and tent with foil for 15 minutes.

Melt butter in a large pan and sauté the pears over medium heat for 2 minutes. Mince 1 clove of garlic and add to pears. Cook until tender but not mushy, about 4 minutes; set aside.

When roast is removed, place the roasting pan on two burners over medium-high heat. When the pork drippings are sizzling add the red wine. Bring to a boil, scraping the brown bits that are in the roasting pan and stirring constantly until the wine is reduced by half. Add the jelly, Worcestershire sauce, vinegar and cayenne. Boil for 4 minutes until the sauce thickens enough to coat the back of a spoon. Pour the sauce over the pears and reheat the pears, if necessary.

Slice the pork into 1-inch slices and spoon pears over the top; serve immediately.

Serves: 6

Nutritional Information per Serving
Calories: 500, Fat: 28 grams, Protein: 35 grams, Carbohydrates: 26 grams, Cholesterol: 125 milligrams, Fiber: 2.6 grams

Wisconsin Brats

A tradition in these parts: pronounced "br-AH-tz"

12 bratwurst (try Johnsonville)
3-4 cans lager beer
2 medium onions
salt and pepper
12 kaiser or hard rolls

"BRAT BATH:"

If you want to have bratwurst "Sheboygan-style" you have to grill them FIRST and THEN soak them in beer! Those who know call this soak mixture the "Brat Bath" which works nicely on that extra side burner on your outdoor grill. As the brats are done, slide them into the bath to stay warm and juicy!

Prepare grill. Oil rack and place 5-6 inches over coals.

Grill bratwursts over glowing coals, turning occasionally, until cooked through and dark golden brown, about 20 minutes. Don't be afraid if they get a little dark, that adds to the flavor.

While bratwursts are cooking, in a 3-quart saucepan heat beer and onions, stirring occasionally, until warm. Keep marinade warm over low heat.

Transfer grilled bratwursts to saucepan and let stand in marinade until ready to serve 15-20 minutes.

Remove bratwursts from marinade with tongs. You can have a single, double, or "butterfly" your brat by cutting in half lengthwise and placing on roll. Using tongs or a slotted spoon, put onions from marinade on brats.

Serve with mustard, ketchup, sauerkraut and pickles.

Serves: 12

Nutritional Information per Serving
Calories: 340, Fat: 21 grams, Protein: 13 grams, Carbohydrates: 25 grams, Cholesterol: 45 milligrams, Fiber: 0 grams

All-Day Barbecued Pork

All day for you to have fun while your slow cooker does the work.

3 pounds pork roast (Boston Butt), rolled and tied
kosher salt
freshly ground black pepper
3 tablespoons butter
1/4 cup minced onion
2 cups ketchup
2/3 cup brown sugar
1/4 cup yellow mustard
1/2 cup cider vinegar
2 teaspoons Worcestershire Sauce
1 teaspoon hot pepper sauce
8 hamburger buns

Heat oven to 200 degrees.

Rub meat with salt and pepper. Place roast in a Dutch oven or covered pot and bake for 7-8 hours. Transfer meat to cutting board and allow to cool for 20 minutes. (Alternative cooking method: Heat grill to medium heat. After applying seasonings to roast, place on grill fat side up, for 3-4 hours. Internal temperature should be 185-190 degrees.)

In a medium saucepan, melt butter; add onions and cook until clear. Add ketchup, brown sugar, mustard, vinegar, Worcestershire sauce and pepper sauce. Simmer for 10 minutes.

Using two forks pull the pork apart into shreds. Discard any large bits of fat. Transfer meat to a large saucepan. Pour 2/3 of sauce over meat and bring to a simmer. Serve the remaining sauce on the side.

Serves: 8

Nutritional Information per Serving
Calories: 400, Fat: 19 grams, Protein: 30 grams, Carbohydrates: 26 grams, Cholesterol: 85 milligrams, Fiber: 0.3 grams

 Make this meal during the week when you need something ready for you when you get home.

EARTH DAY - A WISCONSIN LEGACY

One of Wisconsin's lasting legacies has been its dedication to environmental awareness. This is due largely to the work of Senator Gaylord Nelson, who worked to bring about numerous environmental education programs and changes, including creating Earth Day. Driven to action by the fact that the issue of conserving national resources scarcely received public attention, Nelson came up with the idea of having a national teach-in on the environment. After fundraising and writing letters to government officials and schools, Nelson gained the support of millions of people who all acted to form a collective unit fighting for protection of the environment.

Nelson's environmental activism is remembered and celebrated daily at the University of Wisconsin-Madison, which developed the Gaylord Nelson Institute for Environmental Studies in order to address the need for continued study of environmental issues. Nelson also wrote several books detailing the state of the planet and what changes need to occur to preserve it. Gaylord Nelson's work will undoubtedly have a positive impact on people at the local, state and national levels for generations to come.

Champagne Ham Sandwiches

This is the perfect make-ahead dish for an afternoon buffet.

2 pounds sliced deli ham
6 1/2 cups water
20 whole cloves, bundled and tied together with cheesecloth
2/3 cup sugar
1/3 cup white vinegar
1 1/2 cups ketchup
12 ounces champagne (or 12 ounces lemon-lime soda for non-alcoholic)
1/4 cup cornstarch
8 sandwich buns

In a large saucepan, combine 6 cups water, cloves, sugar, vinegar, ketchup and champagne. Whisk ingredients lightly until incorporated and simmer 2 hours. Sauce will reduce slightly.

In a small bowl, combine cornstarch and 1/2 cup water until cornstarch has dissolved. Whisk cornstarch mixture into saucepan. Sauce will thicken. Add ham to sauce and simmer on low until ham becomes warm to hot.

Serve on buns with mustard, horseradish and mayonnaise.

Serves: 8

Nutritional Information per Serving (without buns)
Calories: 310, Fat: 6 grams, Protein: 23 grams, Carbohydrates: 35 grams, Cholesterol: 50 milligrams, Fiber: 0.6 grams

Notes:

Herb Crusted Lamb with Roasted Potatoes

1 leg of lamb (7-8 pounds)
2 large cloves garlic, slivered
5 tablespoons olive oil
2 tablespoons plus 2 teaspoons dried thyme leaves
2 1/2 tablespoons dried rosemary
2 tablespoons plus 1 teaspoon coarsely ground black pepper
2 tablespoons ground coriander
2 pounds new potatoes, quartered
2 tablespoons chopped fresh rosemary leaves
1 teaspoon coarse salt
1 rosemary sprigs for garnish

Preheat oven to 425 degrees.

With a paring knife, cut slits all over lamb and insert garlic slivers. Brush the lamb all over with 2 tablespoons olive oil.

In small bowl, combine 2 tablespoons thyme, dried rosemary, 2 tablespoons pepper, and coriander; mix well. Pat the herb mixture all over the lamb to form a crust. Place the lamb in a shallow roasting pan.

Place the potatoes in a large bowl. Add the remaining 3 tablespoons olive oil, fresh rosemary, remaining 2 teaspoons thyme, 1 teaspoon pepper and coarse salt. Toss to mix well and arrange around the lamb in the pan.

Place pan on center rack in the oven and roast for 45 minutes. Reduce oven heat to 375 degrees; gently stir the potatoes and cook 30 minutes more.

Remove the pan from the oven and insert thermometer in the thickest part of the meat. It should read 120 for rare. Let the lamb rest, loosely covered, for 15 minutes before carving. The meat will continue to cook a bit more, and the temperature will rise to 135-140 degrees.

Arrange the roast on a serving platter, surrounded by potatoes. Garnish with fresh rosemary sprigs.

Serves: 10

Nutritional Information per Serving
Calories: 680, Fat: 50 grams, Protein: 46 grams, Carbohydrates: 12 grams, Cholesterol: 170 milligrams, Fiber: 1.1 grams

Lamb Burgers

These are a fancy alternative to the normal hamburger cook-out.

2 pounds ground lamb
1 tablespoon chopped parsley
1 tablespoon chopped oregano
3 cloves garlic, minced
2 teaspoon salt
1/2 teaspoon pepper
4 ounces goat cheese, divided into 6 (1/4-inch thick) slices
1/2 cup mint leaves
6 hamburger buns or pita bread

In a medium bowl mix ground lamb with parsley, oregano, garlic, salt & pepper. Use your hands to get spices well mixed with the meat.

Form 6 large patties. Using your hands, scoop off the top and some of the center of each patty. Make sure not to completely hollow out the center of the patty. Take one round of goat cheese and place it in the center of the patty, then cover it with the meat that you scooped off. Press the meat together to seal. You should end up with a burger that is "stuffed" with goat cheese. Repeat for remaining patties.

Prepare barbecue to medium-high heat. Grill patties to desired doneness, about 5 minutes per side for medium. Top each burger with mint leaves and serve on buns or pitas.

Serves: 6

Nutritional Information per Serving
Calories: 620, Fat: 44 grams, Protein: 34 grams, Carbohydrates: 22 grams, Cholesterol: 130 milligrams, Fiber: 0 grams

Notes:

Ginger and Mint Lamb Chops

A quick but elegant meal, perfect for unexpected company.

2 cups cubed, crusty day-old baguette
1/2 cup chopped fresh mint
4 tablespoons minced peeled fresh ginger
3/4 teaspoon salt
7 tablespoons butter, softened, cut into pieces
12 (1 3/4-inch thick) loin lamb chops

Preheat oven to 450 degrees.

In a food processor, blend bread, mint, ginger and salt in until finely chopped. Add butter pieces, one at a time, and process until paste forms.

Place chops on large baking sheet. Press bread mixture firmly on top of chops to adhere. Roast lamb to desired doneness, about 25 minutes for medium-rare. Let stand 5 minutes.

Place 2 chops on each of 6 plates.

Serves: 6

Nutritional Information per Serving
Calories: 660, Fat: 50 grams, Protein: 26 grams, Carbohydrates: 26 grams, Cholesterol: 135 milligrams, Fiber: 1.8 grams

Baked Feta Shrimp

2 medium onions, thinly sliced
1/2 cup of olive oil
2 pounds fresh tomatoes (about 4 large), peeled and chopped
1/4 cup parsley, chopped
2 teaspoons salt
1/4 teaspoon pepper
3 garlic cloves, minced
2 pounds large shrimp, shelled and deveined
12 ounces feta cheese

In a large saucepan or Dutch oven, heat olive oil over medium heat. Add onions and sauté until tender, about five minutes. Add tomatoes, parsley, salt, pepper and garlic. Cover and simmer about 45-60 minutes stirring occasionally.

Preheat oven to 425 degrees.

Notes:

Put sauce and raw shrimp into 6 individual ovenproof dishes. Crumble feta cheese over top. Bake uncovered for 10-15 minutes until shrimp is cooked and cheese is melted.

Time saving tip: To save time you may want to substitute the fresh tomatoes with two 15 ounce cans of diced tomatoes, and the fresh shrimp with thawed frozen, shelled, and deveined shrimp. You may also combine the sauce, shrimp and cheese in a 9x13 baking dish to bake, if you do not care to prepare individual dishes.

Serves: 6

Nutritional Information per Serving
Calories: 520, Fat: 33 grams, Protein: 41 grams, Carbohydrates: 14 grams, Cholesterol: 280 milligrams, Fiber: 2.5 grams

New Orleans Style BBQ Shrimp

Paper towels are a must for this finger-licking good recipe!

3 slices bacon, chopped
1 teaspoon black pepper
1 1/4 sticks margarine or butter
2 cloves garlic, crushed and minced
2 tablespoons Dijon mustard
2 tablespoons crab boil
1 1/2 teaspoons chili powder
1/2 teaspoon oregano
1/2 teaspoon basil
1/2 teaspoon hot pepper sauce
1/4 teaspoon thyme
1/8 teaspoon black pepper, freshly ground
1/4 teaspoon cayenne pepper, optional
1 1/2 pounds medium shrimp, shell on, rinsed and patted dry
flat leaf parsley, roughly chopped, for garnish

Preheat oven to 350 degrees

Fry bacon in large, heavy skillet. Add margarine to bacon and drippings, along with all other ingredients except shrimp. Stir occasionally until margarine is melted and ingredients are thoroughly combined. Put shrimp in 9x11-inch baking dish and pour mixture over. Bake 20 minutes, stirring occasionally.

Serves: 4

Nutritional Information per Serving
Calories: 520, Fat: 40 grams, Protein: 37 grams, Carbohydrates: 3 grams, Cholesterol: 355 milligrams, Fiber: 0.8 grams

Cooking shrimp in their shells seals in flavor and juices, but diners at the table must peel them, a messy job you may want to avoid. Although, some people are known to eat these shrimp whole- shell and all! If you prefer, you may peel off the shells and devein beforehand. Watch the shrimp carefully while baking, though, so you don't overcook. Shrimp are done as soon as they are all curled and opaque.

Confetti Crab Cakes

These crab cakes are excellent!

1 pound fresh or frozen lump crab meat, picked over and
cartilage removed
1 cup cooked corn
3/4 cup onion, finely diced
3/4 cup celery, finely diced
1/2 cup bell pepper, finely diced
1/2 cup mayonnaise
1/2 teaspoon dried, ground mustard
pinch of cayenne pepper, optional
salt and pepper, to taste
1 egg, lightly beaten
1/4 pound (1 sleeve) saltine crackers, crushed to fine crumbs
2 tablespoon olive oil
2 tablespoons butter
Rèmoulade Sauce, recipe follows

Notes:

In a large bowl combine the crab, corn, onion, celery and pepper; mix well.

In a separate small bowl, combine the mayonnaise, mustard, cayenne and salt and pepper. Stir into crab mixture. Once combined, gently fold in the egg and 1/4 of cracker crumbs.

Form the mixture into 12 large patties, if serving as a main course, 24 patties if serving as an appetizer. As you finish making each patty, coat immediately with remaining cracker crumbs and set aside on tray. Cover patties and refrigerate for at least 30 minutes, but no longer than three hours.

Heat oil and butter in a large skillet over medium heat. Cook the crab cakes in batches until golden brown on each side, about three minutes per side. Serve immediately, with Rèmoulade Sauce (page 215).

Serves: 6

Nutritional Information per Serving
Calories: 410, Fat: 27 grams, Protein: 20 grams, Carbohydrates: 22 grams, Cholesterol: 120 milligrams, Fiber: 2.3 grams

Rèmoulade Sauce

1/2 cup chili sauce
1/2 cup mayonnaise
4 tablespoons country Dijon
2 tablespoons fresh lemon juice
2 tablespoons green onions, minced
3 tablespoons drained, chopped capers
1 tablespoon horseradish
dash of pepper sauce, to taste
salt and pepper, to taste

Combine all ingredients in bowl and stir until well mixed. Store in refrigerator.
Best if prepared one day ahead so flavor has a chance to marry.

Nutritional Information per Serving
Calories: 150, Fat: 15 grams, Protein: 1 grams, Carbohydrates: 2 grams, Cholesterol: 10
milligrams, Fiber: 0.5 grams

Baked Tilapia in Tomato-Fennel Sauce

2 tablespoons olive oil
1 medium onion, minced
2 garlic cloves, minced
1 small fennel bulb, diced
1 bay leaf
salt and pepper, to taste
2 (14.5 ounce) cans tomatoes, diced
1 medium carrot, shredded
1/4 cup parsley, chopped
4 tilapia fillets (about 1 1/2-1 3/4 pounds)
1/4 cup lemon juice

Preheat oven to 375 degrees.

Notes:

In a large skillet, heat the olive oil over medium heat. Sauté the onion and garlic and cook about 5 minutes. Add the fennel and bay leaf; add salt and pepper to taste. Cook, stirring occasionally, until vegetables are soft, about 5-8 minutes. Add the tomatoes and cook about 10 minutes, stirring occasionally. Add the carrots and parsley. Cook, stirring until most of the moisture is absorbed, about 10 minutes. (May be prepared in advance – reheat prior to assembling to bake.)

Pour half the sauce into a casserole dish large enough to accommodate the fish in a single layer. Sprinkle the fish with a little salt and pepper, place in the casserole dish, drizzle with lemon juice and cover with remaining sauce.

Bake about 15 minutes.

Serves: 4

Nutritional Information per Serving
Calories: 290, Fat: 8 grams, Protein: 34 grams, Carbohydrates: 20 grams, Cholesterol: 70 milligrams, Fiber: 3.7 grams

Salmon with Chili Mango Salsa

3 tablespoons fresh lime juice
3/4 teaspoon white vinegar
4 teaspoons seeded, coarsely chopped serrano or jalapeño chili
2 teaspoons grated lime zest
2 garlic cloves
4 tablespoons olive oil
2 mangoes, diced
1/2 cup red onion, diced
1/2 cup fresh cilantro, chopped
4 (6 ounce) salmon filets

Prepare grill (medium-high heat).

In a food processor combine lime juice, vinegar, chili, lime zest, garlic and 3 tablespoons olive oil. Process to desired consistency.

Chop mangoes, onion and cilantro by hand, or process lightly so ingredients are not pulverized. Combine processed and chopped ingredients in a small bowl and adjust seasoning to taste with salt and pepper.

Brush salmon with remaining 1 tablespoon olive oil. Season with salt and pepper, to taste. Grill salmon until just opaque in center, about 5 minutes per side.

Serve with salsa.

Serves: 4

Nutritional Information per Serving
Calories: 370, Fat: 19 grams, Protein: 34 grams, Carbohydrates: 15 grams, Cholesterol: 90 milligrams, Fiber: 1.7 grams

Salmon Burgers

Very kid friendly! This can also be prepared with canned salmon, in a pinch.

1 pound salmon
2 shallots, minced
3 tablespoons mayonnaise
1 tablespoon lemon juice
2 teaspoons Dijon mustard
1 teaspoon Worcestershire sauce
1/8 teaspoon cayenne paper
1/2 cup breadcrumbs
2 tablespoons olive oil
1 tablespoon butter

In a food processor coarsely chop salmon until it resembles the consistency of hamburger. In a large bowl combine salmon with shallots, mayonnaise, lemon juice, mustard, Worcestershire sauce and cayenne pepper; blend with a fork. Shape into four patties about 3/4-inch thick and coat with breadcrumbs. Place on waxed paper and refrigerate at least one hour, but not more than six.

In a large, heavy nonstick skillet, heat oil and butter over medium-high heat. Sauté salmon patties for 2-3 minutes, flip and sauté for 1-2 minutes more. Outside should be crispy brown and just cooked through. Serve on bun with lettuce and tartar sauce.

Serves: 4

Notes:

Tartar Sauce

1/4 cup sour cream
1/4 cup mayonnaise
2 teaspoons lemon juice
1 teaspoon Dijon mustard
2 teaspoons chopped fresh dill
2 tablespoons finely diced cucumber
salt and pepper, to taste

Combine all ingredients in a small bowl. Mix well; season with salt and pepper to taste. Cover and refrigerate for at least one hour before serving.

Nutritional Information per Serving (for Salmon Burgers with Tartar Sauce)
Calories: 480, Fat: 36 grams, Protein: 25 grams, Carbohydrates: 14 grams, Cholesterol: 90 milligrams, Fiber: 0.8 grams

Orange Roughy with Shallots and Capers

A great weeknight meal.

6 tablespoons butter
1/2 cup diced shallots
1 1/2-2 pounds orange roughy fillets
1/3 cup capers, rinsed and drained
2 tablespoons fresh minced tarragon
2 tablespoons fresh lemon juice
1 cup dry white wine (Pinot Grigio works well)
1 cup Parmesan, shredded
salt and pepper, to taste

In fry pan melt butter and sauté shallots. In batches, without crowding the pan, add fish and sauté on low to medium heat for about 3-4 minutes. Turn fish over and add capers, tarragon, lemon juice and white wine. Add Parmesan cheese. Cover and cook on low to medium heat for 3-4 minutes. Serve with juice over fish or on side.

Serves: 4

Nutritional Information per Serving
Calories: 480, Fat: 35 grams, Protein: 34 grams, Carbohydrates: 8 grams, Cholesterol: 95 milligrams, Fiber: 0 grams

Tangy Lemon Snapper

2 tablespoons butter or oil
2 tablespoons lemon zest
1 tablespoon brown sugar
1 tablespoon lemon juice
1 teaspoon Worcestershire sauce
1/2 teaspoon salt
4 bay leaves
4 snapper fillets, about 1 1/2 pounds

Mix all ingredients, except fish, together in a small saucepan and bring to a boil. Cool.

Arrange the fish in flat baking dish. Pour the marinade over the fish and let it stand 30 minutes.

Preheat oven to 350 degrees.

Bake for 20 minutes, or until fish is opaque and flakes easily when a knife is inserted.

Serves: 4

Nutritional Information per Serving
Calories: 230, Fat: 8 grams, Protein: 35 grams, Carbohydrates: 4 grams, Cholesterol: 75 milligrams, Fiber: 0.8 grams

Notes:

Roasted Monkfish

This can be substituted with any firm white fish.

4 monkfish fillets, about 2 pounds
salt and freshly ground pepper, to taste
1 teaspoon finely chopped basil leaves
1 tablespoon fresh minced thyme
6-8 shallots, halved plus 2 tablespoons minced shallots
11 garlic cloves, halved if large, left whole if small
flour for dredging
2 tablespoons corn or peanut oil
6-8 Roma tomatoes, quartered lengthwise
1 stalk of celery, cut into 1/2-inch slices
Sprigs of fresh basil, for garnish
Lemon wedges, for garnish

Preheat oven to 400 degrees.

Using a paring knife make several shallow slits lengthwise in the monkfish.
Flatten cuts. Sprinkle both sides of the fillets with 1/2 of the salt, pepper, basil
and thyme. Lay fillets flat on work surface and place the remainder of the basil,
thyme, minced shallots and a clove or two of garlic on one side of each fillet.
Fold the fillets in half from top to bottom enclosing the herbs; fasten with a
toothpick. Dredge in flour, tapping off any extra; set aside.

In a large oven-proof skillet over medium heat, heat the oil until very hot, but
not smoking, and brown the fillets about 3 minutes on each side. Remove fish
and set aside. Add the shallots halves and remaining garlic and cook until just
colored, about 1 minute. Add the tomatoes and celery, tossing to cover and
cooking another 2 minutes. Season vegetables with salt and pepper.

Place the fillets back in the pan, making sure that there is plenty of room
between each fillet, and immediately place in the oven to cook until the fish and
vegetables are a rich brown and the vegetables are slightly caramelized, about
15-20 minutes. If the skillet appears too crowded, place vegetables and fish in a
large roasting pan. It is important that the fish and vegetables have enough
room to allow for the liquids to burn off.

To serve, place the vegetables around the fish on a platter and garnish with the
basil springs and the lemon wedges. Don't forget to remove toothpicks from
fillets before bringing to the table.

Serves: 4

Nutritional Information per Serving
Calories: 335, Fat: 11 grams, Protein: 36 grams, Carbohydrates: 23 grams, Cholesterol: 60
milligrams, Fiber: 2.2 grams

Easy Stuffed Halibut Fillets

1/4 cup butter, plus 1 tablespoon melted butter
1/4 cup chopped onion
1/4 cup diced celery
1/2 teaspoon salt
1/8 teaspoon black pepper
1/4 teaspoon thyme
2 cups soft breadcrumbs
1 tomato, chopped
4 halibut fillets, approximately 1/2-3/4" thick, about 1 1/2 pounds
salt and pepper, to taste

Preheat oven to 450 degrees. Grease a 9x13-inch baking dish.

Notes:

Melt 1/4 cup butter in a large, heavy skillet over low heat. Add onion and celery and sauté for 15 minutes. Mix in salt, pepper and thyme then toss lightly with breadcrumbs. Fold in chopped tomato. Set aside.

Brush fillets with 1 tablespoon melted butter and sprinkle with salt and pepper. Lay two fillets side by side in pan and spread stuffing over both. Lay remaining fillets on top, like a sandwich.

Place in prepared baking dish and bake for 10 minutes per inch of thickness of fish. Bake 20 minutes per inch, if fish is frozen.

Serves: 4

Nutritional Information per Serving
Calories: 725, Fat: 25 grams, Protein: 48 grams, Carbohydrates: 76 grams, Cholesterol: 90 milligrams, Fiber: 0.7 grams

 Savory Swordfish

This marinade makes enough for 3-4 pounds of fish.

1/2 cup olive oil
1/3 cup lemon juice
1/2 cup brandy
1 1/4 cup sesame seeds
2-3 cloves garlic, minced
2 tablespoons soy sauce
1 teaspoon salt
4 pounds swordfish
2 cups Italian breadcrumbs

If possible, make marinade one day ahead, so the flavors get a chance to fully marry. Mix together the oil, lemon juice, brandy, 1/2 cup sesame seeds, garlic, soy sauce and salt in a plastic or glass bowl. Set aside or refrigerate, if making ahead.

Place swordfish in a large glass pan. Pour marinade over fish and refrigerate for 1-2 hours before cooking.

Mix together breadcrumbs and 3/4 cup sesame seeds in a plastic bag large enough to accommodate fish for tossing.

Coat steaks with breadcrumb mixture. Grill approximately 4-5 minutes on each side, for 3/4 inch thick steaks, until firm. Cooking time depends on amount of fish, and thickness.

Serves: 10

Nutritional Information per Serving
Calories: 510, Fat: 28 grams, Protein: 44 grams, Carbohydrates: 20 grams, Cholesterol: 70 milligrams, Fiber: 0.1 grams

 If swordfish is not readily available, substitute another firm, white fish.

Szechwan BBQ Shrimp

This recipe is as dramatic to prepare, as it is to serve. It is important that you make it in a well ventilated area, with your exhaust fan on high! When the Thai peppers hit the hot oil they create a delicate flavor for the sauce, but a potent smell that will cause your guests to cough and their eyes to water. The peppers impart a delightfully subtle heat to the dish that even a person who can only handle mild spice levels will enjoy. Those who like their heat in the nuclear range can eat the peppers themselves.

1 pound extra large or jumbo shrimp, clean and devein
2 tablespoons light soy sauce
2 tablespoons rice wine vinegar
1/3 cup oil
1 tablespoon minced garlic
1 1/2 teaspoons shredded fresh ginger
4 dried Thai red chili peppers

Sauce
1 1/2 cups ketchup
2 tablespoons sugar
2 teaspoons rice wine vinegar
1 teaspoon vinegar
1 teaspoon light soy sauce

2 green onions, sliced on the diagonal, for garnish

Notes:

Split shell along back of each shrimp. Leaving the shell on, pat shrimp dry. Mix soy sauce and rice wine vinegar in a bowl large enough to accommodate the shrimp. Add shrimp to bowl and set aside.

In a small bowl, combine all sauce ingredients, set aside.

In a large, heavy skillet or wok, heat oil over high heat until just smoking. Carefully add garlic, ginger and peppers. Fry for 10 seconds, shaking skillet continuously. Reduce heat to medium-high and add shrimp in one layer. Fry until shells are slightly burnt, turning shrimp over until other side is slightly burnt, as well. Add sauce and stir until slightly brown. Serve with white rice and sprinkle with the sliced green onions.

Serves: 4

Nutritional Information per Serving
Calories: 285, Fat: 3 grams, Protein: 26 grams, Carbohydrates: 38 grams, Cholesterol: 175 milligrams, Fiber: 2.0 grams

Marinated Grilled Shrimp

This shrimp makes for a great surf & turf BBQ.

1/2 cup soy sauce
1 1/2 cups dry white wine
4 tablespoons butter
2 teaspoons lemon juice
2 cloves garlic, crushed
1/2 teaspoon onion salt
1/2 teaspoon black pepper or lemon pepper
2 pounds peeled shrimp

In a medium saucepan mix all ingredients, except shrimp. Cook marinade over medium high heat, to a boil. Remove from heat and cool slightly.

Place shrimp in a glass bowl with marinade and refrigerate 1/2 hour.

Skewer shrimp, and grill for about three minutes per side, brushing with remaining marinade. Shrimp will be done when firm and opaque. Be careful to not overcook, or the shrimp will be tough.

Serves: 4

Nutritional Information per Serving
Calories: 375, Fat: 15 grams, Protein: 48 grams, Carbohydrates: 10 grams, Cholesterol: 375 milligrams, Fiber: 0.3 grams

FISHING IN WISCONSIN

Fishing is an activity that provides all ages with the chance to enjoy the outdoors and appreciate what the beautiful state of Wisconsin has to offer. One of the best things about fishing is that it can be done in a group or solo, giving people the option to spend some solitary time on the lake or catch up with family and friends. Regardless of where people live, there is a good chance a body of water stocked with fish is nearby. This makes it easy to take a day trip to the lake or spend an entire weekend fishing and camping.

Sport fishing is an important part of the industry that generates billions of dollars for the state. Visitors travel from all over to see the wonderful array of plant and animal life Wisconsin has to offer and to catch one of the many types of fish here, such as bass, black crappie, bluegill, bullhead, muskellunge and perch. Fishing is a recreational way to get dinner while enjoying nature and the company of others.

Walleye with Beurre Blanc

This recipe is great with any white, delicately flavored fish. Cod, grouper or snapper are all excellent choices.

1 egg
1 cup dry breadcrumbs
1/4 teaspoon thyme
salt and pepper, to taste
1 1/2 lb. walleye fillets
2 tablespoons butter
2 tablespoons olive oil
fresh thyme, for garnish

Beat egg in a wide bowl, set aside. In a separate wide bowl, combine breadcrumbs, thyme, salt and pepper in another wide bowl.

Rinse fillets and pat dry.

Heat butter and olive oil in a heavy nonstick 12-inch skillet over medium heat. Dip one fillet in egg and then coat with breadcrumb mixture. Repeat for remaining 3 fillets. Transfer fillets to skillet and cook for approximately 4 minutes per side, until firm and cooked through. Fish will be completely opaque and flake easily.

Transfer to warm platter until finished with sauce.

Serves: 4

Nutritional Information per Serving (for Walleye with Beurre Blanc)
Calories: 550, Fat: 35 grams, Protein: 37 grams, Carbohydrates: 22 grams, Cholesterol: 260 milligrams, Fiber: 1.4 grams

Notes:

Beurre Blanc

1/2 cup dry white wine or vermouth
2 tablespoons white wine vinegar
1/4 cup minced shallots
salt and pepper to taste
1 tablespoon heavy cream
6 tablespoons chilled butter, cut into small pieces

Combine wine, vinegar and shallots in a 1-quart saucepan and bring to boil over medium heat. Reduce heat and simmer until cooked down to about three quarters of the original amount, about 5 minutes. Season, to taste, with salt and pepper.

Stir in cream.

Remove sauce from heat. Whisking constantly, add butter one or two pieces at a time. If temperature cools too much, place pan above low heat just long enough to sustain incorporating the butter. You do not want the butter to boil or the sauce will separate and become greasy! Feel free to add a couple more splashes of white wine during the whisking part to cut the butter taste.

Serves: 4

The timing on this recipe is crucial, as the sauce cannot sit for too long. Try doing the first step of the sauce, while preparing the fillets for pan-frying. Finish the sauce while the fillets cook. Plate the fish and pour the sauce over each portion, in equal amounts. Garnish with fresh thyme. This dish is excellent with a delicate risotto and a steamed green vegetable.

Spicy Salmon with Cilantro Salsa

2 large salmon fillets, about 2 pounds
1 lemon, halved
1/2 cup lime juice, approximately 2 large limes
2/3 cup green onions, chopped, white parts only
1/2 jalapeño pepper, seeded and chopped
1 teaspoon kosher salt
3/4 cup fresh cilantro, chopped
1/4 cup fresh spinach, chopped
1/3 cup olive oil

Preheat oven to 350 degrees.

Lay fillets, skin side down in a 9x13-inch baking dish. Squeeze lemon over the fish fillets.

Mix remaining ingredients together in a bowl.

Spread 1/2 cup of the cilantro mixture over each fillet.

Bake for 35–45 minutes. Test fish by inserting knife, fish will flake easily when done. Serve with remaining salsa on side.

Serves: 4

Nutritional Information per Serving
Calories: 445, Fat: 26 grams, Protein: 46 grams, Carbohydrates: 7 grams, Cholesterol: 120 milligrams, Fiber: 0.7 grams

It is important to make this recipe in a timely fashion, as the lemon juice will break down the proteins in the fish and make it mushy.

Notes:

Cod in Court Bouillon

This delicately flavored dish demands a very fresh cut of fish. Consider serving with a white wine based rice side dish, or mashed potatoes.

Mayonnaise Sauce
- 1 cup mayonnaise
- 1 teaspoon paprika
- 2-4 drops of hot pepper sauce
- 2 cloves of garlic, minced
- 1 tablespoon minced fresh parsley
- 1/2 teaspoon of saffron threads

Court Bouillon
- 1 large carrot, thinly sliced
- 1 leek, white and tender green parts well washed, sliced in 1/2 inch pieces
- 1/2 onion, sliced
- 5 cloves of garlic, peeled and roughly chopped
- 1 whole clove
- 2 bay leaves
- 2 tablespoons of extra virgin olive oil
- 1 tablespoon minced fresh parsley leaves
- 1/4 teaspoon freshly ground black pepper
- 1/4 teaspoon salt
- 3/4 cup dry white wine
- pinch of saffron threads
- water, to cover

To finish the dish
- 2 pounds cod fillets, approximately four 6-8 ounce fillets
- 8 springs of fresh basil, for garnish
- 4 wedges of lemon, for garnish

Prepare the mayonnaise sauce at least one hour before serving. Combine all ingredients in a small bowl and refrigerate. The saffron will give it a warm orange gold color.

For the court bouillon, combine all ingredients in a large saucepan, or Dutch oven and cover generously with water. Bring to a boil over medium high heat; reduce heat to medium and cook for 25-30 minutes. Drain broth through a fine sieve or a double layer of cheesecloth; return broth to saucepan.

Place the cod in the simmering court bouillon and cook until firm and white, about 10 minutes. The fish will flake easily and be opaque all the way through when a knife is inserted, if it is done.

Carefully, so as not to break apart the fish, place one fillet on each plate, spooning a little broth over. Place a spoonful of the mayonnaise sauce and a lemon wedge alongside the fish and garnish with fresh basil leaves.

Serves: 6

Nutritional Information per Serving
Calories: 700, Fat: 52 grams, Protein: 43 grams, Carbohydrates: 13 grams, Cholesterol: 130 milligrams, Fiber: 2.1 grams

Feta Shrimp with Farfalle

1 tablespoon butter
2 tablespoons olive oil
2 shallots, finely diced
3 cloves garlic, minced
1 teaspoon dried oregano
1/2 teaspoon dried thyme
1/2 teaspoon dried basil
1 1/2 pound large shrimp, peeled and deveined with tail on
1/2 cup feta cheese
12 ounces farfalle or bow tie pasta, cooked al dente
freshly grated Parmesan cheese for garnish

Heat butter and 1 tablespoon of olive oil over medium heat in a large, heavy nonstick skillet. Add shallots and sauté for approximately 2 minutes, stirring occasionally. Add garlic and sauté for one minute more. Add herbs, stirring until fragrant. Add shrimp and sauté until just pink and curled. Remove all from pan and set aside.

Without cleaning skillet, add remaining 1 tablespoon of olive oil and cooked pasta. Sauté pasta, stirring and shaking pan, until pasta starts to get crisp on the edges. Add feta cheese and toss to combine. Add shrimp mixture back into skillet and combine with pasta and cheese, until heated through.

Place in a serving dish and garnish with freshly grated Parmesan cheese.

Serves: 4

Nutritional Information per Serving
Calories: 625, Fat: 17 grams, Protein: 49 grams, Carbohydrates: 68 grams, Cholesterol: 280 milligrams, Fiber: 2.2 grams

Notes:

Garlicky Crab Linguine

4 tablespoons butter
1 tablespoon extra virgin olive oil
1 large red bell pepper, finely chopped
5 cloves garlic, finely chopped
1/4 teaspoon crushed red pepper
2 drops hot pepper sauce
1/2 cup dry vermouth
1 pound linguine
8 ounce bottle of clam juice
1 pound fresh lump crab meat, picked over
1/3 cup fresh flat-leaf parsley, finely chopped
1/3 cup Parmesan, freshly grated
salt and freshly ground pepper, to taste
1/3 cup pine nuts, toasted

Melt butter and olive oil in heavy large skillet over medium heat. Add bell pepper, cover and cook 2 minutes. Add garlic and crushed red pepper; cover and cook 2 minutes. Increase heat to high; add wine and boil 2 minutes. Set aside.

Cook pasta in large pot of salted water. Drain pasta, reserving 1/2 cup of cooking water.

Return pasta to pot. Add clam juice, 1/2 cup cooking water and bell pepper mixture. Cook over high heat until pasta absorbs half of liquid, about 2 minutes. Add crab and toss until heated through, about 1 minute. Mix in parsley and Parmesan cheese. Season, to taste, with freshly ground pepper and salt. Sprinkle with pine nuts.

Serves: 4

Nutritional Information per Serving
Calories: 800, Fat: 25 grams, Protein: 45 grams, Carbohydrates: 99 grams, Cholesterol: 140 milligrams, Fiber: 4.2 grams

Shrimp and Linguine in Tomato Cream

12 ounces linguine
2 tablespoons extra virgin olive oil
1 pound large shrimp, peeled and deveined
1/4 teaspoon black pepper, freshly ground
1/2 cup finely chopped green onion
1 shallot, diced
2 garlic cloves, minced
1 cup half and half
3/4 cup chicken broth
1/2 cup vermouth
1/3 cup sun sliced dried tomatoes
1 tablespoon tomato paste
1/2 teaspoon basil
1/4 teaspoon oregano
1/4 teaspoon thyme
1/4 teaspoon salt
1/4 cup fresh parsley, chopped
1/2 cup grated Parmesan cheese

Notes:

Boil pasta to al dente and drain. Set aside.

Heat oil in a large skillet over medium high heat. Sprinkle pepper over shrimp. Sauté shrimp, green onion, shallot and garlic for three minutes, or until shrimp is just cooked through. Transfer to a bowl and cover.

Reduce heat to medium. In the same skillet, combine half and half, chicken broth, vermouth, sun-dried tomatoes, tomato paste, basil, oregano, thyme and salt. Cook at a rolling boil until reduced and thickened, about five minutes. Add shrimp and onions to pan and heat through for 2-3 minutes.

Transfer pasta to a large serving bowl. Add shrimp, Parmesan and parsley. Toss and serve immediately.

Serves: 4

Nutritional Information per Serving
Calories: 680, Fat: 21 grams, Protein: 44 grams, Carbohydrates: 79 grams, Cholesterol: 200 milligrams, Fiber: 3.6 grams

Jambalaya with Scallops

This is a great, quick jambalaya. Serve with a salad and you have a healthy, delicious meal.

2 tablespoons oil
1/2 cup onion, chopped
1/2 cup green pepper, diced
2 garlic cloves, minced
3/4 pound cooked, smoked ham, diced
2 (14.5 ounce) cans whole, peeled tomatoes, drained and chopped
1 1/2 cups water
1/2 teaspoon thyme
1/8 teaspoon black pepper
1/8 teaspoon white pepper
1/8 teaspoon cayenne pepper
1/4 teaspoon oregano
1/4 teaspoon basil
1 bay leaf
1 cup uncooked, long grain white rice
3/4 pound large scallops, halved
3/4 pound medium shrimp, shelled and deveined

Heat oil in large stockpot and sauté onion, pepper and garlic. Stir in ham, tomatoes, water, seasonings and rice. Heat to boiling; reduce heat and simmer gently, covered, for 15 minutes, stirring occasionally. Rice should be tender but not sticky. Liquid should be mostly absorbed. Add scallops and shrimp. Cook an additional 5 minutes or until seafood is opaque, but still tender. Remove bay leaf and serve.

Serves: 6

Nutritional Information per Serving
Calories: 370, Fat: 9 grams, Protein: 36 grams, Carbohydrates: 36 grams, Cholesterol: 130 milligrams,
Fiber: 2.4 grams

Lamb Ragu with Pasta

The slow simmer creates a softer taste, which compliments the lamb beautifully.

1/4 cup olive oil
2 pounds lamb stew meat
1/2 cup tomato paste
1 carrot, finely diced
1 stalk celery, finely diced
1 large onion, finely diced
10 cloves garlic, minced
1 (15 ounce) can diced tomatoes
3 bay leaves
2 cups red wine
1 1/4 cups chicken broth
2 dozen sprigs of thyme, plucked and chopped or 2 teaspoons dried
4 sprigs of tarragon, plucked and chopped or 1/2 teaspoon dried
salt & pepper to taste
Pecorino-Romano for grating

Notes:

In a stewing pot large enough to hold all the lamb in one flat layer, heat the olive oil over high heat. As the oil comes to the smoke point, add the lamb to brown. Once a medium brown is achieved add the tomato paste. Lower heat to medium and cook for about five minutes, until the paste begins to caramelize. Add carrots, celery, onion, garlic, tomatoes, bay leaves and red wine. Bring to boil on medium heat, then reduce the heat to simmer, uncovered. Once the alcohol has burned off add chicken broth, just enough to cover the ingredients. Simmer uncovered for roughly 2 hours, until the chunks of lamb crumble between your fingers when pinched. During the simmer stage be sure to stir occasionally.

Once the lamb is done, add the thyme, tarragon and salt and pepper to taste. Simmer for another 10 minutes. Remove the bay leaves. Serve by tossing with pasta of choice. Garnish with grated Pecorino-Romano.

Serves: 8

Nutritional Information per Serving
Calories: 305, Fat: 14 grams, Protein: 27 grams, Carbohydrates: 9 grams, Cholesterol: 75 milligrams, Fiber: 1.8 grams

Serve with fettuccini or rigatoni and a good bottle of Chianti.

Chicken Marengo

3 whole chicken breasts (6 breast halves)
1/2 cup olive oil
1/2 white or yellow onion
2 garlic cloves, crushed
1/2 teaspoon thyme
1 Turkish bay leaf
1/4 cup fresh Italian parsley
1 can artichoke hearts (drained and quartered)
1 cup dry white wine
5 cups chicken broth
1 large can whole tomatoes - drained
1/2 cup cognac
1 cup bow tie pasta, cooked according to directions
1 small can black olives chopped

Bake or sauté chicken breasts. Bone, skin and shred or dice the white meat.

Heat oil in a large skillet or stockpot. Sauté onions and crushed garlic until onions are translucent, 5 minutes. Add chicken, thyme, bay leaf and parsley. Stir in quartered artichokes. Pour in dry white wine, chicken broth, tomatoes and cognac. Simmer for 1 hour. If made 1 day in advance, cover and refrigerate.

Before serving, stir in bow tie pasta and olives and heat through on the stove.

Serves: 6

Nutritional Information per Serving
Calories: 545, Fat: 24 grams, Protein: 36 grams, Carbohydrates: 30 grams, Cholesterol: 55 milligrams, Fiber: 5.3 grams

 Serve on a plate or shallow bowl with crusty sour dough bread and a Caesar Salad (page 120).

Mayor Dave's Chicken on Pasta

Seasoning Mix
2 teaspoons dried thyme leaves
1 1/4 teaspoons ground red pepper
1 teaspoon white pepper
3/4 teaspoon black pepper
1/2 teaspoons dried sweet basil

Rub
1 1/2 tablespoons salt
1 1/2 teaspoon white pepper
1 1/2 teaspoons garlic powder
1 1/4 teaspoons cayenne pepper
1 teaspoon black pepper
1 teaspoon ground cumin (optional)
1/2 teaspoon dried sweet basil

Chicken
1 cup butter, divided
1 cup onions, finely chopped
4 medium sized garlic cloves, peeled and sliced
2 teaspoons minced garlic
2 1/2 cups low sodium chicken bouillon
2 tablespoons Worcestershire sauce
1 tablespoon plus 1 teaspoon Tabasco sauce
2 (16 ounce) cans tomato sauce
2 tablespoons sugar
2 cups finely chopped green onions divided
2 pounds boneless chicken, light and dark meat, cut into 1/2 inch cubes
1 1/2 pounds angel hair pasta

Notes:

In a small bowl, combine all ingredients for the Seasoning Mix and set aside. In another small bowl combine all ingredients for the Rub; set aside.

In a 4 quart saucepan, melt 1/2 cup butter and sauté onions and garlic cloves over medium heat for 5 minutes, stirring occasionally. Add the minced garlic and Seasoning Mix. Continue cooking over medium heat until onions are dark brown, but not burnt, about 8-10 minutes, stirring often. Add 2 1/2 cups chicken stock, Worcestershire sauce and Tabasco sauce; bring to a fast simmer and cook about 8 minutes, stirring often. Stir in tomato sauce, and bring mixture to a boil. Stir in sugar and 1 cup of green onions; gently simmer uncovered for about 40 minutes, stirring occasionally.

Sprinkle the Rub over the cut up chicken, rubbing it with your hands on all sides of the meat. In a large skillet melt 1/2 cup butter over medium heat. Add the remaining 1 cup green onions and sauté over high heat, about 3 minutes. Add the chicken and continue cooking 10 minutes, stirring frequently. When the tomato sauce has simmered 40 minutes, stir in chicken mixture and heat through.

Cook pasta according to directions; drain. Serve chicken mixture on top of the pasta on a large platter or individual plates.

Serves: 6

Nutritional Information per Serving
Calories: 650, Fat: 34 grams, Protein: 46 grams, Carbohydrates: 40 grams, Cholesterol: 170 milligrams, Fiber: 4.1 grams

# Light Fettuccine Alfredo

The old time recipe for fettuccine Alfredo is loaded with calories and fat.
This is a great low-fat adaptation.

1 tablespoon butter
2 cloves garlic, minced
1 tablespoon flour
1 1/4 cups fat free half and half
2 tablespoons 1/3 fat free cream cheese
3/4 cup grated fresh Parmesan cheese
2 tablespoons fresh chopped parsley
1/4 teaspoon white pepper
salt to taste
8 ounces fettuccine
fresh ground pepper to taste

In a medium skillet, melt butter. Add garlic to cook for 1 minute. Add flour and cook, stirring constantly for 2 minutes. Add half and half and cook, stirring constantly until sauce thickens. Stir in cream cheese and Parmesan cheese. Add parsley and season with white pepper and salt. Reduce heat to warm. In a large saucepan, cook fettuccine in boiling water until al dente. Drain well. Stir fettuccine into cheese mixture. Serves: with fresh ground pepper to taste. Pass additional Parmesan cheese if desired.

Serves: 4

Nutritional Information per Serving
Calories: 365, Fat: 9 grams, Protein: 16 grams, Carbohydrates: 55 grams, Cholesterol: 25 milligrams, Fiber: low

 Spinach Manicotti

Sauce
- 4 tablespoons butter
- 4 tablespoons flour
- 2 cups fat free half and half
- 1 1/2 cups chicken stock
- 1/4 teaspoon dried basil
- 1/4 teaspoon mace
- 1/4 teaspoon nutmeg
- salt and pepper to taste

Filling
- 10 ounces frozen spinach, squeezed dry
- 2 cups fat free ricotta cheese
- 4 ounces canned mushrooms, drained
- 1/4 cup chopped green onions
- 12 ounces manicotti pasta shells, cooked and drained

Topping
- 4 ounces low fat cheddar cheese, shredded
- 1/2 cup grated Parmesan cheese

Notes:

Preheat oven to 325 degrees. Grease a 9x13-inch baking pan.

In a medium saucepan, melt butter. Add flour to cook, stirring constantly over medium heat for 3 minutes. Add half and half and broth. Cook stirring constantly, until mixture boils and thickens. Add basil, mace and nutmeg. Add additional broth if mixture is too thick. Adjust seasonings with salt and pepper. Pour one half of sauce in bottom of baking dish and set the remainder aside. In a medium bowl, combine spinach, ricotta cheese, mushrooms and onions. Stir to blend. Stuff cooked manicotti shells with spinach mixture. Lay shells over saucepan. Cover with remaining sauce. Sprinkle with cheddar cheese and Parmesan cheese.

Cover and bake for 60 minutes.

Serves: 6

Nutritional Information per Serving
Calories: 495, Fat: 12 grams, Protein 34 grams, Carbohydrates63 grams, Cholesterol: 40 milligrams, Fiber: 3.6 grams

Pasta Primavera

8 ounces pasta shells or linguine
1 tablespoon olive oil
1 medium onion, finely chopped
1/2 pound fresh mushrooms, sliced
2 cloves garlic, minced
2 cups fresh broccoli florets
1 cup fresh cauliflower florets
1 medium red bell pepper
1 cup snow peas
1/2 cup low fat chicken or vegetable broth
2 tablespoons flour
12 ounces evaporated skim milk or 1 1/2 cups fat free half and half
1/4 teaspoon nutmeg
1 cup grated fresh Parmesan cheese, divided
salt to taste
fresh ground pepper to taste

Cook pasta in a large saucepan of boiling water just until tender. Drain and set aside.

In a large skillet, heat olive oil over medium heat. Add onions and cook until translucent. Add mushrooms and garlic; cook until mushrooms are tender. Add broccoli, cauliflower and snow peas.

In a shaker combine broth with flour. Add broth, milk and nutmeg to vegetables. Cook, stirring constantly until mixture thickens. Reduce heat, partially cover pan and cook 15-20 minutes or until vegetables are very tender. Add cooked pasta and 1/2 cup Parmesan cheese. Heat through. Adjust seasonings with salt and pepper. Top individual portions with remaining cheese.

Serves: 4

Nutritional Information per Serving
Calories: 520, Fat: 13 grams, Protein: 30 grams, Carbohydrates: 70 grams, Cholesterol: 10 milligrams, Fiber: 7.2 grams

Bean Enchilada Casserole

Use a combination of beans to make this fast and easy Mexican dish.

16 (8-inch) corn tortillas
15 ounces kidney beans, rinsed and drained
15 ounce black beans, rinsed and drained
15 ounce white beans, rinsed and drained
15 ounce pinto beans, rinsed and drained
11 ounces cheese soup, condensed
10 ounces enchilada sauce
8 ounces tomato sauce
6 ounces shredded Monterey Jack Cheese
1/2 cup sliced black olives

Preheat oven to 350 degrees. Grease a 9x13-inch baking pan.

Warm tortillas in the oven or microwave to make then soft enough to roll without cracking.

In a large bowl, combine beans and soup. Spoon a portion of bean mixture into each tortilla and roll them up. Place seam side down in the baking pan.

In a small bowl, combine enchilada sauce and tomato sauce. Pour over enchiladas. Cover pan with foil. (Can be made ahead and refrigerated or frozen. Thaw before cooking.)

Bake for 20 minutes. Uncover and top with cheese and black olives. Return to oven for 10 minutes or until cheese is melted.

Serves: 8

Nutritional Information per Serving
Calories: 480, Fat: 16 grams, Protein: 21 grams, Carbohydrates: 64 grams, Cholesterol: 40 milligrams, Fiber: 17 grams

Notes:

Mexican Rice Casserole

This is an easy dish which can be baked ahead and kept in the refrigerator.

2 cups cooked rice
11 ounces corn, drained
15 ounces black beans, drained and rinsed
14 ounces diced tomatoes, undrained
1/2 cup fat free sour cream
1/2 cup salsa or picante sauce
1/2 teaspoon pepper
3 cups mozzarella cheese

Preheat oven to 350 degrees. Grease a 9x13-inch baking pan.

In a large bowl combine rice, corn, beans, tomatoes, sour cream, salsa, pepper and 2 cups of cheese. Mix well. Pour into prepared pan. Top with remaining cheese.

Bake 40-45 minutes, or until lightly brown and set.

Serves: 8

Nutritional Information per Serving
Calories: 300, Fat: 11 grams, Protein: 16 grams, Carbohydrates: 34 grams, Cholesterol: 40 milligrams, Fiber: 5.0 grams

Tangy Thai Chicken Pizza

A great meal for busy families on the go.

Sauce
- 1/2 cup rice wine vinegar
- 1/4 cup low sodium soy sauce
- 3 tablespoons water
- 1/4 cup brown sugar packed
- 2 tablespoons peanut butter
- 1 tablespoon minced fresh ginger
- 4 cloves garlic, minced
- 1/2 teaspoon red hot pepper flakes
- 1/4 cup sliced green onions
- 2 tablespoons finely shredded carrots
- 1 tablespoon fresh, chopped cilantro (optional)

Pizza
- 2 tablespoons olive oil
- 1 pound chicken, cubed
- 1 prepared pizza crust (such as Boboli)
- 1/4 cup Swiss cheese
- 1/2 cup mozzarella cheese

Notes:

Preheat oven to 450 degrees.

Sauce: Mix vinegar, soy sauce, water, brown sugar, peanut butter, ginger, garlic and pepper flakes in a medium bowl. Set aside.

In large sauté pan, heat olive oil over medium high heat. Sauté chicken until cooked through, about 7 minutes. Using a slotted spoon or skimmer, remove chicken from pan and transfer to a plate. In the same pan, add sauce ingredients. Mix with a wire whisk until smooth. Bring mixture to a full boil; reduce heat to a simmer and continue cooking until reduced by half, about 10 minutes. Add the green onions, carrots and cilantro. Add chicken back to sauce mixture and toss until well coated. Remove from heat.

Spread chicken and sauce mixture over the top of pizza crust. Top with both cheeses.

Place on the middle rack of oven and bake for 10-15 minutes. Remove from oven and let stand for 2-3 minutes.

Serves: 4

Nutritional Information per Serving
Calories: 540, Fat: 20 grams, Protein: 40 grams, Carbohydrates: 50 grams, Cholesterol: 85 milligrams, Fiber: 0.8 grams

Blue Cheese, Walnut and Pear Pizza

1/4 cup white wine vinegar
2 cloves garlic, minced
1 tablespoon Dijon mustard
2 sprigs fresh rosemary
1/2 cup olive oil
salt and pepper to taste
1/2 cup blue cheese
2 pears, peeled, and sliced thin
1/4 cup walnuts, toasted
1/3 cup mozzarella cheese - shredded
1 prepared pizza crust (such as Boboli, thin crust)

Preheat oven to 425 degrees.

Combine vinegar, garlic, mustard and rosemary in food processor. When well mixed drizzle in oil to create an emulsion. Add salt and pepper to taste; add 1/4 cup of blue cheese. Combine well.

Place pizza crust in oven for 5 minutes. Remove when crust is slightly crisp on top.

Spread the vinaigrette on the pizza as you would a pizza sauce. Arrange the pears evenly on top of the sauce. Sprinkle toasted walnuts over the pears.

Add the remaining 1/4 cup of blue cheese followed by the mozzarella.

Return pizza to oven for 7-10 minutes or until the mozzarella is completely melted, bubbly and starting to brown. Slice and serve.

Serves: 4

Nutritional Information per Serving
Calories: 565, Fat: 37 grams, Protein: 12 grams, Carbohydrates: 46 grams, Cholesterol: 20 milligrams, Fiber: 2.0 grams

 Try this as an appetizer. Guests will love the unique flavor.

HOLLY HOUSE

In 2001, the Salvation Army opened Holly House, the first transitional home for homeless single women in the greater Madison area. Much more than a roof, Holly House also provides a bed and safe respite along with a comprehensive transitional housing program that gives homeless single women an opportunity to be trained in life and job skills.

While individual goals may differ, each young woman aspires to transform her life from homelessness to hopefulness. The Holly House and Junior League of Madison have worked together to offer residents the tools and programming to make that happen. Most importantly, Holly House offers its residents stability, hope and confidence through supported independence.

"To say that Holly House is the reason I am so changed would be to ignore the great amount of work I have done over the past two years and the dozens of people who have helped me along the way. However, Holly House offered me a place to live, the Salvation Army staff and Junior League volunteers provided encouragement and accountability to help me stay motivated."

-Erika, Holly House resident.

Great Lakes Pizza

This is a deep-dish pizza that is suitable for dinner or as an appetizer.

4 tablespoons olive oil
8 ounces fresh mushrooms, sliced
1 clove garlic, minced
1 (16 ounce) package hot roll mix
1 (12 ounce) jar marinated artichoke hearts, drained, loosely chopped, pulled apart
2 tablespoons crushed red pepper
4 ounces sliced pepperoni
8 ounces grated mozzarella cheese
1/4 cup fresh parsley, chopped

Preheat oven to 400 degrees. Lightly grease a 9x13-inch baking dish.

Over medium heat, warm oil and add mushrooms; cook 6-7 minutes until tender. When mushrooms are almost finished add garlic and cook until golden, stirring constantly, so as not to burn. Remove from heat; set aside.

Prepare hot roll mix using 1 1/4 cups hot water and omitting egg and margarine. After combining roll mix and water allow dough to rest, 5 minutes. Place in prepared pan and, with wet hands, spread the dough on the bottom and up the sides of the pan. Close all seams.

Pour mushroom-garlic mixture over dough and with a pastry brush spread the oil to cover the dough and move mushrooms around to cover evenly. Sprinkle artichoke hearts, red pepper and pepperoni evenly over dough. Top with the cheese and parsley.

Bake 25-30 minutes until cheese is golden.

Serves: 6

Nutritional Information per Serving
Calories: 450, Fat: 28 grams, Protein: 19 grams, Carbohydrates: 31 grams, Cholesterol: 50 milligrams, Fiber: 3.5 grams

Notes:

first rate
finales

Desserts that top the carts

desserts

Almond Tart with Cherry Brandy 265

Apple Cake with Hot Buttered Rum Sauce 267

Badger Cake 268

Baked Caramel Popcorn 286

Bavarian Apple Torte 252

Bucky Bars 282

Caramel Brie 288

Caramel Turtle Brownies 281

Caribbean Coconut Pie 275

Carrot Cake 249

Cherry Pecan Pie 278

Chocolate Chip Mint Cookies 284

Chocolate Coffee Ice Cream Tartufo 272

Chocolate Raspberry Bombe 270

Coconut Pecan Fudge Cake 256

Cranapple Pie 277

Cranberry Pound Cake with Butter Sauce 259

Cranberry Upside Down Sour Cream Cake 259

Double Chocolate Torte 248

Frosted Pumpkin Cranberry Bars 280

Frozen Chocolate-Latte Pie 273

Frozen Tundra Chocolate Crunch 271

Graham Cracker Brownies 283

Lemon-Ginger Sorbet 287

Lydia's Caramel Frosting 288

Mocha Pie 274

Molten Chocolate Cakes 250

Overture Cookies 285

Peanut Butter Fudge Brownies 279

Pumpkin Crisp Pie 276

Pumpkin Marble Cheesecake 262

Pumpkin Ring 255

Raspberry Ripple 269

Red & Blue Trifle 261

Rhubarb Berry Crisp 254

Rhubarb Custard Pie 253

Strawberry-Chocolate Tart 266

Tiramisu Cake 260

Triple Chocolate Cheesecake 263

Warm Fudge Pudding Cake 264

White Chocolate Fruit Tart 251

Nutritional analysis not provided for dessert recipes.

photo courtesy of Wisconsin Dept. of Tourism

Madison –
A Great Place to Call "Home"

When it comes to attracting both residents and visitors to a city, Madison is one of the top choices for recreation and living. Madison is consistently featured in polls and on "Top 10" lists of best places to live and work. *Money* magazine, for example, named Madison the "Best Place to Live" (1998) while *Forbes* magazine (2004) cited Madison as the best metro city for business, one of the best places to live for employment opportunities and one of the best places to obtain a college degree.

It is no wonder Madison is so popular among families, college students and professionals. The city offers an eclectic mix of entertainment, unique shops and eateries, numerous forums for live music, and plenty of outdoor activities. The state capitol often garners attention for Madison both locally and nationally, and is the city's governmental "hub." Madison's combination of natural beauty, cultural diversity, and assorted shops and bars makes it an obvious choice for anyone looking to live in a city with a lot to offer.

But don't just take our word for it, see what recognized publications and organizations across the country have to say about our fair city. See "local flavor" for more categories in which Madison tops the charts.

cocktail party menu

Brie with Port Wine & Cherry Sauce
page 19

Mediterranean Tapenade
page 18

Chicken Satay with Spicy Peanut Sauce
page 32

Double Chocolate Torte
page 248

Overture Cookies
page 285

Chocolate Raspberry Bombe
page 270

Coffee

Double Chocolate Torte

Torte
- 1/2 cup butter
- 6 ounces semisweet chocolate, chopped
- 3 eggs
- 2/3 cup sugar
- 1 teaspoon vanilla
- 1/4 teaspoon salt
- 2/3 cup flour

Glaze
- 1/4 cup butter
- 2 ounces semisweet chocolate, chopped
- 1 cup semisweet chocolate chips
- 2 ounces unsweetened chocolate, chopped
- 1 tablespoon water
- 3 teaspoons honey

CHOCOLATE:

Chocolate has abundant health benefits, particularly for the heart. It is rich in antioxidant polyphenols, which inhibit the oxidation of LDL (bad) cholesterol—lowering the risk of heart attack and stroke.

Preheat oven to 350 degrees. Grease a 9-inch spring form pan.

Torte: In a heavy saucepan, melt butter and chocolate over low heat until smooth. Cool for 15 minutes.

In a medium bowl on high speed, beat eggs, sugar, vanilla and salt until thick, about 3-4 minutes. Add flour; mix well. Pour batter into prepared pan.

Bake 25-30 minutes, until a toothpick placed in the center comes out clean. Cool on a wire rack at least one hour before frosting.

Glaze: Combine all glaze ingredients in a small saucepan. Cook over low heat until smooth. Remove from heat and allow to cool for 10 minutes.

Loosen edges of spring form pan and place torte on serving plate. Drizzle glaze over the top and sides.

Serves: 8

 For a nice touch puree 2 cups fresh or frozen raspberries. Add 2 tablespoons sugar and chill. Spoon sauce over individual servings. Garnish with whipped cream and a berry.

Carrot Cake

Cake
> 2 cups flour
> 2 teaspoons baking powder
> 2 teaspoons cinnamon
> 1 1/2 teaspoons baking soda
> 1 teaspoon salt
> 1/2 teaspoon nutmeg
> 4 eggs
> 2 cups sugar
> 3/4 cup vegetable oil
> 3/4 cup applesauce
> 2 cups grated carrots
> 1 (8.5 ounce) can crushed pineapple, drained
> 1/2 cup raisins

Frosting
> 1/2 cup butter, softened
> 8 ounces low-fat cream cheese, softened
> 2 teaspoons vanilla
> 1 pound powdered sugar, sifted

Preheat oven to 350 degrees. Grease and flour two 9-inch cake pans, set aside.

Cake: Sift together flour, baking powder, cinnamon, baking soda, salt and nutmeg. In a large bowl, beat the eggs with a wire whisk. Add the sugar, applesauce and oil and beat until combined. Stir in the flour mixture until combined. Fold in the carrots, pineapple and raisins; mix well. Pour into prepared pans.

Bake 35-40 minutes, until cakes shrink slightly from the sides of the pans and an inserted toothpick comes out clean. Cool in the pans for 10 minutes. Invert onto racks to cool completely.

Frosting: Combine butter, cream cheese and vanilla, blend until smooth. Add sugar gradually, beating until well incorporated.

Once cooled, use a serrated knife to slice each cake horizontally to create 4 layers. Invert onto racks. Cool if necessary. Spread cream cheese frosting between layers, on top and on sides of cake.

Serves: 12

Molten Chocolate Cakes

This elegant and delicious dessert is always a hit. You can make it one day in advance and then pop it in the oven during dinner for a warm, wonderful dessert! They only look and taste like they were hard to make.

5 ounces bittersweet chocolate, chopped
10 tablespoons unsalted butter
1/2 teaspoon vanilla
3 large eggs
3 large egg yolks
1 1/2 cups powdered sugar
1/2 cup flour
powdered sugar
vanilla ice cream

Preheat oven to 450 degrees. Grease six 1/4 cup soufflé dishes or custard cups.

In heavy medium saucepan over low heat, stir chocolate and butter until melted. Stir in vanilla. Cool slightly.

In a large bowl, whisk eggs and egg yolks until blended. Whisk in powdered sugar; then chocolate mixture. Fold in flour. Divide batter into the six dishes. (This can be made 1 day ahead. Cover and chill. Bring to room temperature before baking.)

Bake 12-14 minutes, until sides are set but center remains slightly soft. Cool 2-3 minutes. Run small knife around cakes to loosen. Invert cakes onto serving plates; gently removing dish from cake. Sprinkle lightly with powdered sugar and serve with a scoop of ice cream.

Serves: 6

Notes:

White Chocolate Fruit Tart

Almost too beautiful to eat.

Crust
3/4 cup butter, softened
1/2 cup powdered sugar
1 1/2 cups flour

Filling
10 ounces vanilla baking chips, melted
1/4 cup whipping cream
8 ounces cream cheese, softened
1 (20 ounce) can pineapple chunks, drained, reserve 1/2 cup juice
1 pint fresh strawberries
1 (11 ounce) can mandarin oranges
2 kiwis, peeled and sliced

Glaze
3 tablespoons sugar
2 teaspoons cornstarch
1/2 teaspoon lemon juice

Preheat oven to 300 degrees. Use an 11 inch tart pan.

Crust: In a large mixing bowl, combine butter and sugar. Gradually add flour; mix well. Press into ungreased tart pan.

Bake for 25-30 minutes, or until lightly browned. Cool.

Filling: In a small mixing bowl, melt vanilla chips until smooth, add cream and mix. Add cream cheese and beat until smooth. Spread over crust. Chill for 30 minutes.

Arrange strawberries, pineapple, oranges and kiwi over filling.

Glaze: In a small saucepan, combine sugar, cornstarch, lemon juice and reserved pineapple juice. Bring to boil over medium heat. Boil 2 minutes or until thickened stirring constantly. Cool, brush over fruit.

Chill 1 hour.

Serves: 12

 Fresh fruit in season can also be used with fantastic results. Try nectarines, peaches, blueberries and raspberries.

Bavarian Apple Torte

This great dessert is surprisingly easy to prepare!

Crust
    1/3 cup sugar
    1 cup flour
    1/2 cup butter
    1/4 teaspoon almond extract

Filling
    8 ounces cream cheese
    1/4 cup sugar
    1 egg
    1/2 teaspoon almond extract

Topping
    1/3 cup sugar
    1/2 teaspoon cinnamon
    1/2 teaspoon almond extract
    6 small baking apples, peeled and sliced
    1/4 cup almonds, sliced

Notes:

Preheat oven to 450 degrees. Use a 9 inch spring form pan.

Crust: In a medium bowl combine sugar with flour. Cut in butter; use a fork to mix until moist dough clumps form. Add almond extract and mix well. Press crust mixture into spring form pan.

Filling: In a medium bowl mix together cream cheese, sugar, egg and almond extract. Pour over crust.

Topping: In a large bowl mix sugar, cinnamon and almond extract. Add apples and toss to coat. Pour over cheese mixture.

Bake 10 minutes. Reduce heat to 400 degrees. Bake an additional 20 minutes.

Sprinkle 1/4 cup almonds over top of apples and bake another 10 minutes.

Serves: 8

 For a nice presentation, layer apples in a circle on top of the torte. If almond extract is not available, use vanilla.

Rhubarb Custard Pie

Prepared with fresh rhubarb from the Farmers' Market, an easy summertime dessert!

3 1/4 cups rhubarb, about 3 large stalks, cubed
1 1/2 cups sugar (divided)
3 eggs
1/4 teaspoon salt
2 heaping tablespoons flour
2 refrigerated pie crusts

Preheat oven to 400 degrees. Use a 9-10 inch pie pan.

In a large bowl mix rhubarb and 1 cup of sugar, set aside. In a separate bowl, combine eggs, 1/2 cup sugar, salt and flour; beat until creamy. Pour cream sauce over rhubarb and stir until combined.

Place refrigerated crust in bottom of pie plate and add fruit and cream mixture. (Do not allow fruit mixture to sit in crust too long as it may become soggy). Add top crust, pinch edges around pie plate and cut several slits in top crust.

Bake 50 minutes. It may be necessary to cover crust around edges with aluminum foil for the first 25 minutes to prevent the crust from getting too brown.

Serves: 8

TOP OF THE CHARTS FOR BUSINESS & CAREERS

- #1 in the nation for business and careers
  – Forbes, May 2004

- #2 medium metro area for doing business in America
  – Inc. Magazine, March 2004

- Best mid-size city in the Midwest for entrepreneurs
  – Entrepreneur Magazine, October 2003

- #5 best places for business and careers
  – Forbes, May 2003

- The most wired city in the country
  – The Media Audit, April 2002

- One of the top 5 cities for entrepreneurial business growth
  – National Commission on Entrepreneurship, March 2002

- #3 city for business owners
  – Business Development Outlook Magazine, November 1999

- #1 America's most wired cities
  – International Demographics, March 1998

- #3 hottest city for growth
  – U.S. News & World Report, April 1995

Rhubarb Berry Crisp

This berry crisp is juicy, soft and crispy all in one bite. Plus, it's easy to make!

Filling
>   3 cups fresh rhubarb, about 3 stalks, diced into 1/2 inch pieces
>   2 cups strawberries
>   1/2 cup raspberries
>   2/3 cup sugar
>   3 tablespoons flour
>   1 teaspoon grated orange zest

Topping
>   1 1/4 cups flour
>   3/4 cup brown sugar
>   1 tablespoon baking powder
>   1/4 teaspoon salt
>   8 tablespoons butter, softened

RHUBARB:

Rhubarb is a very prolific plant – if you need some ideas on what to do with your extra harvest, consider including it in pies, tarts, puddings, breads, jam, jellies or as a sauce served over ice cream.

Preheat oven to 350 degrees. Grease a 9-inch square baking dish.

Filling: In a large bowl combine rhubarb and orange zest and place in prepared pan. Top with berries. Sprinkle with sugar and flour.

Topping: In a small bowl, combine flour, sugar, baking powder and salt. Add butter and mix with fingertips until mixture resembles coarse crumbs. Sprinkle topping over filling.

Bake 35-40 minutes until fruit is soft and bubbly and topping is browned.

Serve warm with vanilla ice cream or whipped cream.

Serves: 6

Pumpkin Ring

Great as a dessert, snack or even breakfast!

Cake

    3 cups biscuit baking mix
    1 cup granulated sugar
    1 cup packed brown sugar
    1/4 cup butter, very soft
    4 eggs
    1 (15 ounce) can pumpkin
    2 1/2 teaspoons pumpkin pie spice
    1/4 cup milk

Glaze

    1 cup powdered sugar
    1 tablespoon milk
    1/2 teaspoon vanilla

Preheat oven to 350 degrees. Grease and flour a 12-cup bundt cake pan or a 10x4-inch angel food cake pan.

In a large bowl with electric mixer on low speed, beat all cake ingredients for 30 seconds. Scrape bowl constantly. Increase to medium speed and beat additional 3 minutes scraping bowl occasionally. Pour into prepared pan.

Bake 45-55 minutes, or until toothpick inserted in center comes out clean.

Cool 10 minutes. Ease a knife along the sides of pan and gently turn over onto serving plate. Cool completely.

In a small bowl, beat all glaze ingredients together until smooth. Drizzle back and forth over cake, until all glaze is used.

Serves: 18

 You can also add 3/4 cup chocolate chips for a taste of chocolate!

Coconut Pecan Fudge Cake

A wonderful birthday cake for someone special. It's worth the effort!

Cake

    1/2 cup shortening
    6 tablespoons cocoa
    1 cup boiling water
    1/2 cup buttermilk
    1 1/2 teaspoons baking soda
    2 cups sugar
    2 eggs
    2 cups flour
    1/2 teaspoons salt
    1 teaspoon vanilla

Fudge Frosting

    2 3/4 cups powdered sugar
    1/2 cup butter, melted
    2/3 cup cocoa powder
    1/3 cup milk
    2 teaspoons vanilla extract

Coconut Pecan Frosting

    1 egg
    2/3 cup evaporated milk
    2/3 cup sugar
    1/4 cup butter
    dash of salt
    1 1/3 cups flaked coconut
    3/4 cup chopped pecans
    1 teaspoon vanilla

Cakes: Place rack in center of oven and preheat oven to 350 degrees.

Generously grease two 8 or 9-inch round pans with shortening and dust with flour. Shake out excess flour and set pans aside.

In a small bowl, mix shortening, cocoa and boiling water; let cool.

In another small bowl, mix buttermilk with baking soda; set aside.

In a large bowl, using an electric mixer, combine sugar, eggs, flour, salt with cocoa mixture and buttermilk mixture. Add vanilla and beat until smooth. Divide batter between the prepared pans. Smooth batter with a rubber spatula.

Notes:

Put cakes in oven side by side. Bake cakes until inserted toothpick comes out clean and sides are starting to pull away from the sides of the pan.

For 8-inch pans, bake 35-40 minutes. For 9-inch pans, bake 28-30 minutes.

Remove the pans from oven and place on a cooling rack for 10 minutes. Run a knife around edges and invert each layer on rack. Invert layers again, so they cool right side up. Cool cakes completely, approximately 30 minutes.

Fudge Frosting: In a large mixing bowl, combine butter and cocoa until thoroughly mixed and smooth. Add one cup of sugar at a time, alternating each cup with some of the milk. Beat on medium speed until smooth and of spreading consistency. Add vanilla and more milk, if necessary, to achieve desired consistency.

Coconut Pecan Frosting: In a saucepan beat the egg slightly. Stir in milk, sugar, butter and salt. Place pan over medium heat and stir constantly until thickened and bubbly, about 7 minutes. Stir in vanilla, coconut and pecans. Cool thoroughly.

Assembly: Using a serrated knife, slice each cake layer in half horizontally, creating 4 layers. For the first layer, place the cut side down and spread with fudge frosting. Place the next cake layer, cut side down, on frosting. Repeat steps with remaining cake layers, ending with coconut pecan frosting on top. Us the fudge frosting, frost around outside of cake. Use a decorator's bag and star tip to decorate top and bottom edges with piped fudge frosting.

Serves: 12

Spread a tablespoon of fudge frosting on the cake plate then place the first layer over it. The frosting serves to anchor the bottom layer.

TOP OF THE CHARTS FOR HEALTH & FITNESS

• One of the best walking cities
— *Prevention,* April 2004

• Healthiest city for men
— *Men's Health,* November 2003

• #2 mid-size city in the country for cycling
— *Bicycling,* November 2001

• #5 fittest city in America
— *Shape,* September 2000

• #10 University for women athletes
— *Sports Illustrated for Women,* August 1999

• #4 best bicycling cities
— *Bicycling,* August 1997

• #1 healthiest city for women
— *American Health,* January 1997

Cranberry Pound Cake with Butter Sauce

2 cups flour
2 teaspoons baking powder
1 cup sugar
1/2 teaspoon salt
1 cup milk
3 tablespoons melted butter
2 cups whole fresh or frozen cranberries

Butter Sauce
1 cup sugar
1/2 cup butter
1/2 cup whipping cream
1 teaspoon vanilla

Notes:

Preheat oven to 350 degrees. Use a 5x7-inch loaf pan.

In a large bowl, mix flour, baking powder, sugar and salt. Add milk, butter and cranberries. Mix until well blended. Pour into loaf pan.

Bake 1 hour, or until inserted toothpick comes out clean.

Sauce: In a small saucepan, mix all the ingredients well and bring to a boil. Pour warm sauce over bread slices, and serve.

Serves: 10

This recipe can be doubled and made in a 9x13-inch pan.

Cranberry Upside Down Sour Cream Cake

Topping
  1/2 cup butter
  1 1/2 cups sugar
  1/4 cup water
  1 teaspoon ground cinnamon
  12 ounces fresh or frozen cranberries, about 4 cups

Cake
  1 1/2 cups cake flour
  1/2 teaspoon baking soda
  1/8 teaspoon salt
  6 tablespoons butter, softened
  1/2 cup sugar
  1/2 cup light brown sugar, packed
  2 large eggs
  3/4 cup sour cream
  2 teaspoons vanilla

Preheat oven to 350 degrees. Grease a 9-inch spring form pan and wrap outside with foil.

Topping: Melt butter in a heavy saucepan over medium heat. Add sugar, water and cinnamon. Boil, stirring frequently, until sugar dissolves, about 4 minutes. Stir in the cranberries. Pour mixture into spring form and spread evenly. Set aside.

Cake: Sift flour, baking soda and salt. Set aside. With an electric mixer, beat butter until smooth and then add sugars, beating until fluffy. Add eggs, one at a time, until well incorporated. On low speed; stir in half the flour mixture and mix until combined. Add sour cream, vanilla and stir until combined. Add remaining flour mixture and stir until smooth.

Transfer to spring form, scraping batter over cranberries as evenly as possible and then smoothing. Be careful not to let the batter sink to the bottom of the pan.

Place springform pan on a baking sheet in oven and bake 50 minutes, or until inserted toothpick comes out clean. Cool on rack for 10 minutes.

Run a knife around edge, to loosen cake. Place serving plate over spring form and invert cake. Remove ring, foil and pan bottom. If kept in airtight container this cake can be made a day ahead.

Serves: 10

Tiramisu Cake

A very attractive cake that's very simple to make.

8 ounces cream cheese
1 3/4 cups whipping cream (divided)
2 tablespoons sour cream
1/2 cup sifted powdered sugar (divided)
1/4 cup plus 5 tablespoon coffee liqueur (divided)
1/4 cup sifted powdered sugar
10 inch round angel food cake
3/4 cup strong coffee

Mocha Fudge Sauce
1/4 cup fudge ice-cream topping
3 tablespoons coffee liqueur

HOW TO WHIP CREAM:

Chill metal or glass bowl and beaters in freezer for 5 minutes before making. Pour heavy cream into chilled bowl and use mixer on medium speed for 1 minute. Increase to high speed until soft peaks form, about 3-4 minutes. Add sugar and vanilla to taste.

Chill a medium bowl and beaters of an electric mixer.

In a large bowl combine cream cheese, 1/4 cup whipping cream and sour cream. Add 1/2 cup powdered sugar and 3 tablespoons coffee liqueur. With electric mixer, beat on medium speed until smooth.

In the chilled bowl combine remaining whipping cream, 1/4 cup powdered sugar, and 2 tablespoons coffee liqueur, beat until stiff peaks form. Fold 1/2 cup of the whipped cream mixture into cream cheese mixture. Set aside.

Using a serrated knife cut cake into three layers. Place layers on a baking sheet. With a long-tined fork or skewer, poke holes in tops of layers. In a small bowl, combine coffee and 1/4 cup coffee liqueur and drizzle over each layer.

Assembly: On a serving platter, place the first layer and top with half of cream cheese filling. Add second layer and remaining filling. Add third layer. Frost with remaining whipped cream mixture. If desired, cover and chill up to three hours.

Mocha Fudge Sauce: In a microwave or small saucepan, heat 1/4 cup fudge ice cream topping until warm. Stir in 3 tablespoons coffee liqueur to make a drizzling consistency.

Drizzle top and sides of cake with mocha fudge sauce. Drizzle additional sauce on serving plates.

Serves: 10

Red & Blue Trifle

The perfect dessert for your 4th of July party.

1 cup low-fat ricotta cheese
8 ounces light cream cheese, room temperature
1 cup powdered sugar
1 cup low-fat sour cream
4 tablespoons Frangelico or Framboise liqueur or 3 tablespoons orange juice
8 ounces heavy or whipping cream
1 quart fresh raspberries
1 quart fresh blueberries
10 inch round angel food cake

Chill a large bowl and beaters of an electric mixer. In a food processor fitted with metal blade or in blender, process ricotta cheese until smooth. Add cream cheese, sugar, sour cream; mix just enough to blend ingredients. Pulse in liqueur; set aside.

In chilled bowl, whip cream. Using spatula, fold cheese-sour cream mixture into whipped cream to blend; set aside.

Scrape golden brown crust from surface of angel food cake and discard. Cut cake into 1-inch cubes and place in large mixing bowl. Pour cheese mixture over cake cubes, stirring gently to combine.

In a large glass trifle dish or 4-quart glass bowl place 1/3 of cubed cake mixture. Place 1/2 of raspberries evenly over cake layer; top with another 1/3 of cake mixture. Arrange all of the blueberries over this layer then top with remaining 1/3 of cake mixture. Top with remaining 1/2 of raspberries. Cover with plastic wrap.

Refrigerate at least 4 hours. Serve chilled in clear glass bowls.

Serves: 16

Pumpkin Marble Cheesecake

A new alternative to the traditional pumpkin pie.

Crust
>   2 cups gingersnap cookie crumbs
>   1/3 cup melted butter

Cake
>   16 ounces cream cheese, room temperature
>   1/2 cup sugar
>   1 teaspoon vanilla
>   3 eggs
>   1 cup canned pumpkin
>   1/4 cup sugar
>   3/4 teaspoon cinnamon
>   1/4 teaspoon nutmeg

Notes:

Preheat oven to 350 degrees. Grease a 9-inch spring form pan.

Combine gingersnap crumbs and butter in a food processor until mixed; press into bottom of prepared pan.

Bake 10 minutes. Cool on rack.

In a mixing bowl, combine cream cheese, 1/2 cup sugar and vanilla. Mix at medium speed until well blended. Add eggs one at a time, mixing well after each and scrapping down sides of bowl often. Set aside 1 cup of this batter.

Pour the remaining batter into a large bowl; add 1/4 cup sugar, pumpkin, cinnamon and nutmeg and mix well. Pour half this pumpkin batter over the crust. Pour the reserved cup of batter over the top in a swirl pattern. Pour remaining half of pumpkin batter over the top, again using a swirl pattern. Smooth together with a butter knife to finish marble effect.

Bake 50 minutes. Cool.

Serves: 10

 Drizzle top with small amount of melted chocolate for garnish. Cool at least three hours before serving.

Triple Chocolate Cheesecake

Slice this dessert very thin because it is quite rich. It will definitely satisfy your chocolate craving!

Crust
>   8 tablespoons lightly salted butter
>   2 cups very finely ground chocolate wafer crumbs (about 36 cookies)
>   1/4 cup sugar

Filling
>   2 pounds cream cheese
>   1 1/4 cups sugar
>   1 tablespoon rum
>   1 1/2 teaspoons vanilla
>   3 1/2 ounces German chocolate squares, melted
>   pinch salt
>   4 large eggs
>   1 cup mini chocolate chips

Topping
>   2 cups sour cream
>   1/2 cup sugar
>   1/2 teaspoon almond extract

Preheat oven to 350 degrees. Use a 10-inch spring form pan.

Crust: In a medium saucepan, melt butter. Add wafer crumbs and sugar, stir until well blended. Using the back of a teaspoon, press mixture over bottom and up 1 inch of the side of spring form pan.

Filling: In a large mixing bowl, combine cream cheese and sugar; beat 2 minutes. Add rum, vanilla, salt and melted chocolate; blend thoroughly. With mixer at lowest speed, add eggs one at a time. Mix just until egg has been incorporated. Stir in chocolate morsels. Pour filling into crust.

Bake 40 minutes. Remove and let stand 10 minutes. Keep oven on.

Topping: In a small bowl, combine sour cream, almond extract and sugar. Spread evenly over top of baked filling.

Return pan to 350 degree oven for 10 minutes. Remove from oven and place in refrigerator immediately, to prevent cracking.

Serves: 16

 To prevent messes in your oven, put foil under the spring form pan and curl up the edges to catch drips.

Warm Fudge Pudding Cake

This is a quick dessert that everyone will love!

1 cup flour
3/4 cup granulated sugar
2 tablespoons cocoa
2 teaspoons baking powder
1/4 teaspoon salt
1/2 cup milk
2 tablespoons vegetable oil
1 teaspoon vanilla
1 cup chopped nuts
1 cup packed brown sugar
1/4 cup cocoa
1 3/4 cups hot tap water

Preheat oven to 350 degrees.

Notes:

In an ungreased 9x9x2-inch baking pan, mix flour, granulated sugar, cocoa, baking powder and salt. Mix in milk, oil and vanilla with fork until smooth. Stir in nuts. Spread evenly throughout pan.

In a small bowl, mix together brown sugar and 1/4 cup cocoa; sprinkle evenly on top. Pour hot tap water over batter.

Bake 40 minutes. Let stand 15 minutes; spoon into dessert dishes and then invert onto dessert plates. Serve with ice cream.

Serves: 9

Almond Tart with Cherry Brandy

A light dessert!

3/4 cup sugar
1/2 cup unsalted butter, room temperature
1 (7 ounce) package almond paste, cut into pieces
2 large eggs
1 tablespoon kirsch or cherry brandy
1/2 teaspoon almond extract
1/4 teaspoon salt
1/3 cup cake flour
1/2 teaspoon baking powder
powdered sugar

Preheat oven to 350 degrees. Grease and flour an 8-inch cake pan.

In a large bowl, mix sugar and butter until light and creamy. Add almond paste, 1 piece at a time, beating well after each addition. Beat in eggs one at a time. Mix in kirsch, almond extract and salt.

In a small bowl, mix flour and baking powder; add to batter. Beat just until blended. Spoon into prepared pan, smooth top of batter.

Bake 35 minutes or until top is golden brown and tester inserted into center comes out clean. Cool in pan on rack. The cake does not rise very much. It will appear low in the pan.

Transfer cake to platter. Dust with powdered sugar and serve. (Cake can be made a day ahead; store in an airtight container at room temperature.) Serve with fresh raspberries on the side for garnish.

Serves: 8

TOP OF THE CHARTS FOR SPORTS & LEISURE ACTIVITIES

- #1 best college sports town
  - *Sports Illustrated on Campus,* September 2003

- Madison Children's Museum, ranked among the 10 best children's museums
  - *Child,* February 2002

- #2 of 25 great towns for raising an outdoor family
  - *Outdoor Explorer,* September 1999

- 1 of 3 "Star Farmers' Markets"
  - *Food and Wine,* September 1996

- #1 of 10 top canoe towns in the U.S.
  - *Paddler,* October 1995

- 1 of 5 top farmers' markets
  - *Good Housekeeping,* August 1995

- #1 "dream town"
  - *Outside,* July 1995

- Best mid-sized city travel getaway
  - *Midwest Living,* August 1994

Strawberry-Chocolate Tart

Crust
> 1 1/2 cups chocolate wafer cookie crumbs
> 6 tablespoons unsalted butter, melted
> 1/4 cup sugar

Filling
> 1 1/2 pint fresh strawberries
> 1/2 cup sugar (divided)
> 2 tablespoons water
> 1 teaspoon fresh lemon juice
> 1 (8 ounce) container mascarpone cheese (room temperature)
> 1/2 cup heavy whipping cream
> 1/4 teaspoon vanilla

Topping
> 1 pint fresh strawberries, hulls removed and berries cut in half
> 1/3 cup seedless strawberry preserves

Notes:

Preheat the oven to 350 degrees. Use a 9-inch round tart pan with removable bottom.

Crust: Combine cookie crumbs, melted butter and sugar in a food processor and process until the crumbs are moistened. Press the mixture into the bottom of tart pan.

Bake 10 minutes, until set. Cool on a wire rack.

Filling: In a food processor, combine the strawberries, 1/4 cup sugar, water and lemon juice. Puree until smooth. To remove the seeds, pour through a strainer set over a bowl to extract as much liquid as possible. Discard the seeds.

In a mixing bowl, combine the mascarpone cheese, whipping cream, vanilla and the remaining 1/4 cup sugar. Beat until mixture is smooth and stiff peaks form. Fold in the strawberry puree. Spread filling over the cooled crust. Cover and refrigerate overnight.

Topping: Arrange fresh strawberries on tart. Stir the strawberry preserves in a small saucepan over medium low heat until melted to form a glaze. Brush glaze over fresh strawberries. Refrigerate tart at least 1 hour.

Remove the tart pan sides, slice into wedges and serve.

Serves: 8

 Mascarpone cheese is an Italian cream cheese generally found with other specialty cheeses.

Apple Cake with Hot Buttered Rum Sauce

A real homemade cake with apples and apple pie spices served with a warm brown sugar rum sauce.

1/4 cup butter
1 cup sugar
1 egg
1/2 teaspoon salt
1 teaspoon baking soda
1/2 teaspoon cinnamon
1/4 teaspoon ginger
1/4 teaspoon nutmeg
1 teaspoon vanilla
1 cup flour
2 cups apple, peeled and finely diced
1/2 cup walnuts, chopped

Topping
1/4 cup evaporated milk
2 tablespoons butter
1/2 cup brown sugar
1 tablespoon rum

Preheat oven to 325 degrees. Grease a 7x11-inch baking pan.

In a large bowl beat butter and sugar until creamy. Add egg and beat until smooth. Add salt, baking soda, cinnamon, ginger, nutmeg and vanilla. Beat until well mixed. Stir in flour and mix just until smooth. Stir in apples and nuts. Pour into pan.

Bake 25-30 minutes until cake is lightly brown and the middle springs back when touched lightly with your finger.

Topping: In a small saucepan combine evaporated milk, butter, brown sugar and rum. Stir over medium heat until mixture just comes to a boil. Immediately remove from heat. (Mixture will curdle if allowed to boil rapidly.)

Drizzle warm topping over individual pieces of cake.

Serves: 6

 To use a 9x13-inch pan, prepare 1 1/2 times the recipe.

Badger Cake

Cake
- 2 1/2 cups self-rising flour
- 1 cup buttermilk
- 1 1/2 cups vegetable oil
- 1 teaspoon baking soda
- 1 teaspoon vanilla extract
- 1/4 cup red food coloring (the ONLY way to get "Badger Red")
- 1 1/2 cups granulated sugar
- 1 teaspoon unsweetened cocoa powder
- 1 teaspoon white vinegar
- 2 large eggs

Frosting
- 3/4 cup butter, softened
- 10 ounces low-fat cream cheese, softened
- 1 pound confectioner's sugar
- 1 1/2 cups pecans, chopped

In the words of Marie Antoinette, "Let them eat cake!"

Heat oven to 350 degrees. Grease three 9-inch round cake pans.

In a large mixing bowl, combine all cake ingredients. Divide batter equally into three prepared pans.

Bake 20 minutes, until toothpick comes out clean. Cool layers in pans on wire racks for 10 minutes. Carefully remove layers from pans to racks to cool completely.

Frosting: In a large bowl, combine butter and cream cheese. Gradually add confectioner's sugar. Beat until fluffy; fold in pecans.

Frost each layer and sides. Refrigerate at least 1 hour before serving.

Serves: 16

Raspberry Ripple

Excellent dessert for the holidays!

1/2 cup sugar
2 cups flour
pinch of salt
1 cup butter
1 egg yolk
1/2 cup raspberry jam
1/4 cup sliced blanched almonds
1/2 teaspoon vanilla

Preheat oven to 350 degrees.

In a large bowl, combine flour, sugar and salt; cut in butter. Add egg yolk and work in with your hands to form a ball. Divide into 3 equal balls.

On an ungreased cookie sheet, shape each third into 12x3-inch strips. Place each strip 4 inches apart. With back of a spoon, make a depression 1/2-inch deep down the center of each strip.

In a small bowl, combine jam, almonds and vanilla. Spread 1/3 of mixture into each depression. Refrigerate 30 minutes.

Bake 20 minutes, until light golden. Cool slightly on baking sheet. Cut each strip into 1-inch diagonal slices.

Makes: 30 pieces

TOP OF THE CHARTS FOR QUALITY OF LIFE

- #2 best small city to live
  – *Men's Journal,* June 2004

- Friendliest city in the Midwest
  – *Midwest Living,* June 2003

- #2 among America's best places to live and work
  – *Employment Review,* June 2003

- #2 among America's best places to live and work
  – *Employment Review,* June 2002

- #2 best place to live and work in America
  – BestJobsUSA.com, May 2002

- #1 best small city for women
  - *Ladies Home Journal,* March 2002

- One of America's most environmentally friendly cities
  – ENN.com, *Environmental News Network,* September 2000

- One of the nation's best small cities for families
  – *Family Fun,* September 2000

- Runner up top retirement site in the U.S.
  – *Money,* June 2000

- Best city for quality of life
  – *Business Development Outlook,* October 1999

- Top 10 cities to have it all
  – *A&E Network,* September 1999

- #1 best place to live in America
  – *Money,* July 1998

- #1 best city for women
  - *Ladies Home Journal,* November 1997

- #1 of 10 best cities for working moms
  – *Redbook,* June 1996

- #3 safest of nation's 100 largest cities
  – *Morgan Quinto Press,* January 1996

Chocolate Raspberry Bombe

This is a deliciously rich dessert best prepared one day in advance.

Brownies
1/2 cup unsalted butter, cut in pieces
2 tablespoons strong coffee
8 ounces semisweet chocolate, chopped
2 large eggs, room temperature
3/4 cup sugar
1 teaspoon vanilla
1/4 cup flour

Crust
1 (9 ounce) package chocolate wafer cookies, crushed
6 tablespoons unsalted butter, melted

Truffle Sauce
1/2 cup plus 1 tablespoon whipping cream
1/4 cup unsalted butter, cut up
12 ounces semi-sweet chocolate chips
1 teaspoon vanilla

Pie
1 quart raspberry sherbet, softened
1 quart vanilla ice cream, softened

BABCOCK
ICE CREAM:

The UW-Madison Babcock
Dairy Plant has been making
"top of the charts" gourmet ice
cream for decades on campus.
People line up to get a taste of
the award-winning Babcock ice
cream that comes in 70
different flavors including:
Union Utopia, Grainger Granite
Crunch with Academia Nuts
and Praise to Thee,
Our Almond Mocha.

Preheat oven to 325 degrees. Use an 8-inch square pan and 9-inch spring form pan.

Brownies: Line square pan with foil extending over sides of the pan. Butter foil, or spray with cooking spray.

In a medium saucepan, warm 1/2 cup butter and coffee over medium heat until butter is melted. Reduce heat to low. Add chocolate and stir until melted and smooth. Cool 5 minutes. Set aside.

In a large bowl, beat eggs with sugar and vanilla until thick, about 2 minutes. Stir in chocolate mixture. Mix in flour. Transfer batter to pan.

Bake 25 minutes, until brownies are cracked around edges. They will be very soft. Refrigerate. Leave oven on.

Crust: Grease a 9-inch springform pan. Mix wafer crumbs with 6 tablespoons melted butter until moist. Press in bottom and 1-inch up sides of spring form pan.

Truffle Sauce: In heavy medium saucepan, bring whipping cream and butter to just simmering. Remove from heat. Add semisweet chocolate chips and vanilla extract. Whisk until sauce is smooth.

Bake 10 minutes. Cool.

Assembly: Place raspberry sherbet in bottom of pan. Top with 1/2 of cut up brownies and 1/2 of chocolate sauce. Top with vanilla ice cream. Place remaining brownies on top of vanilla ice cream. Drizzle remaining chocolate sauce on top of brownies. Serve immediately or freeze until ready to serve.

Serves: 16

Frozen Tundra Chocolate Crunch

This is a guaranteed winner. Everyone will all want the recipe!

2 cups powdered sugar
1 1/2 cups evaporated milk
2/3 cup chocolate chips
1/2 cup butter
1 teaspoon vanilla
1 (15 ounce) package chocolate cream filled cookies
1/2 cup butter, melted
1/2 cup Spanish peanuts
1/2 gallon vanilla ice cream, softened

Use a 9 x 13-inch cake pan.

In a medium saucepan combine powdered sugar, evaporated milk, chocolate chips, 1/2 cup butter and vanilla. Bring to a boil and continue to boil for 8 minutes, stirring constantly. Cool.

In a large bowl, crush chocolate cream filled cookies; add 1/2 cup melted butter and combine. Spread in pan. Sprinkle 1/2 of the peanuts over cookie mixture and refrigerate 30 minutes, until set.

Spread 1/2 softened vanilla ice cream over peanuts. Cover with 3/4 of the chocolate mixture and remaining vanilla ice cream. Drizzle with the rest of the chocolate mixture. Chop remaining peanuts and sprinkle on top. Freeze overnight. Top with a few Spanish peanuts if desired.

Serves: 12

Chocolate Coffee Ice Cream Tartufo

2 pints vanilla-bean ice cream, softened slightly
1 cup almonds, toasted, chopped
1 1/2 pints coffee chip ice cream, softened slightly
1 cups whipping cream (divided)
1/8 cup light corn syrup
12 ounces bittersweet (not unsweetened) or semisweet chocolate, chopped
3 ounces semisweet chocolate, chopped
1 teaspoon vanilla extract
1/2 teaspoon almond extract

STORING
ICE CREAM:

To prevent ice crystals from forming on ice cream, place a piece of wax paper directly over surface of ice cream container and replace lid before placing it in the freezer.

Line 9x5x2 1/2-inch metal loaf pan with plastic wrap, leaving a 3-inch overhang on all sides.

Using small flexible spatula quickly spread softened vanilla-bean ice cream evenly over bottom and up sides of prepared pan. Freeze about 30 minutes. Sprinkle 1/4 cup chopped almonds over ice cream in bottom of pan. Return to freezer for an additional 30 minutes or until ice cream is firm.

Spread softened coffee chip ice cream over vanilla ice cream, filling pan completely. Smooth over the top so it is level. Freeze until ice cream is firm, about 1-2 hours.

Ganache: In a medium saucepan, over medium heat, bring 3/4 cup cream and corn syrup to a simmer in medium saucepan. Remove from heat. Add both chocolates and whisk until smooth. Whisk in both extracts. Cool ganache to room temperature, about 45 minutes, whisking occasionally.

Spread 2/3 cup chocolate ganache over top of ice cream. Freeze until chocolate is very firm, about 2 hours.

Rewarm chocolate ganache over low heat just until fluid if necessary. Cool to room temperature (mixture will thicken slightly.) Line baking sheet or serving tray with waxed paper. Run small knife around sides of loaf pan to loosen ice cream loaf. Invert loaf onto prepared sheet; peel off plastic wrap. Working quickly and using small flexible spatula, spread 1 cup chocolate ganache over top and sides of ice cream loaf, covering ice cream completely and forming 1/4-inch-thick chocolate coating. Refrigerate remaining ganache. Sprinkle remaining 3/4 cup chopped almonds over top of chocolate-covered ice cream loaf.

Freeze until chocolate is firm, at least 1 hour. Cover completed tartufo with plastic wrap and keep frozen. Can be made 1 week ahead.

To serve: Add remaining 1/4 cup cream to ganache and rewarm over low heat to use as sauce. Cut tartufo into 1/2-inch-thick slices. Cut each slice diagonally in half, forming 2 triangles. Place 2 triangles on each plate in a criss-cross pattern. Drizzle with warm ganache.

Serves: 16

 Frozen Chocolate-Latte Pie

Crust
  1 1/2 cups chocolate wafer cookie crumbs
  6 tablespoons unsalted butter, melted
  1/4 cup sugar

Filling
  1 1/2 quarts coffee ice cream, half of it softened
  1/3 cup milk
  1/4 teaspoon cornstarch
  4 ounces bittersweet or semisweet chocolate, chopped
  2 tablespoons coffee-flavored liqueur

In a medium bowl, mix crumbs and butter; add sugar. Press in the bottom and up sides of a 9-inch pie pan.

Spread softened ice cream evenly in crust; smooth top. Freeze, uncovered, 1 hour, until firm to touch.

In a 2-quart saucepan, stir milk and cornstarch until smooth. Over medium heat, stir mixture until bubbling, about 2 minutes; remove from heat. Stir in chocolate and coffee liqueur until melted and smooth. Let cool.

Spoon 3 tablespoons sauce into a small, unpleated zip-lock bag. Press all of the air out of the bag and seal. Set remaining sauce aside.

Spread reserved sauce over ice cream in crust. Drop 8 equal scoops or spoonfuls of firm ice cream around rim of pie. Snip the corner of the bag of chocolate sauce. Squeeze sauce decoratively onto pie.

Serves: 8

Mocha Pie

A sophisticated dessert for a dinner party.

1/3 cup hot water
4 teaspoons instant coffee granules, divided
1/2 (20.5 ounce) box fudge brownie mix, about 2 cups
2 teaspoons vanilla extract
2 large egg whites
cooking spray
3/4 cup milk
3 tablespoons, Kahlua
1 (3.9 ounce) package chocolate-flavored instant pudding mix
3 cups frozen reduced-calorie whipped topping, thawed
chocolate curls

BROWNIES:

To make brownies from remaining mocha pie ingredients, combine 2 cups brownie mix, 1/4 cup water and 1 lightly beaten large egg white in a bowl. Stir just until combined. Spread into an 8-inch square pan coated with cooking spray. Bake at 350 degrees for 23 to 25 minutes.

Preheat oven to 325. Grease a 9-inch pie pan.

Combine hot water and 2 teaspoons coffee granules in a bowl; stir well. Add 2 cups brownie mix, 1 teaspoon vanilla and egg whites; stir until well-blended. Pour mixture into prepared pie pan.

Bake 22 minutes. Brownie will be fudgy when tested with a toothpick. Let cool completely on a wire rack.

In a medium bowl, combine milk, 2 tablespoons Kahlua, 1 teaspoon coffee granules, 1 teaspoon vanilla and pudding. With mixer at medium speed, mix 30 seconds. Gently fold in 1 1/2 cups whipped topping. Spoon pudding mixture onto brownie crust; spread evenly.

Combine 1 tablespoon Kahlua and 1 teaspoon coffee granules in a small bowl; stir well. Gently fold in 1 1/2 cups whipped topping. Spread whipped topping mixture evenly over pudding mixture. Garnish with chocolate curls, if desired. Serve immediately or store loosely covered in refrigerator.

Serves: 8

 Store remaining 2 cups brownie mix in a zip-lock plastic bag in refrigerator. Reserved brownie mix can be used for another pie or to make a small pan of brownies.

Caribbean Coconut Pie

This decadent dessert will have you thinking of steel drums and warm breezes.

1 (9-inch) refrigerated piecrust
1/2 cup chocolate chips
1/4 cup butter, melted
1 2/3 cup evaporated milk
1 1/2 cup sugar
3 tablespoons cornstarch
1/8 teaspoon salt
2 large eggs
1 teaspoon vanilla
1/2 cup chopped pecans
1 1/3 cup flaked coconut

Preheat oven to 375 degrees.

Press pie crust into 9-inch pan. Sprinkle chocolate chips on pie crust.

In a large bowl, mix melted butter with evaporated milk. Add sugar, cornstarch and salt. Add the eggs, one at a time, beating well between each addition. Add the vanilla. Pour into the pie crust. Sprinkle with nuts and coconut.

Bake 45 minutes. Allow to cool at least 4 hours before serving.

Serves: 8

Pumpkin Crisp Pie

Add a new twist to Thanksgiving dessert by using this alternative to pumpkin pie.

2 eggs
1 (15 ounce) can pumpkin
1 (14 ounce) can sweetened condensed milk
1 teaspoon ground cinnamon
1/2 teaspoon ground ginger
1/2 teaspoon ground nutmeg
1/4 teaspoon ground cloves
1/2 teaspoon salt
2 egg whites
1 (9-inch) unbaked pie shell
2 tablespoons flour
1/4 cup packed brown sugar
1 1/2 teaspoons ground cinnamon
2 tablespoons butter, chilled
1 cup chopped pecans

Notes:

Preheat the oven to 425 degrees.

Using two small bowls, separate egg yolks from whites. Set aside.

In a large bowl, mix pumpkin, sweetened condensed milk and egg yolks. Stir in cinnamon, ginger, nutmeg and salt. In a large glass or metal bowl, whip egg whites until soft peaks form. Gently fold into pumpkin mixture with a rubber spatula. Pour filling into pie shell.

Bake 15 minutes.

Streusel topping: In a small bowl, combine flour, brown sugar and cinnamon. Cut in the cold butter with a fork or pastry blender until the mixture resembles coarse crumbs. Mix in the chopped nuts. Remove the pie from the oven and reduce the oven temperature to 350 degrees. Sprinkle topping over the pie and return to the oven and bake an additional 40 minutes, until set.

Serves: 8

Cranapple Pie

1/4 cup currants
1/4 cup brandy
1 1/2 cups fresh or thawed frozen cranberries
1 1/4 cups granulated sugar
6 tablespoons, plus 1 cup flour
1 tablespoon grated orange peel
3/4 teaspoon ground cinnamon
1/2 teaspoon ground nutmeg
1/4 teaspoon salt
6 cups Granny Smith apples, peeled & sliced, about 2 1/4 lbs
1 (10-inch) unbaked refrigerated pie crust
2/3 cup firmly packed brown sugar
1/2 cup butter, chilled

Preheat oven to 375 degrees. Place rack on bottom rack of oven.

Clean cranberries and discard any that are bruised or bad. Rinse and
drain berries.

In a small bowl, combine brandy and currants. Cover and let stand until currants
are plump, at least 1 hour or up to 1 day.

Press pie crust into pie pan. Set aside.

In a large bowl, mix 1 1/4 cups granulated sugar, 6 tablespoons flour, orange
peel, cinnamon, nutmeg and salt. With a slotted spoon, lift currants from
brandy and reserve brandy. Add currants, cranberries and apples to sugar
mixture and mix well. Taste and add more granulated sugar if desired. Pour
filling into pie crust in pan. Drizzle remaining brandy evenly over pie.

In small bowl, combine 1 cup flour and brown sugar. Cut in butter with a pastry
blender or mix with fingers until mixture resembles coarse crumbs. Sprinkle
topping evenly over filling. Set pie on a foil-lined 12-inch pizza pan or large
baking dish and place on bottom rack of the oven. Bake.

After 30 minutes check to see if pie is browning too quickly. If so, cover loosely
with foil. Bake an additional 30-35 minutes until juices bubble around edges and
through the topping.

Set pie, uncovered, on a rack to cool, about, 2-3 hours.

Serves: 10

Cherry Pecan Pie

Crust
- 1 cup flour
- 2 tablespoons powdered sugar
- 1/2 cup butter

Filling
- 2 eggs
- 1 teaspoon vanilla
- 3/4 cup sugar
- 1/4 cup flour
- 1/2 teaspoon baking powder
- 1/2 teaspoon salt
- 1/2 cup coconut
- 3/4 cup pecans, roughly chopped
- 1 (14 ounce) can tart cherries

Notes:

Preheat oven to 350 degrees.

Crust: In a large bowl, with a pastry blender or 2 forks, combine flour, sugar and butter until mixture resembles coarse, pea-sized crumbs. Press mixture into the bottom and sides of a 9-inch pie pan, working quickly so the butter doesn't start to melt.

Bake 25 minutes.

While piecrust cools, increase oven temperature to 375 degrees and make filling.

Filling: In a large bowl, beat eggs slightly. Add vanilla, sugar, flour, baking powder and salt to combine. Stir in coconut, pecans and cherries. Pour into cooled pie shell.

Bake 30 minutes, until filling is set.

Serves: 8

Peanut Butter Fudge Brownies

This is a wonderful peanut butter and chocolate combination.

Batter
   2 cups sugar
   1 cup butter, softened
   2 teaspoons vanilla
   4 eggs
   1 1/2 cups flour
   3/4 cup cocoa
   1 teaspoon baking powder
   1/2 teaspoon salt
   1 cup mini peanut butter chips

Topping
   3/4 cup peanut butter
   1/3 cup butter
   1/3 cup sugar
   2 tablespoons flour
   2 eggs
   1 teaspoon vanilla

Frosting
   3 ounces unsweetened chocolate (pre-melted packets)
   3 tablespoons butter
   2 2/3 cups powdered sugar
   1/4 teaspoon salt
   1 teaspoon vanilla
   4 tablespoons water

Preheat oven to 350 degrees. Grease a 9x12-inch pan.

Batter: In a large bowl combine sugar, butter, vanilla and eggs, beating well after each. Gradually add flour, cocoa, baking powder and salt. Mix well. Stir in peanut butter chips. Set aside.

Topping: In small bowl cream topping ingredients and blend until smooth.

Spread 1/2 of batter in prepared pan. Spread topping mixture over the batter mixture. Spread remaining 1/2 batter mixture over the top. Gently swirl a knife through the layers to marble.

Bake 40 to 50 minutes. Cool.

Frosting: In medium saucepan, melt chocolate and butter over a low heat, stirring constantly. Remove from heat and stir in powdered sugar, water and vanilla until smooth. Spread over brownies.

Makes: 36 brownies

Frosted Pumpkin Cranberry Bars

Cranberries add a new twist to these classic bars.

Bars
  1 1/2 cups flour
  1 1/4 cups sugar
  2 teaspoons baking powder
  2 teaspoons cinnamon
  1 teaspoon baking soda
  1/2 teaspoon ginger
  3 eggs
  1 (15 ounce) can pumpkin
  3/4 cup melted butter
  3/4 cup dried cranberries

Frosting
  4 ounces fat-free cream cheese, chilled
  1/4 cup butter
  1 teaspoon grated lemon rind
  1 teaspoon vanilla extract
  3 1/2 cups powdered sugar

Notes:

Preheat oven to 350 degrees. Grease a 15x10-inch baking pan.

Bars: In a medium bowl, combine the dry ingredients. In another bowl, whisk the eggs, pumpkin and butter; stir into dry ingredients until well combined. Stir in cranberries. Spread into prepared pan.

Bake 20-25 minutes, until a toothpick comes out clean. Cool on a wire rack.

Frosting: With an electric mixer at medium speed, beat first 4 ingredients until smooth. Gradually add sugar to butter mixture; beat at low speed just until blended.

Spread frosting on cooled bars.

Makes: 24 bars

Caramel Turtle Brownies

These chewy, rich brownies will have you going back for more!

1 (18.5 ounce box) German chocolate cake mix
2/3 cup evaporated milk
3/4 cup softened butter
1 cup walnuts or pecans
14 ounces caramels
12 ounces semisweet chocolate chips
cooking spray

Preheat oven to 350 degrees. Grease a 13x9-inch pan.

In a large mixing bowl, beat cake mix, 1/3 cup evaporated milk and softened butter. Blend until mixture holds together. Stir in nuts. Press 1/2 of cake mixture into prepared pan. Set aside remaining mixture.

Bake 6 minutes.

Meanwhile, combine caramels and remaining evaporated milk in a double boiler over medium-low heat. Stir mixture until melted.

When cake has baked for 6 minutes, remove from oven and sprinkle chocolate chips on top. Pour melted caramel evenly over the top of the chocolate chips. Spread remaining cake mixture over caramel. This works best by spraying your hands with cooking spray, or dampening your hands with water, and using your hands to spread out the mixture.

Return to oven for additional 15-20 minutes. Cool slightly and cut into bars.

Makes: 28 bars

TOP OF THE CHARTS FOR ARTS & INSPIRATION

- One of the best designer cities in the country
  – *HOW Design,* December 2003

- One of five top cities that inspire
  – *Delicious Living,* March 2003

- #1 small-size city for creativity
  – *The Washington Monthly,* July 2002

Bucky Bars

Don't go tailgating without these bars!

Oatmeal Batter
- 1 cup butter
- 2 cups sugar
- 2 eggs
- 2 teaspoons vanilla
- 2 1/2 cups flour
- 1 teaspoon baking soda
- 1 teaspoon salt
- 3 cups oatmeal, quick or regular

Filling
- 12 ounces chocolate chips
- 1 (14 ounce) can sweetened condensed milk
- 2 tablespoons butter
- 1/2 teaspoon salt
- 2 teaspoons vanilla
- 1 cup walnuts

Notes:

Preheat oven to 350 degrees. Grease a 15x10x1-inch pan.

Oatmeal Batter: In a large bowl, mix together all the ingredients; set aside.

Filling: Combine chocolate chips, sweetened condensed milk, butter and salt in a double boiler; melt. When chocolate mixture is smooth, add vanilla and nuts.

Spread 2/3 of the oatmeal batter in prepared pan. Cover with chocolate filling. Dot with remaining oatmeal mixture.

Bake 25-30 minutes. Let cool, cut into bars.

Makes: 36 bars

 Wrap your hand with wax paper for neat and easy spreading.

Graham Cracker Brownies

Yummy take-along snacks for boating or a picnic!

1 1/4 cups crushed graham crackers, about 18 crackers
3/4 cup pecan pieces
1 (15 ounce) can sweetened condensed milk
1/4 cup melted butter
1/2 cup semi-sweet chocolate pieces
1/4 teaspoon salt

Preheat oven to 350 degrees. Grease an 8-inch square pan.

In a large bowl, combine all ingredients. Mix well. Spoon into prepared pan.

Bake 30-35 minutes. Cool completely.

Cut into squares. Wrap and store in tightly covered container.

Makes: 16 brownies

Chocolate Chip Mint Cookies

1/2 cup unsalted butter
3/4 cup brown sugar
3/4 cup sugar
2 eggs
2 teaspoons vanilla
1 1/2 teaspoons peppermint extract
2 cups flour
1 teaspoon soda
1 teaspoon salt
2 cups chocolate chips

Preheat oven to 375 degrees.

Cream together butter, brown sugar and sugar. Beat in eggs, vanilla and peppermint extract. Sift together flour, soda and salt. Gradually add dry ingredients to the creamed mixture. Stir in chocolate chips.

Bake 8-10 minutes.

Convection Ovens: If using a convection oven, be prepared to get addicted to these cookies, which are done from start to finish in less than half hour! Just adjust cookie size so you can get the whole batch divided among three cookie sheets and bake them all at once, checking at four minutes to make sure they are baking evenly. If trays look uneven, switch and rotate all trays. Check again at eight minutes. They should never take longer than nine minutes to bake.

Makes: 36 cookies

Notes:

Overture Cookies

Great "dunking" cookies in milk or coffee.

1 cup butter
1 cup brown sugar
1 cup sugar
2 eggs
2 teaspoons vanilla
2 cups flour
1 teaspoon baking powder
2 teaspoons baking soda
1/2 teaspoon salt
2 cups oatmeal
2 1/2 cups cornflakes
1 cup coconut
1/2 cup wheat germ
1/2 cup raisins
1/2 cup pecans or almonds, chopped

Preheat oven to 350 degrees.

Cream together butter and sugars until light & fluffy. Add eggs and beat in well until sugars are no longer grainy. Add vanilla. Sift together flour, baking powder, soda and salt and add to creamed sugars on low speed. Fold in remaining ingredients. Drop by teaspoonful 3 inches apart on lightly greased cookie sheets.

Bake 10 minutes, until light brown. While still warm, carefully remove from cookie sheet and cool on rack.

Makes: 36 cookies

Baked Caramel Popcorn

The perfect treat for a weekend movie night.

cooking spray
1 cup packed dark brown sugar
1/2 cup light corn syrup
1/3 cup butter
1 tablespoon light molasses
1 1/2 teaspoons vanilla extract
1/2 teaspoon baking soda
1/2 teaspoon salt
12 cups popcorn, air popped without salt or fat

Preheat oven to 250 degrees. Coat a large jellyroll pan with cooking spray.

Combine sugar, corn syrup, butter and molasses in a medium saucepan; bring to boil over medium heat. Cook 5 minutes, stirring a couple times. Remove from heat; stir in vanilla, baking soda and salt.

Place popcorn in a large bowl; pour sugar mixture over popcorn in a steady stream, stirring to coat. Spread popcorn mixture into prepared pan.

Bake for 1 hour, stirring every 15 minutes.

Remove from oven; stir to break up any large clumps. Cool 15 minutes. Serve warm or at room temperature. Store in airtight container up to 1 week.

Serves: 10

Notes:

Lemon-Ginger Sorbet

This light dessert is also excellent as a tingling palate cleanser to serve between courses.

1 1/2 cups sugar
2 tablespoons peeled and minced fresh ginger
2 tablespoons finely grated lemon zest
4 cups water
1/2 cup fresh lemon juice

In a medium saucepan, over medium heat, combine the sugar, ginger, lemon zest and water. Bring to a boil, stirring often. Boil uncovered, over medium heat, for 10 minutes. Cool mixture then stir in lemon juice.

Freeze in a freezer-proof container for about 6 hours, or until almost frozen solid. Remove from container and, in a food processor, process until smooth. Freeze for 2 more hours until firm.

Serves: 8

RONALD MCDONALD HOUSE CHARITIES OF MADISON

"The Junior League of Madison has been an important part of our 'family' since before the Ronald McDonald House opened its doors in 1993.

Members of the Junior League were instrumental in fundraising initiatives to build the House, have organized special events to celebrate the House's milestone birthdays and have provided our families with dozens of home-cooked meals over the years. But most importantly, Junior League volunteers have generously donated thousands of hours to assist us in providing warmth, comfort and compassion to the families with critically injured and ill children that we serve. The very fabric of the Ronald McDonald House is laced with the kindness and good work of the Junior League of Madison. On behalf of the children and families that are touched by your efforts...thank you."

Sandra L. Lampman
Executive Director, Ronald McDonald
House Charities of Madison

Caramel Brie

Consider this for a cheese-dessert course at the end of your meal.

8-10 ounces Brie
1/2 cup chopped salted nuts
1/2 cup dried cranberries or craisins
3/4 cup butterscotch or caramel ice cream topping
thin ginger cookies

Soften Brie at room temperature. In a small bowl mix nuts and cranberries.

Pour ice cream topping over the cheese. Top with nut mixture. Serve with thin ginger cookies.

Serves: 8

Lydia's Caramel Frosting

This is an old recipe from Madison's Vilas family. It is wonderful on a yellow cake.

1/2 cup butter, melted
1 cup brown sugar
1/4 cup milk
1 cup powdered sugar

Cook butter and brown sugar over low heat for 2 minutes, stirring constantly. Add milk and continue to cook and stir until mixture comes to a boil.

Remove and cool. When cool add the powdered sugar and spread.

Covers one 9x12-inch cake.

This recipe is named for Lydia Aberle, a former cook to Francis and Joseph W. Vilas. The Vilas family's lakeside home remains today at 69 Cambridge Road, Maple Bluff.

no reservations

Favorite restaurant recipes to make at home

restaurant favorites

Blue Marlin
Sea Scallops 297

The Madison Club
Cranachan 304

Café Continental
Bananas Foster
French Toast 292

Maple Bluff Country Club
Cream of Shiitake
Mushroom Soup 296

Captain Bill's
Coconut Shrimp 295

Marigold Kitchen
Blackberry Vinaigrette 293

Eldorado Grill
Wisconsin Four Cheese
Chile Rellenos 298

Nakoma Golf Club
Pecan Beet Salad 294

Fyfe's Corner Bistro
Key Lime Pie 305

Ocean Grill
Deviled Crab 299

Lombardino's Italian
Restaurant and Bar
Shrimp alla
Sambuca 303

Restaurant Magnus
Lamb Chops with
Sunchoke Puree
and Vegetables 300

Louisianne's, Etc.
Chicken and Sausage
Jambalaya 301

Wollersheim Winery
Prairie Fumé Salmon Tourte 302

Nutritional analysis not provided for restaurant recipes.

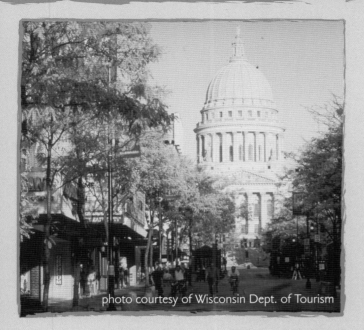

photo courtesy of Wisconsin Dept. of Tourism

State Street - That Great Street

Madison's own melting pot is located right at the heart of the city. State Street is the location where all points of Madison come together— a slew of ethnically diverse restaurants, the UW-Madison campus, diverse shopping venues, the Madison Art district and the State Capitol.

State Street is a pedestrian concourse that starts at the University campus and is a potpourri of color, smells and energy that runs into the State Capitol. At any given time, on any given day, you will find restaurants ranging from college-fare-take-out to uptown European cuisine, boutiques with upscale, designer gifts to gag gifts and cheese heads.

On the State Capitol end of State Street you will find the most powerful figures in state government walking among school-age children taking tours of the Capitol. Along State Street to the other end at Bascom Hill, college students, locals and visitors enjoy the vast array of eateries and eclectic shops that line the street.

State Street provides Madisonians and visitors with a perfect snapshot of the diversity and the uniqueness that makes Madison a great place to be.

dinner party menu

Tomato Basil Bisque
page 82

Pear, Arugula and Endive Salad with Candied Walnuts
page 112/113

Pork Tenderloin with Herbed Breadcrumb Crust
page 197

Garlic Mashed Potatoes
page 154

Beans with Basil
page 142

Molten Chocolate Cakes
page 250

Café Continental
Bananas Foster French Toast

Sauce
- 1/2 cup butter
- 1 1/4 cups brown sugar
- 1 1/4 cups heavy cream
- 4 bananas sliced
- 1 ounce of rum (optional)

Toast
- 8 slices of French bread, cut 3/4-inch thick
- 8 eggs
- 1/3 cup sugar
- 1 1/2 cups milk
- 1 1/2 cups heavy cream
- butter
- powdered sugar (optional)

Notes:

Sauce: In a medium saucepan, melt butter; add brown sugar and cook until smooth. Whisk in cream. Bring mixture to a boil and simmer until slightly thickened. (Sauce can be made 1 day ahead and refrigerated.)

French Toast: In a large bowl, combine eggs, sugar, milk and cream. Whisk until sugar is dissolved. Dip bread in egg mixture until lightly soaked. In a large skillet over medium heat, sauté bread in butter until golden brown, turning once.

Transfer sauce to a large sauté pan; bring to a boil. Add sliced bananas and flambé with rum, if desired. Spoon over French toast, sprinkle with powdered sugar and serve.

Serves: 8

 You can substitute blueberries or fresh-sliced strawberries for bananas. The topping can also be used over ice cream.

Marigold Kitchen
Blackberry Vinaigrette

Marigold Kitchen suggests using this vinaigrette over a mix of baby greens, toasted hazel nuts, thinly sliced red onions, bleu cheese and diced fresh pears.

    2 cups fresh or frozen blackberries
    3 tablespoons sugar
    1/2 cup water
    2 shallots, minced
    1/2 cup champagne vinegar
    2 cups canola oil
    2 tablespoons Dijon mustard
    salt and ground black pepper to taste

In a medium saucepan, combine blackberries, sugar and water. Bring to a boil and simmer over low heat. Stir until berries have broken down and reached a consistency of a loose jam. Be careful not to over-reduce.

Transfer berry mixture into a large mixing bowl and whisk together the blackberries, minced shallots, champagne vinegar and Dijon mustard.

Finish by whisking in canola oil in a slow, steady stream until fully combined. Season with salt and pepper.

Serves: 4

 Always season the salad mix with a touch of salt and pepper before adding your vinaigrette. Make sure not to over-dress your salad. Be creative, mix and match your favorite ingredients to create your own signature salad.

Nakoma Golf Club
Pecan Beet Salad

Salad
> 2 medium red beets
> 2 medium yellow beets
> 2 heads Bibb lettuce
> 1 head California red leaf lettuce
> 2 cups baby spinach
> 1/2 cup crumbled gorgonzola cheese
> 2 Roma tomatoes
> 1 yellow bell pepper

Dressing
> 3/4 cup pecan halves, toasted (divided)
> 1/4 cup cider vinegar
> 3/4 cup vegetable oil
> 2 teaspoons salt
> 1 teaspoon white pepper
> 1 teaspoon sugar

Notes:

In a medium-sized pot cover beets with water and bring to a boil. Reduce heat to a simmer and cook until fork tender, about 20 minutes. Cool beets in an ice water bath. Peel beets and julienne.

Rip lettuce by hand into bite-sized pieces and remove large stems from spinach. Wash mixture in salad spinner or colander and drain. Remove seeds from tomatoes and yellow peppers. Julienne tomatoes and yellow peppers.

In a blender add 1/2 cup pecan halves, reserving the rest for garnish. Add the vinegar, salt, white pepper and sugar. Blend until smooth; in a slow, steady stream add the vegetable oil.

Divide the lettuce mixture among 4 large plates. Arrange tomatoes and yellow peppers on top of the lettuce. Place the beets and the gorgonzola on next. Top with about 2 1/2 ounces of dressing and the remaining pecan halves.

Serves: 4

Captain Bill's
Coconut Shrimp

Sauce
    1 cup mayonnaise
    1 1/2 cups honey
    1/2 cup Dijon mustard
    1/2 cup horseradish

Shrimp
    65 raw medium shrimp, peeled and deveined
    2 cups flour
    1/2 quart Drake's Fry batter mix
    6 ounces coconut milk
    8 ounces coconut flakes
    oil for frying

Combine sauce ingredients; set aside.

In a heavy saucepan, heat oil to 375 degrees. Dredge shrimp in flour to coat. Mix Drake's Fry batter and coconut milk together, adding water, if necessary, to create cake-batter consistency. Dip shrimp in batter mixture. Roll shrimp in coconut flakes to cover and deep fry to golden brown.

Serve with honey mustard horseradish sauce.

Serves: 20 if served as appetizer; 8 if served as dinner

 If Drake's Fry is not available, any box of store-bought fry batter mix with flour, cornmeal, salt and spices will work.

FRIDAY NIGHT FISH FRY

One of Wisconsin's oldest dining traditions is the Friday Night Fish Fry. It is a time-honored tradition dating back over a century. Though the origins of the fish fry are not exact, we can only assume it is a result of the plentiful perch and cod supply from Wisconsin's many lakes.

There are a number of stories as to why fish fries are celebrated on Fridays. One is linked to the huge Catholic population in the state during the early part of the 20th century. A fish fry was – and continues to be - one way to satisfy the religious ban on eating meat on Fridays.

It is largely agreed that the elements of the perfect fish fry include: beer-battered fried cod, potatoes, coleslaw, rye bread and a cold beer. Today, even the most elegant restaurants offer their version of this Midwest comfort food. But the truly authentic Friday Fish Fry is still a tasty family-style meal found in neighborhood taverns, local restaurants, church basements and American Legion Halls.

Maple Bluff Country Club
Cream of Shiitake Mushroom Soup

Roux
3 tablespoons clarified butter
3 tablespoons flour

Soup
1 ounce clarified butter
3 medium stalks celery, diced
1 medium onion, diced
8 ounces shiitake mushrooms, stems removed, sliced
8 ounces domestic mushrooms, sliced
2 quarts beef stock or canned consommé
1 small bay leaf
1 small sprig fresh thyme
2 cups heavy cream
1/8 teaspoon Worcestershire sauce
salt and pepper to taste
cooked roux to thicken

ROUX:

When adding roux to soup, whisk briskly to thoroughly incorporate cooked roux into soup. This will help eliminate flour lumps. Add small amounts of roux until desired thickness is achieved. Soup will continue to thicken slightly after each addition of roux. Be sure to cook soup for five minutes after final addition of roux. If soup becomes too thick add a little extra cream, to adjust the viscosity.

Roux: Heat butter in saucepan over medium heat. When the butter is hot, but not smoking, carefully and quickly add the flour. With a wooden spoon carefully, but quickly mix the flour and butter together to combine thoroughly. Reduce heat, cook flour and butter for 3 minutes stirring constantly. Remove from heat and stir to cool. After cool, store in air tight container and use to thicken soups, sauces and gravies.

Soup: Place butter in small soup pot or large saucepan and melt over medium heat (do not brown). When butter has melted, add diced celery and onions. Sweat over medium heat stirring frequently until softened. Add sliced mushrooms and cook until mushrooms have released all their juices. Add beef stock or consommé. Bring to a boil and reduce heat to a simmer. Add the bay leaf. Simmer slowly for 10 minutes. Add fresh thyme sprig. Add heavy cream, Worcestershire sauce and salt and pepper.

Using a wire whisk, incorporate small amounts of roux into the soup to thicken to desired viscosity. After thickening soup to the desired consistency with roux, allow to simmer for 5 minutes to thoroughly cook flour.

Serves: 8

 Using a cooked roux to thicken soups, sauces and gravies will result in a velvety smooth texture with no flour lumps.

Blue Marlin
Sea Scallops

1/4 cup brown sugar
1/4 cup brandy
3 slices smoked bacon (we use Applewood)
3 U-10 (colossal) fresh sea scallops
1-2 tablespoons fresh lemon juice

In an 8 inch sauté pan, render bacon until nearly crispy. Pushing bacon to the side of the pan, add scallops and sear until golden brown. With sauté pan away from stove, add 1/4 cup of brandy and allow 30 seconds to burn off. Add a tablespoon fresh lemon juice. Add 1/4 cup brown sugar.

Remove scallops at medium rare to medium and allow sauce to reduce.

Plate scallops and drizzle sauce over scallops.

Serves: 1

Eldorado Grill
Wisconsin Four Cheese Chile Rellenos

This recipe combines a traditional Southwestern chile relleno with Wisconsin feta, cheddar and Monterey Jack cheeses.

12 (5-inch) poblano chiles
1/2 pound Wisconsin feta cheese, crumbled
1/2 pound Wisconsin white cheddar cheese, shredded
1/2 pound Wisconsin Monterey Jack cheese, shredded
1/2 pound cream cheese
1 tablespoon fresh lime juice
4 scallions or green onions, thinly sliced
1 tablespoon black pepper
canola oil as needed
8 eggs, separated
1 1/2 cups all purpose flour

Notes:

Roast whole chiles over open flame, turning frequently, until blackened and blistered. Put into ice-water bath to cool; peel skin off under running water. Cut a slit in side of each chile, making a pocket.

In a large bowl, mix cheeses, lime juice, green onions and black pepper. Stuff 2 ounces of cheese mixture into each chile.

In a 10-inch skillet, pour 3/4 inch of oil and heat to 325 degrees. While oil heats, beat egg whites until stiff. Add yolks to whites and mix until blended, 5-10 seconds more.

Roll stuffed chiles in flour, coating entire chile. Coat chiles with egg mixture and fry, 3-4 at a time, until both sides are golden brown. Remove onto paper towels. Repeat process with remaining chiles. Serve with salsa.

Serves: 12

Ocean Grill
Deviled Crab

1/4 cup breadcrumbs
1/4 cup grated Parmesan cheese
1/2 cup unsalted butter
1 shallot, minced
2 cloves garlic, minced
2 plus tablespoons flour
2 tablespoons Dijon mustard
2 cups heavy whipping cream
1-2 dashes Tabasco sauce, to taste
1 pound canned lump crab meat, picked over
1/2 pound canned crab leg meat, picked over
2 tablespoons fresh dill, minced

Preheat oven to 350 degrees.

In a small shallow bowl combine bread crumbs and Parmesan cheese. Set aside.

Melt the butter over low heat; gently cook the shallot and garlic until just starting to brown. Stir in the flour, to form a loose roux. Increase heat to medium, and cook for 2 minutes. Whisk in the mustard, and gradually add the cream. Cook, whisking continuously, until a thick sauce forms. Add Tabasco. Fold in the crabmeat and dill.

Season with salt and pepper.

Transfer to a 1-quart oven-proof casserole dish. Top with bread crumb-cheese mixture.

Bake for 7-10 minutes, until the cheese is melted and the top is browned. Serve with crackers or crostini.

Serves: 4 as an appetizer

TASTE OF MADISON

Madison restaurants have long been known for their exciting flavors, diversity and unique style. As the summer draws to an end each year, restaurants from all over the city come together for a two day food festival known as the Taste of Madison.

Each year, this beloved city tradition brings thousands of people to the city center for a culinary adventure. The Capitol perimeter is lined with over 55 vendors who provide samples of their most popular menu features. The cuisine options range from classic steak house fare to unique ethnic cuisine to favorites from the local greasy spoons.

The intoxicating smells entice people from all over to gather with family and friends, enjoy the sounds of live music and indulge in a culinary journey.

Restaurant Magnus

Lamb Chops with Sunchoke Pureé and Vegetables

4 lamb chops
pink, white and black peppercorns
1/4 pound sunchokes (Jerusalem artichokes)
1 quart half and half
2 tablespoons butter
8 ounces black trumpet mushrooms, sliced
12 ounces red potatoes, diced
1 medium red onion, chopped
1/4 pound fresh spinach

Topping
Chilean cherries
balsamic vinegar
pinch of sugar

SUNCHOKES:

The sunchoke is a lumpy, brown-skinned tuber that resembles a gingerroot. The white flesh of this vegetable is nutty, sweet and crunchy. Sunchokes can be found at the Farmers' Market in early spring. Buy sunchokes that are firm and fresh looking, not soft or wrinkled. Store in a plastic bag in refrigerator for up to one week.

Preheat oven to 450 degrees.

In a heavy skillet, sear lamb chops with pink, white and black peppercorn. Sear approximately 1 1/2 minutes per side. Place chops in oven for four minutes. Let rest for 3 minutes at room temperature.

In a medium saucepan, bring sunchokes and half and half to a simmer. Cook sunchokes for about 10 minutes or until they are fork tender. Cool slightly. In a blender or food processor, puree sunchokes to a smooth consistency.

In a medium sauté pan melt butter. Add mushrooms, red potatoes, red onion and spinach. Sauté for 3-6 minutes.

Topping: Soak cherries in balsamic vinegar with a pinch of sugar.

To prepare plates: Place 1/4 cup of sunchoke puree on plate. Place the lamb chops on the puree. Place the mushrooms, potato, red onion and spinach in the center of the plate. Finish with 1/2 teaspoon of cherries on top of each lamb chop.

Serves: 4

Louisianne's, Etc.
Chicken and Sausage Jambalaya

1/4 cup olive oil
2 medium onions, chopped
4 ribs celery, chopped
4 cloves garlic, minced
2 medium bell peppers, seeded and chopped
2 small zucchini, halved lengthwise and sliced 1/4-inch thick
2 teaspoons salt
2 teaspoons chili powder
2 teaspoons ground black pepper
1/2 teaspoon ground white pepper
1 tablespoon oregano leaves
1 tablespoon thyme leaves
1 teaspoon rubbed sage
1 teaspoon garlic powder
5 dashes cayenne pepper sauce
12 ounces fresh mushrooms, sliced
1 pound chicken breasts, cut in 1/2-inch cubes
1 (14 ounce) can chicken broth
1 smoked sausage (4 ounces), sliced into 1/4 inch pieces
1 (14 ounce) can cut okra
2 (14.5 ounce) cans diced tomatoes
2 (8 ounce) cans tomato sauce
1 (6 ounce) can tomato paste
6 cups cooked rice

Place oil in a 6-quart pot over medium heat. Add onions, celery, garlic, bell peppers, zucchini, salt, chili powder, black pepper, white pepper, oregano, thyme, sage, garlic powder and cayenne pepper sauce. Cook stirring occasionally until the onions are transparent. Add the mushrooms and cook 2 minutes more. Add the chicken, cook and stir 5 minutes more. Add the chicken broth, sausage, okra, diced tomatoes, tomato sauce and tomato paste. Simmer at least 30 minutes.

Remove from heat and add the cooked rice. Mix well and let stand 5 minutes.

Serves: 8-10

 This is a great dish for using leftovers! Substitute sausage with cut up beef, chicken or pork. Cooked shrimp and other seafood should be added in the last 5 minutes of simmering.

Wollersheim Winery
Prairie Fumé Salmon Tourte
This recipe should be started 1 day in advance.

2 pounds fresh or frozen salmon
1 medium onion, chopped
1/2 bottle Prairie Fumé wine
2 puff pastry sheets (17 ounce package)
1 (10 ounce) package frozen chopped spinach
2 cups sour cream
2 cups grated Swiss cheese
salt, pepper
1 (6 ounce) can tomato paste
1 teaspoon honey

MARINARA SAUCE:

To make fresh marinara sauce, combine 1 (14.5 ounce) can diced tomatoes; 1 clove garlic, minced; 1 pinch sea salt and 1 tablespoon olive oil in a blender and puree until smooth.

Prepare salmon by cleaning off skin and cutting into 1-inch chunks. (Works best when fish is partially frozen.) Place fish chunks in glass bowl with onion and wine. Cover and marinate in refrigerator overnight.

Preheat oven to 400. Grease a 14-inch deep-dish pizza pan.

Roll one sheet puff pastry to fit the bottom and sides of prepared pizza pan. Place dough on bottom and up sides of pan.

Drain salmon and onion and reserve wine marinade. Spread salmon and onion on pastry. Cook spinach and drain well. Layer spinach, sour cream and Swiss cheese over salmon. Season with salt and pepper.

Roll out top layer of pastry dough and cut a design in the center. Lay on top and seal edges of pastry dough.

Bake 50-60 minutes.

Meanwhile, prepare sauce. Heat reserved wine marinade in saucepan with tomato paste. Simmer for 15 minutes to thicken. Adjust acidity by adding few drops of honey. Add one more tablespoon Prairie Fumé just before serving. Season with salt and pepper.

Allow tourte to cool for 15 minutes before serving with warm Prairie Fumé tomato sauce on the side.

Serves: 10

Lombardino's Italian Restaurant and Bar
Shrimp Alla Sambuca

This versatile dish can be served as a first course with crostini, or as an entree by adding steamed potatoes and zucchini.

12 jumbo shrimp, peeled and deveined
2 tablespoons olive oil, plus more for sautéing
1 small fresh fennel bulb, sliced
1/4 cup kalamata olives, halved
1/4 cup shrimp stock
1/4 cup marinara sauce (recipe for fresh marinara on page 302)
kosher salt and fresh ground pepper to taste
2 ounce shot black Sambuca
1/4 cup freshly chopped Italian parsley

Heat saute pan for a minute or so; drizzle about 1 ounce of extra virgin olive oil into the pan and swirl to coat. Add the shrimp and toss continually for 30 seconds, or until nicely seared. Add the fennel and olives. Add the shrimp stock and marinara sauce, which lowers the temperature of our hot pan and slows down the cooking in order to maintain tender, perfectly cooked shrimp. Turn the flame to medium-low and cover the pan: this will let the shrimp gently steam until done.

When the shrimp are fully cooked season with salt and pepper and swirl in the sambuca. Top with chopped parsley and serve.

Serve with olive oil-grilled or toasted crostini.

Serves: 4 as an appetizer

This dish is prepared and served rather quickly. It is important to start with a hot sauté pan in order to achieve an initial sear on the body of the shrimp: this translates into pure flavor. The whole dish should take 2-3 minutes start to finish.

OUR CITY COOKS - MADISON ORIGINALS

Madison Originals is a grassroots confederation of more than four dozen independently-owned restaurants dedicated to preserving the Madison area's unique local flavor amid the onslaught of national chains.

Members believe that their varied menus, attentive service and hometown civic responsibility offer a genuine alternative to the "saming" of America.

The group's mission is to call attention to the concept of eating locally through modest collective marketing efforts, fun and occasionally frivolous special events and sponsorship of charitable causes.

Several restaurants featured in "No Reservations" are Madison Originals.

The Madison Club

Cranachan

Cranachan is a typical Scottish dessert. It is simple to put together and yet very elegant: with a name that allows you to savor a taste of Scotland!

1 cup oatmeal
1 cup heavy cream
4 tablespoon of Scotch whisky
1 teaspoon almond extract
2 tablespoons honey
1 pint fresh raspberries
2 tablespoons powder sugar

Preheat oven to 350 degrees.

Place oatmeal on a baking pan. Toast oatmeal for 10-15 minutes, or until golden brown. Let cool.

Whip cream gradually adding whisky, almond extract and honey until soft peaks appear.

In 4 red wine glasses begin layering, starting with oatmeal, then raspberries and then whipped cream. Repeat layering one more time.

Finish with raspberries and dust with powdered sugar as a garnish.

Serves: 4

Notes:

Fyfe's
Key Lime Pie

Crust
3 1/2 cups graham cracker crumbs
1/4 cup sugar
1 cup butter, melted

Filling
6 (14 ounce) cans sweetened condensed milk
16 ounces Nellie and Joe's Key Lime Juice
     (or other fresh key lime juice)
24 egg yolks

Garnish
fresh whipped cream
1 lime, circularly sliced

Preheat oven to 350 degrees. Use 10-inch pie plates.

Combine graham cracker crumbs, sugar and butter in a large bowl; mix well. Divide crust between two pie plates. Bake crust for 8-10 minutes or until set.

Place condensed milk, lime juice and egg yolks in a bowl and mix well. Divide filling between both crusts and bake for 18-25 minutes or until firm.

Cool pies and refrigerate overnight. Cut into 8 wedges, per pie. Garnish each slice with a dollop of freshly whipped cream and a lime wedge or dusting of zest.

Makes 2 Pies.

Serves: 16

SCHOOL, PARENTS AND READING CONNECTION (SPARC)

School, Parents and Reading Connection (SPARC) has been implemented in area elementary schools with help from the Junior League of Madison. The SPARC program provides backpacks to first and second grade children with theme-based books and educational activities. Students take the backpacks home to complete the activities with brothers, sisters and parents.

"When parents get involved, it shows kids how important school is. It's helped a lot of our students, particularly those who don't have the materials at home. It's great to see how excited they are to learn."

-Michelle Torre,
Midvale Elementary School teacher

glossary

● ● ● COOKING TERMS ● ● ●

Blanch
To plunge food (usually vegetables and fruits) into boiling water briefly, then into cold water to stop the cooking process. Blanching is used to firm the flesh, to loosen skins (as with peaches and toma- toes) and to heighten and set color and flavor (as with vegetables before freezing). See also parboil. 2. This term also refers to the horticultural technique whereby the leaves of plants are whitened or prevented from becoming green by growing them in complete darkness. It's this labor-intensive process that makes Belgian endive so expensive.

Bechamel
Also called by its Italian name, balsamella, this basic French white sauce is made by stirring milk into a butter-flour roux. The thickness of the sauce depends on the pro- portion of flour and butter to milk. The proportions for a thin sauce would be 1 tablespoon each of butter and flour per 1 cup of milk; a medium sauce would use 2 tablespoons each of butter and flour; a thick sauce, 3 tablespoons each. Béchamel, the base of many other sauces, was named after its inventor, Louis XIV's steward Louis de Béchamel.

Braise
A cooking method by which food (usually meat or vegetables) is first browned in fat, then cooked, tightly covered, in a small amount of liquid at low heat for a lengthy period of time. The long, slow cooking develops flavor and tenderizes foods by gently breaking down their fibers. Braising can be done on top of the range or in the oven. A tight-fitting lid is very important to prevent the liquid from evaporating.

Broth
The difference between broth and a stock is that broth is prepared using a whole chicken or chicken parts simmered in water with vegetables and seasoning until done. Stock uses the bones to achieve its flavor.

Brown Sauce
Known in France as espagnole sauce, brown sauce is used as a base for dozens of other sauces. It's traditionally made of a rich meat stock, a mirepoix of browned vegetables, a brown roux, herbs and some- times tomato paste.

Chiffonade
A method of cutting basil or other herbs by stacking and rolling the basil leaves into a cylinder and cut thinly crosswise into a chiffonade or ribbon.

Clarify
To clear a cloudy liquid by removing the sediment. The most common method is to add egg whites and/or eggshells to a liquid (such as a stock) and simmer for 10 to 15 minutes. The egg whites attract any parti-

cles in the liquid like a magnet. After cooling for about an hour, the mixture is poured through a cloth-lined sieve to strain out all residue. Rendered fat can be clarified by adding hot water and boiling for about 15 minutes. The mixture is then strained through several layers of cheesecloth and chilled. The resulting top layer of fat should be almost entirely clear of residue.

Consommé

A consommé is a clarified stock and is used in the preparation of clear soups.

Demi-Glace

This is a half-glaze. It is used as the foundation in meat and poultry sauces as well as a glaze. When cooking poultry and meats, all you need to do is deglaze your pan with reserved marinade or wine and bring to a boil. Add demi-glace, fresh vegetables and hers and serve immediately.

Extra Virgin Olive Oil

This is the cold-pressed result of the first pressing of the olives, and is only 1 percent acid. It's considered the finest and fruitiest of the olive oils.

Fold

A technique used to gently combine a light, airy mixture (such as beaten egg whites) with a heavier mixture (such as whipped cream or custard). The lighter mixture is placed on top of the heavier one in a large bowl. Starting at the back of the bowl, a rubber spatula is used to cut down vertically through the two mixtures, across the bottom of the bowl and up the nearest side. The bowl is rotated a quarter turn with each series of strokes. This down-across-up-and-over motion gently turns the mixtures over on top of each other, combining them in the process.

Flambé

Sprinkled with brandy or a liqueur and ignited.

Glace De Viande (Meat Glaze)

Start with 1 quart of brown stock. See recipe on page. This is a rich stock reduction used to enhance meat sauces in both flavor and depth. To make glace de viande reduce brown stock by three-fourths or until it coats the back of a spoon. Be careful not to burn the stock. You may want to transfer to a smaller pot to complete the process. Once the glace is made, it should be stored in an airtight container and chilled. Glace de viande will keep indefinitely when stored properly and can also be used on its own as a meat glaze.

Julienne

Food cut in very thin strips.

Macerate

To soak a food (usually fruit) in a liquid in order to infuse it with the liquid's flavor. A spirit such as brandy, rum or a liqueur is usually the macerating liquid. See also marinate.

glossary

Marinate

To soak a food such as meat, fish or vegetables in a seasoned liquid mixture called a marinade. The purpose of marinating is for the food to absorb the flavors of the marinade or, as in the case of a tough cut of meat, to tenderize. Because most marinades contain acid ingredients, the marinating should be done in a glass, ceramic or stainless-steel container—never in aluminum. Foods should be covered and refrigerated while they're marinating. When fruits are similarly soaked, the term used is macerate.

Parboil

To partially cook food by boiling it briefly in water. This timesaving technique is used in particular for dense foods such as carrots. If parboiled, they can be added at the last minute with quick-cooking ingredients (such as bean sprouts and celery) in preparations such as stir-fries. The parboiling insures that all the ingredients will complete cooking at the same time. See also blanch.

Poultry Stock

You can substitute veal bones for the chicken bones to achieve a white veal stock. When the poultry stock has reduced it turns a golden brown and has a great flavor. White veal stock should not be reduced to the point that it will change color.

Puree

Any food (usually a fruit or vegetable) that is finely mashed to a smooth, thick consistency. Purees can be used as a garnish, served as a side dish or added as a thickener to sauces or soups. This can be accomplished by one of several methods including using a food processor or blender or by forcing the food through a sieve.

Ragout

A derivative of the French verb ragoûter, meaning "to stimulate the appetite," ragoût is a thick, rich, well-seasoned stew of meat, poultry or fish that can be made with or without vegetables.

Reduce

To boil a liquid (usually stock, wine or a sauce mixture) rapidly until the volume is reduced by evaporation, thereby thickening the consistency and intensifying the flavor. Such a mixture is sometimes referred to as a reduction.

Render

To melt animal fat over low heat so that it separates from any connective pieces of tissue, which, during rendering, turn brown and crisp and are generally referred to as cracklings. The resulting clear fat is then strained through a paper filter or fine cheesecloth to remove any dark particles. The term try out is used synonymously with render.

Roux

A mixture of flour and fat that, after being

slowly cooked over low heat, is used to thicken mixtures such as soups and sauces. Types of roux: White and blond are made with butter. Cook the former just until it begins to turn beige and the latter until pale golden. Use to thicken cream and white sauces and light soups. Thee fuller-flavored brown roux can be made with butter, drippings or pork or beef fat. It's cooked to a deep golden brown and used for rich, dark sauces and soups. Cajun and Creole dishes use a lard-based roux, which is cooked (up to an hour) until a beautiful mahogany brown.

Sauté

To cook food quickly in a small amount of oil in a skillet or sauté pan over direct heat.

Scald

A cooking technique—often used to retard the souring of milk—whereby a liquid is heated to just below the boiling point. To plunge food such as tomatoes or peaches into boiling water (or to pour boiling water over them), in order to loosen their skin and facilitate peeling. Also referred to as blanch.

Stock

In the most basic terms, stock is the strained liquid that is the result of cooking vegetables, meat or fish and other seasoning ingredients in water. A brown stock is made by browning bones, vegetables and other ingredients before they're cooked in the liquid. Most soups begin with a stock of some kind, and many sauces are based on reduced stocks.

Zest

The perfumy outermost skin layer of citrus fruit (usually oranges or lemons), which is removed with the aid of a citrus zester, paring knife or vegetable peeler. Only the colored portion of the skin (and not the white pith) is considered the zest. The aromatic oils in citrus zest are what add so much flavor to food. Zest can be used to flavor raw or cooked and sweet or savory dishes.

● ● ● HERBS & SPICES ● ● ●

Allspice

Spicy berries that taste like a blend of cloves, cinnamon and nutmeg. Add to beef dishes, yellow vegetables, breads, relishes, pickles, cakes and pies.

Aniseed

The small round seeds of the anise plant. They have a licorice flavor. Enliven beef and pork dishes, fruits, breads, cakes, and biscuits.

Basil

A member of the mint family. The fresh green leaves are full of flavor. Crumbled and dried leaves are less aromatic. Use in chicken, fish, and tomato dishes, pasta sauce and salads; also use for soups, stuffings, pesto sauce and salad dressings.

glossary

Bay Leaf

Belonging to the bay laurel family, leaves are dried for use. Remove bay leaves before serving a dish; they remain tough and their edges sharp, even after cooking. Add to poached fish or poultry dishes as well as to stocks, soups, stews, casseroles and pasta sauces.

Caraway Seed

Small crescent-shaped seeds commonly found in rye bread. Use to perk up pork, carrots and coleslaw, as well as egg and cheese dishes.

Cardamom seeds

If seeds are in pods extract them with your fingers. The seeds are also sold ground, or you can grind your own in a coffee mill or by crushing them between two spoons. Use cardamom pods whole in coffee or add ground cardamom to breads, cakes and biscuits.

Celery Seeds

Stronger tasting than fresh celery, these seeds have an intense celery flavor. Complement beef, lamb, and vegetable stews, egg salads and barbecue sauces.

Chervil

Similar to a combination of parsley and tarragon, chervil is available fresh or dried. Excellent in roast meat, poultry, fish, vegetable and egg recipes as well as salads.

Chilli Powder

Made from hot red chilies, chilli powder may also contain cumin, oregano and garlic. The hotness varies, so use it with caution. As well as main-course dishes, it adds zest to barbecue sauces, dips, spreads, salad dressings, bread and croutons

Chives

The long, slender tubular leaves of chives have a delicate onion flavor. More fragrant than sharp. Sprinkle fresh snipped chives on any mildly seasoned egg, cheese, fish, poultry, vegetable or salad dish.

Cinnamon

The sweet, reddish brown bark of the East Indian cassia tree, cinnamon is sold either ground or as rolled sticks. Best suited to sweetened bean dishes, yellow vegetables, cooked fruits and baked desserts.

Cloves

These dried buds, whole or ground, give a warm, pungent flavor to foods, both sweet and savory. Cloves are strong - use sparingly. Glazed hams can be studded with whole cloves when baked. Use ground cloves in baking, fruit desserts and in spicy meat dishes.

Coriander

Coriander is sold in bunches. It has a biting grassy taste and an almost piercing fragrance. Coriander seeds, whole or ground, have a different, lemony flavor. Coriander and coriander seeds are not interchangeable. Add fresh coriander to soups and egg, cheese, fish, and poultry dishes. Add ground coriander or crushed coriander seeds to beef soups and stews and to curries.

Cumin Seeds
Whole or ground, these seeds have a powerful musky aroma and flavor. Complement meat and rice dishes, curries, Mexican dishes and potato casseroles.

Curry Powder
A mixture of many spices, the different brands vary in color, flavor and hotness. Use to season meats, poultry, fish, fruits, vegetables and cream soups and sauces.

Dill
The fresh fronds of dill have a slightly lemony, salty flavor. Dried dill is much more intense; use it sparingly. Add to fish, lamb, poultry and vegetable dishes, as well as to salads, dressings and sauces.

Fennel Seeds
Either ground or whole, these seeds have a sweet aniseed flavor. Used in Malay and Indian curries, they can be added to fish, egg dishes and stews as well as to salads, dressings and sauces.

Ginger
This fresh underground plant stem has a peppery, lemony flavor. Ground ginger is less aromatic, more biting. Enhances meat, poultry, seafood, and vegetable stir fries as well as cakes, biscuits, pies, and breads.

Mace
The casing around nutmeg, mace is sold ground or as dried 'blades'. It tastes like nutmeg but is more delicate. Use in poultry, fish, vegetable and cheese dishes and in fruit desserts, custards, cakes, and biscuits.

Marjoram
Both the fresh and dried leaves of marjoram have a strong, savory flavor. Suitable for veal, lamb, and poultry dishes, green vegetables and tomatoes.

Mint
Although Mint comes in flavors such as pineapple and peppermint, spearmint is the variety most used. Enhances green peas and new potatoes and is used fresh in salads, mint sauce and as a fragrant garnish.

Nutmeg
Available in whole seeds, but usually sold ground, nutmeg has a warm, sweet flavor. Add to beef soups and stews, yellow vegetables, breads, cakes and fruit desserts.

Oregano
Related to marjoram, the dried leaves of oregano are available crumbled or ground. Use in tomato dishes, pasta sauces and salad dressings.

Paprika
A red powder ground from dried red cap-

glossary

sicum pods, paprika varies from nutty and sweet to hot. Can be used to garnish, or as a seasoning for goulashes, fish, poultry and potato dishes.

Parsley
A member of the carrot family, curly parsley has a mild taste; the flat-leaf, or Italian variety is more pungent. Parsley enhances meat, poultry, fish and vegetable dishes, and is good in omelets, stuffings and herb bread.

Poppy seeds
Tiny gray seeds with a nutty flavor. Use only fresh seeds; they turn rancid quickly. A favorite in cakes, biscuits, breads, sweet pastries and salad dressings.

Rosemary
An aromatic herb, rosemary has needle-like leaves that give off a rich, resinous scent whether fresh or dried. Roast meat, poultry, fish, green peas, carrots, stuffings, gravies and casseroles all benefit from its hearty flavor.

Saffron
An expensive yellow spice, sold in thread or powder form, saffron has a strong but delicate flavor. Used sparingly, saffron enhances chicken, rice and seafood dishes.

Sage
The fresh, ground or dried grey-green leaves have a pungent lemony flavor, sage can be bitter if overused. Sage is traditional in meat and poultry stuffings and is also delicious in cheese dishes.

Savory
Dried whole or ground leaves with a grassy aroma, savory has a light, fragrant flavor. Add to egg, rice, vegetable and poultry dishes.

Sesame seeds
Pearly flat seeds with a mild nutty flavor. Add to stir fries and bread; use as a garnish for chicken, fish, and vegetables.

Tarragon
Fresh or dried, this herb retains its mild licorice flavor well. Enlivens fish and poultry dishes, especially with wine or cream.

Thyme
Fresh or dried, thyme has a pungent aroma similar to sage. Discard any stems. Equally at home with meat, poultry, seafood, eggs, cheese, vegetables and salad.

Turmeric
The powdered yellow root lends a peppery pungency to curry powder, mustards and pickles. Use this pungent spice in small quantities in curries, and in chicken and egg dishes.

• • • RESOURCES • • •

The following valuable resources were used to gather the snipits of "local flavor" about the Madison area and the helpful tips, tricks and trivia that are sprinkled throughout.

American Players Theatre Web site,
www.americanplayers.org

Arts on Campus Web site, www.arts.wisc.edu

"Badger State Showmen: A History of Wisconsin's Circus Heritage" by Fred Dahlinger, Jr. and Stuart Thayer.

Better Homes & Gardens Cookbook

Botham Vineyard

Circus World Museum Web site,
www.circusworldmuseum.com

www.co.dane.wi.us/commissions/lakes/
lakesandstreams.html

Columbia County Economic Development Corporation Web site, www.ccedc.com

Dane County Farmers' Market Web site,
www.dcfm.org

Dane County Lakes & Watershed Commission

Downtown Madison, Inc. Web site,
www.downtownmadison.org

www.epicurius.com

Essen Haus Restaurant

www.food.com

www.geography.wisc.edu/sco/maps/WIstatistics.php

Greater Madison Chamber of Commerce

Greater Madison Convention & Visitors Bureau Web site, www.visitmadison.com

Green Bay Packers Web site, www.packers.com

Henry Vilas Zoological Society Web site,
www.vilaszoo.org

Hoofers Web site, www.hoofers.com

www.infoplease.com

Joseph Huber Brewing Company Web site,
www.huberbrewery.com/brewery

Kehl School of Dance

Madison Magazine

Madison Museum of Contemporary Art Web site,
www.madisonartcenter.org

Monona Terrace Convention Center Web site,
www.mononaterrace.com

Monroe Chamber of Commerce & Industry Web site, www.farmtofeast.com &

wicip.uwplatt.edu/green/ci/monroe/about/history.htm

New Glarus Chamber of Commerce Web site,
www.swisstown.com

Olbrich Botanical Gardens Web site,
www.olbrich.org

Georgia O'Keefe Museum Web site,
www.okeefemuseum.org

Overture Foundation Web site,
www.overturefoundation.org

www.producepete.com

Taste of Home magazine

University of Wisconsin Athletics Web site,
www.uwbadgers.com

University of Wisconsin Web site;
wiscinfo.doit.wisc.edu/arboretum

UW-Madison Communications Web site,
www.news.wisc.edu/9222.html

UW-Madison Dept. of Food Science Web site,
www.wisc.edu/foodsci/store/dairyplant.html

UW Marching Band Web site, www.badgerband.com

Weber's Big Book of Grilling

www.whfoods.com

Wisconsin Alumni Association Web site,
www.uwalumni.com/askabe/traditions.html

Wisconsin Department of Tourism

Wisconsin Department of Transportation Web site,
www.dot.wisconsin.gov

Wisconsin Milk Marketing Board Web site,
www.wisdairy.com

Wisconsin State Cartographer's Office Web site,

Wisconsin State Journal

acknowledgments

It truly takes a village to produce an extraordinary cookbook. We know we could not have done it without the countless hours of volunteer time, the generous support of our Junior League corporate sponsors, the financial contributions of a dedicated group of Junior League women and the commitment and willingness of Junior League members as well as their friends and family who collected and tested the recipes for this first edition of *Mad About Food*.

Hats off to the more than three hundred Junior League members, friends and family who contributed excellent recipes, conducted multiple testings and helped in various ways to ensure the highest quality content for *Mad About Food*.

Ruth Acker	Andrea Blader	Dan Chin	Karen DeTienne
Cindy Alvarez	Laura Blakeslee	Amy Christianson	Sara DeTienne
Virginia Amann	Mary Blanchard	Curt Christianson	Kitty Dettman
Chuck Angevine	Michelle Blang	Karen Christianson	Veronica Dickmann
Peggy Angevine	Patricia Bleakley	Dave Cieslewicz	Gail Docken
Sharon Anundson	Wilma Bliss	Dorothy Cipolla	Kristin Dollhopf
Joyce Apfel	Marianne Bolz	Peggy Comerford	Jan Dowden
Jon Aranoff	Marcia Bon Durant	Susie Conley	Nancy Dryburgh
Jane Arduser	Michelle Bonnarens	Jennifer Conlin	Mara Dublin
Mary Argall	Renee Bordner	Barb Cooper	Dave Duchow
Vicky Ausman	Gwen Bosben	Barb Coulson	Ellie Duchow
Silvana Avedon	Sarah Botham	Dee Joy Coulter	Polly Duchow
Sue Bakke	Ann Boyer	Janet Crnich	Roger Duchow
Andrea Ball	Kelly Brandt	Laura Crosby	Heather Duncan
Michelle Ballweg	Kathy Bullock	Katy Culver	Julie Dunlap
Chris Barker	Lorinda Cain	Lisa Danford	Sarah Duren
Mary Bartzen	Teressa Campbell	Bonnie Darda	Maureen Durick
Jule Belling	Mrs. Gary Cannalte	Laura Davidson	Nancy Eifert
Jennifer Bergman	Mary Jane Carpenter	Russell Davidson	Sue Ela
Chris Berry	Hillary Carr	Joan Dawson	Amy Ellestad
Mary Pat Berry	Patricia Carroll	Megan Decker	Pamela Eyrick
Kim Bethea	Sheri Carter	Trish DeAmicis	Kari Fisher
Amy Bina	Valarie Chicy	Andy DeTienne	Barb Folco

Cate Furay
Tracy Gallager
Jane Gardner
Marilyn Getscher
Lauren Gmender
Paige Graham
Jaclyn Gregoire
John Gregoire
PJ Gregoire
Rachel Gregoire
Sandi Gregoire
Connie Grogan
James Hackworthy
Michelle Hackworthy
Beth Hatton
Maggie Healy
Liz Heinrichs
Lori Heinrichs
Rebecca Heiting
Rebecca Helms
Stephaanie Herbst-Lucke
Jenny Hiltbrand
Jean Herzberg
Teri Horton
Kirsten Houghton
Nancy Hueber
Ken Huxhold
Dana Jacobs
Jane Johnson
Diane Joy
Sue Joy-Sobota
Jennifer Kahl
Rachel Kammer
Pam Katz
Chris Kennedy
Katie Kennedy
Carla Kinny
Katherine Klinke
Elizabeth Kluesner
Jennifer Kohn
Connie Kolpin
Sharon Kopinski
Diane Kouba

Larry Kouba
Susan Kouba
Jodi Kowalski
Darlene Kozarek
Shari Kuemmel
Katie Kunz
Leslie Ladd
Uli Lake
Susan Lang
Mary Lang Sollinger
Robyn Lawler
Kelly Leigel
Cathy Lemkuil
Linda Lemkuil
Barb Lessner
Kelly Liegel
Jane Linstroth
Krista Linstroth
Anne Lucke
Gloria Lund
Susan Luskin
Dennis Lynch
Mary Lynch
Rich Lynch
Nancy Lynch
Amy Maher
Margaret Maher
Barb Malchow
Elaine Malter
Stephanie Marquis
Lois Marsh
Jean Marty
Sandy McClure
Penny McDonough
Ann McIvor
Cynthia McKenna
Sally McKittrick
Anne Merfeld
Kay Mergen
Jana Meyers
Patsy Miller
Sue Miller
Zoe Miller

Adam Mills
Bill Mills
Connie Mills
Eric Mills
Grant Mills
Alissa Minor
Elizabeth Misel
Kritin Mitchell
Sue Mohoney
Megan Moline
Mary Morton
Kelly Mortrud
Tammy Moyer
Julie Murawski
Terry Murawski
Kelly Murdoch
Lori Murphy
Jeannine Muschinski
Amy Newton
Jan Niebur
Candice Nielsen
JoWayne Nunberg
Bea Nyenhuis
Jennifer O'Donnel
Michelle Ogilvie
Gail Olson
Norene Oppriecht
Sue Ossmann
Sheree Castro Paradise
Renee Pasciak
Judy Patterson
Melinda Pellino
Colleen Penwell
Joanne Peterson
Nan Peterson
Marcia Phillips-Hyzer
Kathi Preboske
Meg Prestigiacomo
Tricia Prodoehl
Char Purtell
Marlene Pytlik
Beth Ravenscroft
Pam Reichelderfer

Contributors (continued)

Tracy Reichenbacher
Susan Reynolds
Laurel Rice
Mike Richards
Susan Richardson
Pat Richter
Renee Richter
Sue Ring-Wagner
Laurie Robertson
Robert Rodman
Tracie Rodman
Vergene Rodman
Cindy Rogerson
Julie Roehrig-Wagner
Luanne Romvald
Carrie Roquet
Vicki Rowe
Nilka Sanderson
Elizabeth Sax
Rob Sax
Heidi Schaefer
Janie Schaefer
Jen Scheller

Renee Schinder
Marianne Schlecht
Ruth Ann Schoer
Liz Schumacher-
Commello
Debbie Schwartz
Wendy Seay
Christy Seaholm
Steve Shattuck
Lisa Sheehan
Jeremey Shepherd
Val Simpson
Dee Sjolund
Carmen Skilton
Melinda Slingsby
Patti Smith
Susan Smith
Vicki Spatt-Ballweg
Carol Spreitzer
Charlie Spreitzer
Charles Spreitzer
Jennifer Spreitzer
Mary Spreitzer

Sarah Spreitzer
Mindi Stassi
Susan Stoehr
Carol Straubel
Jodi Sweeney
Linda Sykes
Penny Symes
Paula Thill
Ellen Thom
Jennifer Tiedeman
Heidi Tjugum
Hillary Tjugum
Sherry Topp
Nina Toutant
Angie Tuckwood
Michele Tuong
Kay Turgeson
Sara Uttech
Susan Van Sicklin
Jan Von Haden
Ellis Waller
Ann Wann Stross
Charlene Warner

Mara Warner
Mary Warren
Wendy Warren
Donna Weihofen
Nadine Weske
Sally Whiffen
Suzie Wilkinson
Zane Williams
Amy Windsor
Lynn Wiskowski
Kathleen Woit
Dawn Wood
Jim Wood
Kennan Wood
Lynn Wood
Cindy Young
Ginny Yuska
Sue Zaleski
Marykay Zimbrick
Peggy Zimdars
Heidi Zoerb
Amy Zumwalt

We extend much gratitude to the following Junior League women who committed funds to help defray costs and ensure that the majority of proceeds raised could be used to support community programs.

Chefs

Cindy Alvarez
Sue Bakke
Mary Pat Berry
Susie Conley
Mary DeNiro
Sandy McClure
Nancy Meadows
Susan Reynolds
Laurel Rice
Cynthia Rogerson

Sous-Chefs

Peggy Angevine
Mary Argall
Mary Bartzen
Vincia Carlstrom
Sheri Carter
Gail Docken
Julie Dunlap
Shari Kuemmel
Uli Lake
Shirley Lightner
Susan Luskin
Nancy Lynch

Jane McMurray
Connie Mills
Patsy Miller
Josie Pollock
Carole Ruiz De Chavez
Vicki Rowe
Janie Schaefer
Susan Stoehr
Paula Thill
Mary Jo Tierney
Jan Von Haden
Suzie Wilkinson
Kathleen Woit

Special thanks to the following corporate sponsors who have generously given to the Junior League of Madison through financial or in-kind contributions. Their donations, along with the funds raised through this and other fund-raising activities of the Junior League help ensure that the needs of women and children in need in our community can be met.

Champion for Women and Children
anew
Capital Newspapers
Charter Communications
Wood Communications Group

Guardian for Women and Children
Wisconsin Capital Management
Two Men and A Truck

Advocate for Women and Children
The Duchow Family
Wells Fargo Bank

Patron of Women and Children
The Alvarez Family
Rybdahl's Classic Kitchens
M&I Bank
Magic 98
106-FM

Supporter of Women and Children
State Bank of Cross Plains
Sub-Zero Freezer Company, Inc.
Zander's Interiors

Friend of Women and Children
Bark & Wag
Bergstrom Automotive, Inc.
The Madison Club
DI Financial Group
Schorr Construction
US Bank

index

H

J

L

M

◦ ◦ ◦ **R** ◦ ◦ ◦

notes

notes

Junior League of Madison, Inc.
P.O. Box 44726
Madison, WI 53744-4726
888-894-1414
Order through our website: juniorleagueofmadison.com

Name: _____

Address: _____

City: _____ State: _____ Zip: _____

   Number of copies _____   @ $26.95 per copy_____

   Sales tax   @ $1.49 per copy _____

   Shipping and handling   @ $4.00 per copy _____

       Total: $

☐ Check enclosed (payable to the Junior League of Madison-Cookbook)

☐ Visa Card _____ : _____ : _____
      (card number)   (expiration date)   (signature)

☐ MasterCard _____ : _____ : _____
      (card number)   (expiration date)   (signature)

--------------------------✂--------------------------✂--------------------------

Junior League of Madison, Inc.
P.O. Box 44726
Madison, WI 53744-4726
888-894-1414
Order through our website: juniorleagueofmadison.com

Name: _____

Address: _____

City: _____ State: _____ Zip: _____

   Number of copies _____   @ $26.95 per copy_____

   Sales tax   @ $1.49 per copy _____

   Shipping and handling   @ $4.00 per copy _____

       Total: $

☐ Check enclosed (payable to the Junior League of Madison-Cookbook)

☐ Visa Card _____ : _____ : _____
      (card number)   (expiration date)   (signature)

☐ MasterCard _____ : _____ : _____
      (card number)   (expiration date)   (signature)